GENERATING
CHANGE

DOUG WALTON, PHD

GENERATING CHANGE

Anywhere, Anytime, by Anybody

Practical approaches for creating change
in organizations and communities

ROOSTER PRESS

P.O. Box 1654
Pleasanton, CA 94566
www.roosterpress.com

ISBN: 978-1-949378-00-9

First printing, 2018.

Printed by CreateSpace in the United States of America.

Cover design by Ana Grigoriu-Voicu at books-design.com

Copyediting by Delores Peterson and Geri Walton

Contents

Part III: Design **77**

5. **The Design of People Systems**................................. **79**

    Understanding the Desired Outcome 81

    Innovating Solutions... 82

    Analyzing the Context of the People System........................... 83

    Optimizing Existing Systems.. 84

    Evolving New Systems 87

    Cheat Sheet 93

6. **Architecting Collaboration**................................... **96**

    Authentic Collaboration.. 97

    Collaborative Idea Flow 104

    Alignment Workshops 112

    Cheat Sheet 122

7. **Engaging Stakeholders** **123**

    Who Are the Stakeholders? 124

    Contacting Stakeholders.. 131

    Methods of Collecting Stakeholder Information 132

    Analyzing the Stakeholder Perspectives 136

    Cheat Sheet 141

8. **Developing Change Success Indicators** **143**

    The Success Indicator 144

    Lightweight Development Process...................................... 149

    Using Success Indicators... 152

    Cheat Sheet 153

Part IV: Involve **155**

9. **Mobilization Strategy** **157**

    Ensuring Change Readiness 158

    How People Adopt a Change... 158

    Building the Mobilization Strategy................................... 162

    Cheat Sheet 174

Preface

Most books about social and organizational change are written for executives, professional consultants, or academics. But in the modern world, change is becoming pervasive, and this means it is happening throughout communities and organizations, on many levels, now involving everyone. Executives and outside experts cannot develop, manage, or control all aspects of human change in even a modestly sized community or company.

So, this book is offered to anyone who wants to make a difference in their part of the world. You are not required to have any specific background, career, or role in the community or an organization. You simply need the intention and the will to carry it out.

These are the answers to the hundreds of questions I have been asked regularly in my consulting practice. Based on extensive research in the field and two decades of experience, I have sought to put the best, most fundamental approaches that are effective into this book.

Much of the existing literature, some of which remains highly popular, is based on debunked concepts and assumptions from times gone by. This is the stuff that works, based on experience and science. I hope you find it immensely valuable.

Regards,

Doug Walton

https://www.empowerbase.com

PART I: Intention

All intentional change starts with an individual making a commitment to do something different

---

1

Casting Stones

I alone cannot change the world, but I can cast a stone across the waters to create many ripples.

—Mother Teresa

We all live in communities like businesses, families, churches, and governments. At times, our communities are only a handful of people. At other times, they could involve millions. These communities often operate the way we wish. But, when they stop serving our needs, we want to change them. That is what this book is about.

Change is accelerating everywhere in the modern world, and the conditions that enabled you, your company, or even your community to be successful in the past are likely to change soon. Technology is changing our means to communicate and deliver products. Modern science is changing our assumptions about the best foods for health, how to make decisions, and what motivates people to act. This means you can either be impacted by change or create it. Perhaps, you might want to generate more value for your customers, provide better support for homeless people, improve the national healthcare system, or get your school board of directors to treat the teachers better. These intentions require human behavior changes. But, whereas smartphones and new clothing styles are accepted willingly, these social or organizational changes are often strongly opposed by major segments of the community, even powerful ones.

Regardless of the presence of initial opposition, our communities and organizations can be changed for the better. Many people have done it, even against formidable challenges. In 1982, a small group of people in Arkansas were concerned about the state's chronic food insecurity, so they started a program to at least provide rice to starving Arkansans. This program, called the Arkansas Rice Depot, then expanded to all kinds of food. Later, when a school counselor noted behavioral problems in the classroom might be related to the kids not having enough food at home, the Arkansas Rice Depot developed a program to provide the children with backpacks of food to take home for the weekend. The children's school behavior began to improve, and the program is so successful that it is now widely modeled by "backpack clubs" all over the United States.[1,2]

Anyone can learn to be a successful change maker. You do not have to be the CEO or have special authority. Nor do you have to start with enormous amounts of money or other resources. Mainly, you need three things: an unwavering intention to create something good, a steadfast determination, and a willingness to learn the basic methods of successful change. Then, as Mother Teresa advocated, you can be the catalyst for waves of change emanating outward from you, like the ripples from a cast stone hitting a still pond. The basics of how to mobilize those waves are covered in this book.

The False Promise of Mandates

People who are frustrated about the progress of a change effort often say, "If only we could get the CEO to make a mandate." This sentiment exposes the underlying assumption many people have that communities or organizations change by having powerful people tell the rest of the community what to do. In an organization, the people holding this belief want the senior leadership team to show strong sponsorship and create a clear vision. Then, if the leader of the organization tells the employees to change, they must do it, right?

Not exactly. Influence from powerful people is important, but not the complete solution. I will tell a quick story to show why. About 10 years ago, I experienced this vividly while working in the IT organization of a Fortune 500 networking equipment manufacturer. One of the IT teams had discovered that software applications were being made and deployed to production servers at an accelerating rate. But many of these applications had very low usage. The net effect was escalating support costs with little added value.

The root cause of this proliferation of applications was what is called in IT "a solution looking for a problem." This means the application development teams were creating and deploying applications based on a seemingly promising idea, rather than a solid understanding of the user's needs. To counteract this situation, the CIO was petitioned to make a public statement advocating developers to ensure they were conducting proper analysis before making applications.

The announcement was made at a strategic planning offsite comprising 300 IT managers, directors, and vice-presidents. The offsite was a big, expensive show—a multi-day conference held at a large casino resort in Reno, Nevada. Managers flew in from all over the world to attend the event, which was a kick-off for the next fiscal year. There were carefully prepared presentations, high-profile industry speakers, professional audiovisual production, lavish entertainment, and the clear presence of investment in time and resources in an important company event. One of the main themes was how the IT department could improve itself.

On the first morning, the CIO took the stage and clearly explained that the IT department tended to build and deploy applications without a full understanding of the problem to be solved. The CIO showed a graph with a steeply rising line depicting hundreds of IT applications being produced every year, and he noted a considerable number of those applications had little usage. Over the ensuing two days of the conference, the recurring theme was that IT managers should ensure applications were not developed without a clear value case.

The IT managers returned to their home offices in various parts of the world. About a week later, I was in a project planning meeting with a director and some managers who had been at the Reno meeting. The conversation went as follows:

```
DIRECTOR: We need to get this skills inventory ap-
plication going as quickly as possible.

PROJECT MANAGER: We'll need to do some research on
the requirements and put together a program plan.

DIRECTOR: Okay, that's fine, but we don't want to
have "paralysis by analysis."

PROJECT MANAGER: But without the analysis, we
might be building an application that doesn't get
used.

DIRECTOR: I'm not saying we shouldn't do analysis,
but we don't want to get stuck in it and not get
anything done. It's clear that this application is
needed.
```

Everyone nodded, and the conversation moved on to discussing dates for completing various parts of the design of the skills inventory database *without doing the requirements analysis.* So, without a conscious decision, the group completely dropped the idea to explore the value case, even though the CIO of the company had thoroughly demanded more thorough analysis of requirements only a week earlier.

Was the director at fault? It depends on how you look at it. He did not follow the expectations of the CIO. But he may not have even been conscious of having affirmed the status quo, and no-one else dared speak up. Most likely, the director believed he was doing what was best for the company.

What could have happened instead? There are at least two possibilities.

- The director could have proactively evaluated the impacts of taking time to incorporate a more rigorous planning process and renegotiated expectations with others. However, the director probably did not consider that step, nor did he believe that doing more planning would be worthwhile.

- The program manager could have taken a stronger stance or tried to negotiate a mutually acceptable way of conducting the analysis. But, the program manager either did not feel safe in challenging the director or did not have the skills to do it safely.

The fact that certain behaviors occurred, and other behaviors did not, is the result of conditioning. This conditioning happens in all relationships and involves the subconscious and automatic reactions people have in response to situations they encounter throughout the day. Most of these reactions occur on auto-pilot, without much consideration of the underlying assumptions, which might have changed. Thus, this story illustrates a core tenet of organizational change to always keep in mind:

> *All change in an organization or society ultimately comes down to change in individual behavior and relationships.*

Systems of People

How does an organization work? Probably most people think of a hierarchy with the CEO or president at the top. Ideally, the CEO is highly charismatic and visionary, along the lines of Steve Jobs or Elon Musk. In this kind of system, a mandate seems to make sense. It is an intuitive, yet somewhat deceiving, concept of how organizations work.

First, while people frequently remember the big-name, celebrity leader more favorably, those leaders are not necessarily the most successful, especially if a big ego is driving them. Research by author Jim Collins found, "In more than two-thirds of the comparison companies, we noted the presence of a gargantuan ego that contributed to the demise or continued mediocrity of the company."[3] Instead, Collins found the most successful leaders are characterized by humility and firm resolve.

Second, our ability to see how change can work is often constrained by our mental models of organizations. Organizations are complex, and nobody has the mental capacity to comprehend everything about an organization or community of any size. So, we create simplified mental models in our heads and on paper to make them easier to grasp.

The most pervasive and enduring model of an organization was initiated around 1854 when Daniel McCallum, the general superintendent of New York and Erie Railroad, came up with an ingenious solution to

Figure 1-1. First Organizational Chart

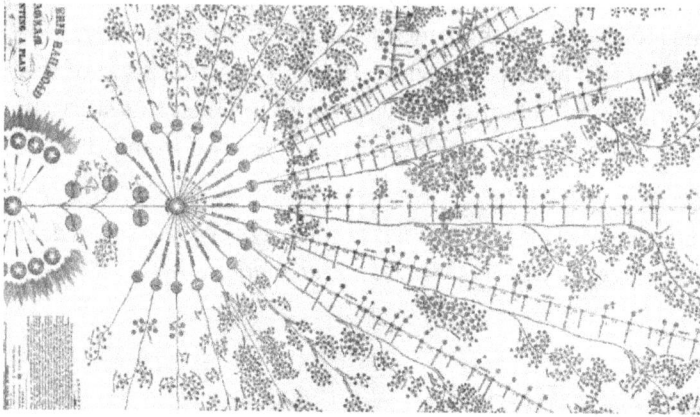

simplifying the complexity of rail operations. McCallum — a Scottish-born, self-educated engineer, inventor, and Union general — found himself faced with rising costs for transporting goods. He believed these rising costs were caused by inefficiencies arising from not knowing who was responsible for what duties in the organization. He thus had a large, tree-like diagram created, part of which is shown in Figure 1-1. His position was at the center of the tree, shown on the left side of the drawing, and the positions of all his staff were on branches that radiated outward. McCallum's drawing was one of the first *organization charts.*[4]

Although it took decades for the concept to catch on, and the chart was ultimately depicted more often as a pyramid like that shown in Figure 1-2. The organization chart is now used in almost every organization of any size. However, the ubiquity of the organization chart is also a barrier to how we think about changing organizations. When we have used a model for so long, we can fall into the trap of believing it is reality, rather than just a representation of reality. As the famous philosopher of general semantics Alfred Korzybski observed in a 1931 conference paper, "the map is not the territory."[5] Maps are abstractions of reality: They simplify it, so we can focus on what is perceived to be important at the expense of over-looking other things. Too often, the map is confused for the territory.

As we saw in the story of the director who shut down proper pro-ject planning, the territory of an organization—meaning the structure of relationships and influence—is much more nuanced than an organiza-tional chart reveals. Besides the CEO, people are influenced by many other people. In an organization, this might include colleagues, partners, stake-holders, direct reports, and a direct manager. Or, in a family, this might involve children, relatives, neighbors, spouses, and parents.

Figure 1-2. The Classic Organization Chart

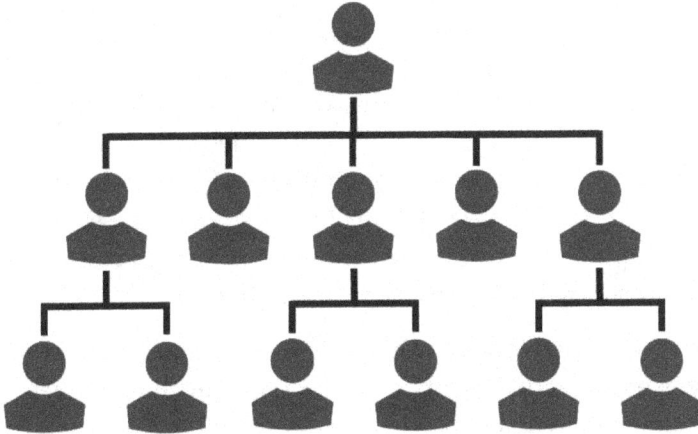

The advent of social media has made us much more aware of this. Popular platforms like Facebook can show diagrams of who is connected to whom among your friends. This kind of view enables us to conceptual-ize our community as a social network, as shown in the diagram below. Our relationships create a *people system*.

We begin to see that many other people influence a person beyond just the people in the management chain. The hierarchical reporting rela-tionships shown in an organizational chart still exist, as shown by the square lines in the middle of the diagram. But other relationships exist con-currently. So, while the organization chart remains useful, it is only one of many possible views.

Figure 1-3. Organization as System of Relationships

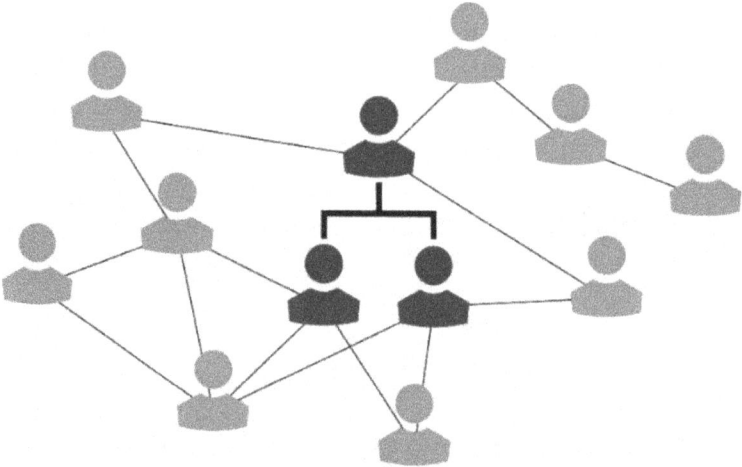

Besides the network view that we have been discussing, we could also look at the organization as a process model, which focuses on flows of value and communications through group of stakeholders. As author and systems-scholar Dr. Bela H. Banathy often asserted, seeing the world through multiple models, or lenses, in fact gives a much more comprehensive view, much like having two eyes versus one.[6]

The social network view helps us see forms of influence other than power, so we can realize we often attribute too much to the person at the top. We can get more insights when we focus on the relationships of a set of stakeholders who share a common purpose. This purpose might be to provide a web application, deliver hot meals to the homeless, or just emotionally support each other and have fun as a family. This leads us to an important new definition:

> *When people work together toward a shared purpose, they form a network of relationships called a people system.*

Change Resistance

The relationships in people systems create certain regular dynamics. One of these dynamics is to maintain the stability of the system. As shown in the story of the director who discouraged proper project planning, the existing people system is maintained through seemingly ordinary comments made by countless people in situations occurring throughout the daily activities of the organization or community. These comments serve to herd wayward people back to the status quo. Thus, those questioning the accepted approaches are shut down, and innovative ideas are declared too complex or risky. People who might provide a fresh perspective are not invited to meetings because they might be too disruptive.

The people who discourage change are likely not conscious of doing so. They usually believe, often based on past success and education, that their decisions are for the good of the company. Moreover, during regular business operations, they may be doing exactly what is needed for the company. They are keeping product flowing, getting projects done, and ensuring revenue comes in. They are trying to maintain order.

So, these relationships tend to keep the system stable. They compensate for things that are out of whack that might threaten the system. They maintain harmony in families and keep companies making money. Yet, while these stabilizing actions are essential to order, they can also keep the community from changing. In the context of a change, the people who are maintaining the existing system are obstructionists. The effect of their efforts to maintain order is often called *resistance to change*.

What is interesting about people systems is that the relationships are maintained by perceptions and beliefs, not physical laws. These perceptions arise from what we believe other people think. Other people are acting per reality as they perceive it now, but it can change. This is where we must be careful about projecting our incorrect beliefs on others and making attributions about their motives. Our beliefs about others can make change seem impossible or take us down strange paths.

For example, in our previous story, no doubt some people would argue the director was not following "orders" or being "accountable." But thinking the problem is the director's lack of accountability would fall into what is called the *fundamental attribution error*. This is the tendency where we attribute the failings of others to presumed personality flaws, while attributing our own failings to external factors we had no control over.

If we consider the situation from the perspective of the director in our earlier story, we can see how blaming the director could be an instance of the fundamental attribution error. The director was under pressure from clients to deliver a solution, and people around him had universally agreed the solution sounded like the right thing to do. He thought, "Doing research will only waste time in getting to what we already know we need to do. There isn't time to wait." Even though he agreed in principle with the approach of defining the requirements clearly, he simultaneously believed everyone around him agreed the decision was obvious. In his view, he was doing what was best for the company. And he was not alone. The same decision was made many times over by many other managers in various settings over the weeks following the leadership offsite as they acted within a system of well-conditioned expectations and relationships.

Thus, to create positive change, we must take an empathetic attitude toward others. We must avoid labeling them as change resistors, and assume they are doing their best given their current understanding of the situation. This opens the door to productive conversation and exploration of assumptions. To avoid falling into the fundamental attribution error oneself, it is critical to internalize this:

> *Assume that others are doing their best, given the current understanding of the situation, unless there is substantial evidence to the contrary.*

Change Adoption

Habitual relationships can hinder change, but those same relationships can also help create change. This occurs because our perceptions of the world are formed by the information we receive. Since we cannot practically conduct our own original research for everything, we watch the news, talk to our friends, read books, and observe what other people do. Thus, most of the information we get is from other people, whether directly or via some media. While certain people are completely unknown to us — journalists and scientists for example — others are relatives and friends we have known for years.

It's often said, "People don't change." It is true that they might not change dramatically or frequently, but they do in fact change, sometimes rapidly. A 2015 *Bloomberg* article by Alex Tribou and Keith Collins charted the pace of change of several major social attitudes over the last 200-plus years. This analysis showed how attitudes toward interracial marriage, prohibition, women's suffrage, abortion, same-sex marriage, and recreational marijuana changed very rapidly once the change got underway.[7] The acceleration of change typically happens in a pattern we refer to as "viral" in the Internet age.

To understand how this works in a fun and simplified way, we can examine how a viral video occurs. The basic behavior to be adopted is watching the video. We will explore: How does a person decide to watch it? And how does watching it become an epidemic?

For our case study, consider the 2007 internet sensation, "Leave Britney Alone," by Tennessee teen Chris Crocker. The video was one of the most famous (or infamous) viral videos of the year, and both the video maker and its subject were highly controversial.

Viral Adoption

The video conveys Crocker's highly emotional appeal for ending media criticism of pop singer Britney Spears. At the time, Spears was subjected to intense media interest, as she was one of the most searched for names on the Internet and the target of continuous pursuit by paparazzi.[8] Beyond her music success, her personal life had become of such great public interest that details of her divorce and increasingly erratic behavior routinely made national news. During this time, she gave a widely-panned performance at the 2007 MTV Video Music Awards, and the subsequent withering condemnation compelled Crocker, presenting himself as a transgendered teen at the time, to make a tearful, crying video in her defense where he implored the media to "leave Britney alone!"

Crocker posted the first part of the video on his Myspace account and a second part on YouTube.[9] He had already posted some 60 videos on assorted topics and had a sizable following.[10] The YouTube version was the one that got considerable attention.

At first, the video only got the attention of his subscribers and some portion of people who searched for Britney Spears. We will call this group the first adopters. Then, this group liked and shared the video with their friends. Not only did this increase the sphere of adopters, but also raised the visibility of the video in YouTube rankings, bringing it to the attention of more people.

The increased adoption of the video created a "snowball effect" where more adopters leads to even more adopters. This is because the visibility is raised. When more people see the video on "top video" rankings, the likelihood of them hearing about it from a friend or even more than one friend is higher. This effect increases even more because there begins to be a sense of being left out—now everyone has seemingly seen it but you, so you are more compelled to watch it.

In Crocker's case, there was soon so much attention that the national news began covering the video. Crocker was then interviewed by several prominent news organizations. And of course, this led to even more adopters.

Along the way, other secondary effects began. Besides the supporters, there were detractors, either against Spears or the quality of the video. Moreover, because Crocker appeared transgendered, his personality created controversy as he became a symbol for some groups and the object of hatred by others. This was based on his apparent transgendered message, not having anything to do with the video itself. These groups further fueled the notoriety and exposure of the video.

Ultimately, there was a limit to the number of people who had any interest in the story, and the adoption rate died off. The pattern though, like almost all change has followed the classic S curve as shown in Figure 1-4. It had a slow start with a few first adopters followed by rapid acceleration and then leveling off as the number of remaining possible adopters were depleted. The same pattern was followed with social changes like abortion legalization, as mentioned above. The differences are in the rate of acceleration, the ultimate number of adopters, and whether the adoption is sustained.

The 'viral video' is an example of **diffusion**, which is explained by **diffusion theory**, which focuses on how an innovation, such as a product or behavior, is adopted across a population of individuals. This dynamic has been extensively studied by researchers, and the seminal work in the field is Everett Rogers' *The Diffusion of Innovations*.[11] In this work, Dr. Rogers synthesizes many studies conducted over 50 years. This work, in addition to the work of Mark Granovetter on threshold levels,[12] has proven out numerous times in practice and should be considered a bedrock understanding about how change works.

Figure 1-4. S Curve

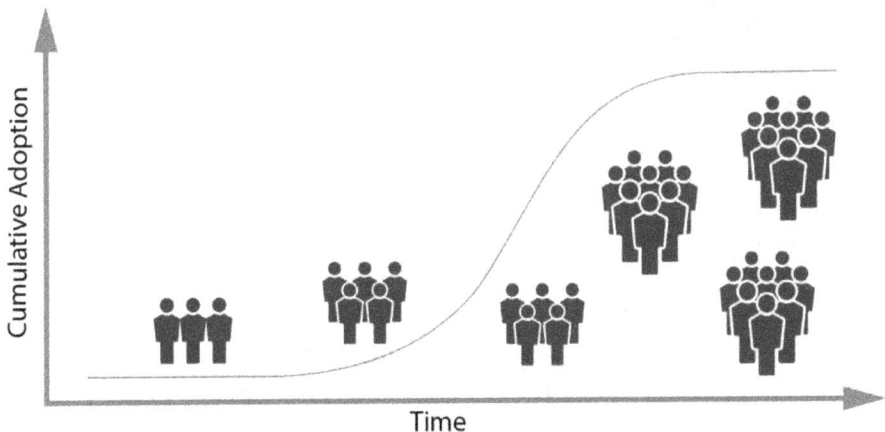

So, change practitioners should remember the following:

Change occurs through a diffusion process involving several groups of adopters who engage each other in a sequence mainly driven by interpersonal influence.

Personal Appeal

We have discussed how watching the video propagated, but why were people interested at all? We will use the term ***stakeholders*** to refer to people who have an interest—favorable or unfavorable—in some potential change. We can then look at how stakeholders might react through some of the factors outlined in the work of Harvard psychologist Howard Gardner.[13]

- **The right narrative.** When a story is found that stakeholders can see themselves in, then attitudes begin to shift. At the time of Crocker's video, there was great interest in Britney Spears in general. There was also an emerging interest in transgender issues, so Crocker's message gave voice to several different stakeholder groups.

- **Timing.** A change message needs to come at the right time. Other situational factors can be at play—during a crisis, attention might be focused elsewhere. In the case of Crocker's video, odds are that had it been released even a few months earlier or later, it might have gone unnoticed. The interest in Spears would likely have been less, or other national news might have been more attention grabbing.

- **Real benefits.** There should be benefits to the stakeholders. In the case of the video, it was on the surface just entertaining. But, it temporarily then became a way to connect with others and to introduce issues of media influence and attitudes toward transgenderism.

- **Rationality.** The narrative needs to make sense. Stakeholders are often attracted based on feeling, but ultimately the proposed change needs to be plausibly rational. While Crocker's style and presentation were extreme, his basic argument was reasonable. During that time, talk of too much media and paparazzi attention was pervasive. The death Anna Nicole Smith was fresh; other promising stars like Lindsay Lohan were also exhibiting outlandish behavior that many attributed to excess media attention; there were concerns about dangerous paparazzi behavior, such as dangerous driving that allegedly contributed to the death of Princess Diana.

Issues of motivation and stakeholder perceptions are a deep topic we will explore further in later chapters. For now, it is important to keep in mind that our target audience is the stakeholder, who can be defined this way:

Stakeholders are expected to adopt new, ongoing behaviors.

Sustainability

Notice that our definition of a stakeholder included the word "on-going." While viral videos are useful for demonstrating some key dynamics of change, there are crucial differences between viral videos and real change in organizations and communities. One of those key differences is the ongoing adoption of a behavior. That is, a person usually only watches a video a few times at most. For example, see Figure 1-5 which shows the hits for Crocker's video. [14] There was a rapid acceleration at first, so fast you that you hardly see the S shape, and then it quickly drops off.

In real change, we need the behavior to be ongoing, or sustained. To explore this further, we can look at the case of residential recycling in the United States. Prior to the 1970s, residential recycling in the United States was largely unknown. There were bottle-return deposits and people tended to re-use items more than simply throw them out. But these were relatively few cases. When concern grew about the huge amount of waste was being generated by modern consumer society with its prevalence of

Figure 1-5. Rise and Fall of "Leave Britney Alone" Video

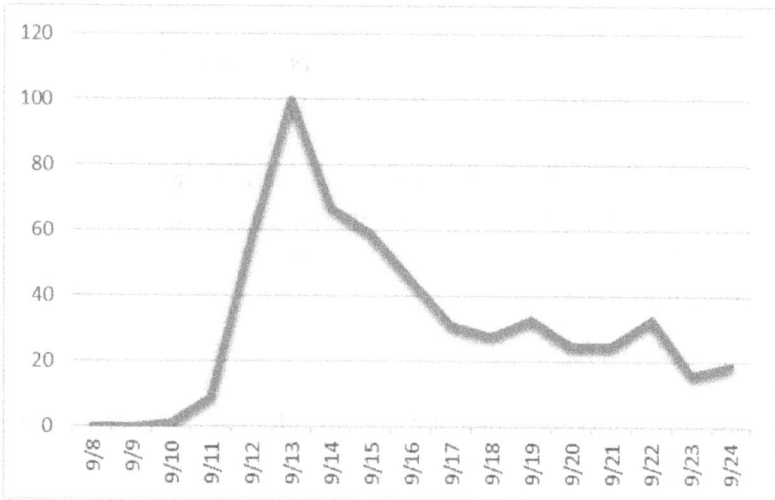

disposable products, several organizations, both commercial and non-profit, as well as politicians, organized to raise awareness of the problem. These parties created a new narrative calling for citizens to be at least partially responsible for the waste that was being created. This resulted in events like Earth Day and the beginning of community-based curbside collection programs for recyclable materials.[15]

Since the 1960s, the recycling rate has climbed and maintained, even though it is largely a cost to stakeholders.[16] The benefit is feeling good about helping sustain the environment, even though the individual may never personally experience the benefit. This has happened because a self-supporting system of mutual relationships has formed, replacing the old conditioned relationships. Some of the factors are as follows:

- **Easier.** Over time, it has become easier to recycle. Rather than collecting items and taking them to a recycling center or remembering to take bottles back to get your deposit, many communities, restaurants, and businesses have specific containers available for sorting and collecting recyclable material. In the beginning, you had to cut the little cellophane windows out of the envelopes, but later it wasn't necessary, so it became as simple as throwing it in the right bin, which was colored. Recyclable items began being marked with the recycle icon.

- **Expectations developed.** As more people recycled, peer pressure was created on others. If you do not follow along, you look out of place or not supportive of the community.

- **Integration.** Beyond the curbside collection, recycling is further integrated in people's lives. Besides the waste collection methods, recycling is taught in schools. Many disposable containers are now made of materials that are easier to recycle.[17]

- **Incentives.** Although the motivation to recycle is largely altruistic, there are incentives in place. Many communities and programs offer incentives for recycling, such as bottle deposits, battery deposits, and so on. Some communities have passed laws requiring recycling.[18]

A change that is not sustained is probably not worth the effort to put in place. For this reason, it is important to remember:

> *A change program that is not embedded in the ongoing behaviors of the stakeholders is not finished.*

Building the Plane While Flying It

Apart from knowing how people adopt a change spontaneously, we must be able to manifest it intentionally. Soon after I completed a doctorate in organizational systems in the early 2000s, I set out to immediately to apply the techniques and research I had learned at the major computer networking company. I thought amazing change would happen. Yet, I got no traction on this at all. Even more, my performance was questioned, and I nearly got canned.

Of course, as a certified expert, I thought everyone was wrong — at first. But after listening to a lot of difficult feedback, I began to realize that while I was still right in many ways, I was also a wrong in a key way. That key problem was that a lot of the research in the field was not directly feasible in real life because the research assumed pristine conditions, perfect communications, and a step-by-step approach to change. These approaches made nice books and satisfy our rational minds but could not be further from reality.

In real change situations, there is never enough time for a pristine initiative and conditions are always changing. Deadlines are driven by external factors. A lot of poor decisions get made that are outside your control. New requirements and needs arise unexpectedly. The solution changes, budgets get reduced, and conflicting priorities limit the program.

Here is one way to look at it. The traditional approach embodies an assumption that the change process is like an aircraft construction project, where some engineers (the executives) create a plan and implement the plan. Metal, windows, fittings, electronic gear and myriad other pieces are gathered. The frame is created, engines are installed, and controls are put in place. Everything is tested, and actions are checked off along the way to track progress. The newly constructed aircraft is rolled out of the hanger to great fanfare as a completed project. But, an organization is like a plane that is already in the air: Ongoing operations must be maintained; services must continue to be designed, built, and delivered; contracts must be met; payrolls must be distributed. Thus, in a real situation, we must "build the plane while flying it."

This reality inspired me to think: **What kind of a change approach could deal with inherent chaos?** I came up with these key organizing principles.

- **Responsiveness.** The approach must offer a way to sense the conditions.

- **Flexibility.** To deal with inherent ambiguity, the approach needs to be malleable with the ability to be right-sized to the situation.

- **Modularity.** There must be modularity, to avoid completely redesigning the approach every time the situation changes. Consistent modules must be available that can be applied like building blocks when appropriate.

- **Aptness.** The approach should not ask for more than the organization can do. We should meet them where they are at. This means offering approaches that others can understand without a large time investment upfront. It also means focusing on delivering what is needed and not more.

In the next section, we look at a model that would embody these principles.

The Generating Change Model

With the principles outlined in the preceding section, our model should be driven by understanding what is needed to advance the change, not by the next step to be checked off. As discussed, the change is advanced by a diffusion process, or dynamic between people who influence each other and provide social proof that that the change is good and safe. Note that while a top-down leadership directive might start the change off, it is not the sole dynamic which determines if the change is propagated.

Using diffusion theory and other research to be discussed further later, we can identify some *critical success factors*, or interim outcomes, that are necessary for success. These are as follows:

- *Clarity and alignment* on the intended outcome by a core group of *formal and informal leaders*. Clarity creates focus. Moreover, it is very difficult to achieve results wen acting alone, without the support of influential people.

- A viable *design* for what is to be changed. The change must be adoptable by the target population, and it is often best designed by working participatively with stakeholders.

- *Involvement of early adopters* in successfully using the change.

- *Support for the early adopters* in scaling their influence on others.

- *Evolving and embedding* the framework that provides the support for large-scale adoption.

While these critical success factors suggest states, they do not remain static in real life. That is, the clarity and alignment of leadership waxes and wanes; seemingly good designs suddenly exhibit flaws. So rather than treating these like steps to be completed, you must organize on going actions, or *functions*, to keep the critical success factors in place. You create a people system that continuously galvanizes your supporters to action, creates the narrative, designs the changes, influences the first adopters to engage others, and embeds incentives. You create a *change system*, which is a type of people system, that generates change in the target people system.

For simplicity, we can group the actions needed in our change system into four major ongoing activities, or *functions*. These are Align, Design, Involve, and Evolve. Each function moves the adoption progress forward along the diffusion S curve, as shown in the figure below.

Figure 1-6. Generating Change Model

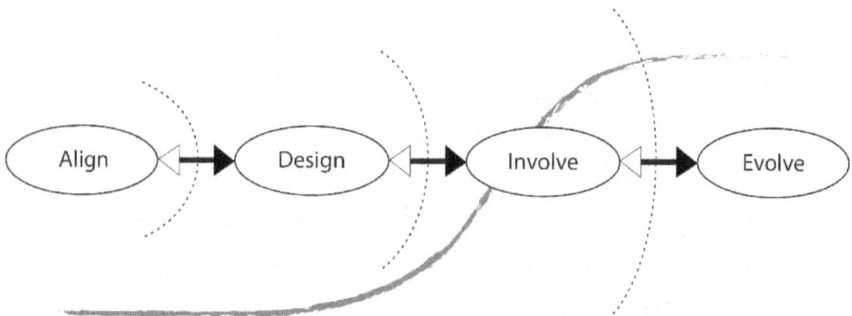

As shown by the arrows in the figure, each function propagates influence toward the right. For example, clear ideas lead to better, more detailed designs, and better designs lead to better engagement of first adopters. But, this is not strictly unidirectional; rather, as each function operates, discoveries happen, and learning occurs. So, the function can also inform the outcomes of the function on its left, as indicated by the hollow arrows.

I call this the Generating Change Model, and the remaining four parts of this book are organized to cover each of the major change functions of the model. Within each part, there are several chapters providing specific instruction on how to employ the relevant module of organizational change best practices. While those new to organizational change might benefit by reading from the beginning, it is not necessary. Each chapter is designed to detail the application of a specific organizational change practice. Experienced practitioners can likely use the chapters in a standalone fashion to address their current challenges.

Moreover, the model is designed to assess the critical success factors of the situation and design the appropriate methods that are needed to move the change forward. This is shown in Figures 1-7 and 1-8.

Learning the material in this book takes an investment of time and study. Moreover, you will need to get out in the world, observe what is happening from a new perspective, try things, and consider what you have learned. To facilitate this learning process, most chapters have a summary in the form of a "cheat sheet" of key points you can keep in your back pocket, laptop bag, or smart phone. Then, you can pull these out as a reminder when you are in the heat of the moment.

Cheat Sheet

This chapter looked at some of the core dynamics of creating change. This consideration led to the set of guiding ideas summarized below.

Figure 1-7. The Generating Change Assessment

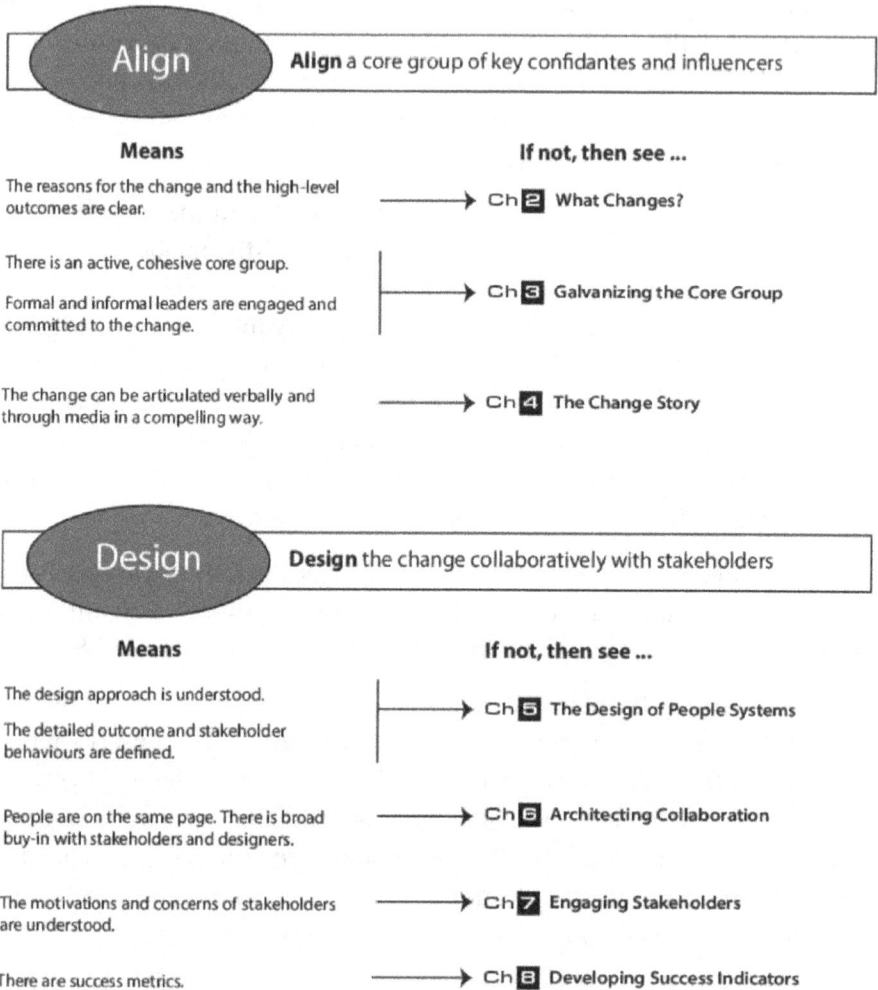

| Align | Align a core group of key confidantes and influencers |

Means	If not, then see ...
The reasons for the change and the high-level outcomes are clear.	→ Ch **2** What Changes?
There is an active, cohesive core group. Formal and informal leaders are engaged and committed to the change.	→ Ch **3** Galvanizing the Core Group
The change can be articulated verbally and through media in a compelling way.	→ Ch **4** The Change Story

| Design | Design the change collaboratively with stakeholders |

Means	If not, then see ...
The design approach is understood. The detailed outcome and stakeholder behaviours are defined.	→ Ch **5** The Design of People Systems
People are on the same page. There is broad buy-in with stakeholders and designers.	→ Ch **6** Architecting Collaboration
The motivations and concerns of stakeholders are understood.	→ Ch **7** Engaging Stakeholders
There are success metrics.	→ Ch **8** Developing Success Indicators

- All change in an organization or society ultimately comes down to change in individual behavior and relationships. People behave the way they do because they believe their behavior is the best approach to the situation as they perceive it. People exist in systems of relationships that place expectations on them and require specific skills to manage.

Figure 1-8. The Generating Change Assessment(cont.)

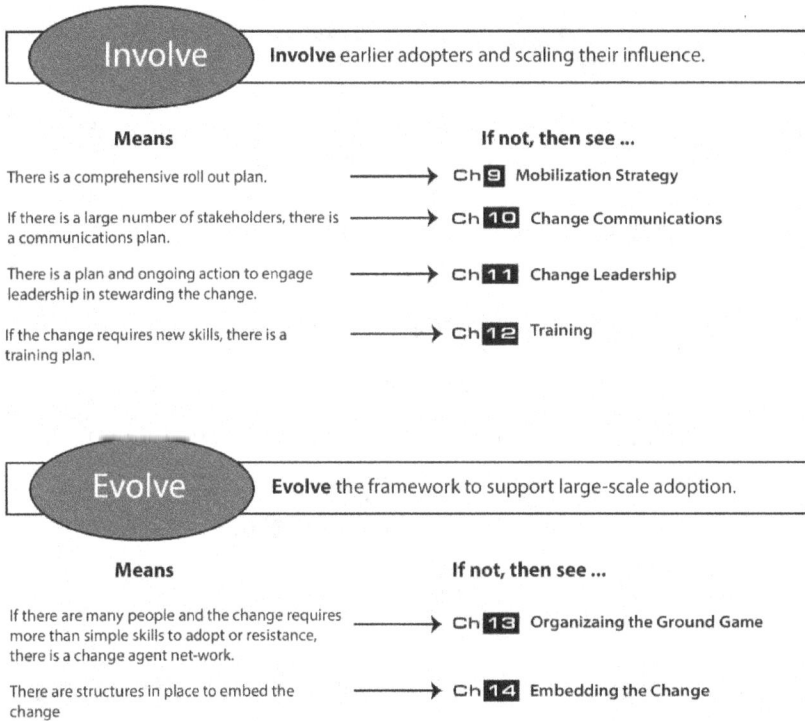

Involve **Involve** earlier adopters and scaling their influence.

Means   **If not, then see ...**

There is a comprehensive roll out plan. ⟶ Ch **9** Mobilization Strategy

If there is a large number of stakeholders, there is ⟶ Ch **10** Change Communications
a communications plan.

There is a plan and ongoing action to engage ⟶ Ch **11** Change Leadership
leadership in stewarding the change.

If the change requires new skills, there is a ⟶ Ch **12** Training
training plan.

Evolve **Evolve** the framework to support large-scale adoption.

Means   **If not, then see ...**

If there are many people and the change requires ⟶ Ch **13** Organizaing the Ground Game
more than simple skills to adopt or resistance,
there is a change agent net-work.

There are structures in place to embed the ⟶ Ch **14** Embedding the Change
change

- When people work together toward a shared purpose, they form a network of relationships called a ***people system***.

- Assume that others are doing their best, given the current understanding of the situation, unless there is substantial evidence to the contrary. Organizations respond to change attempts and seek to maintain the status quo. While inherently, organizations must maintain stability of operations to survive, this also means the organization will tend to cancel out change attempts if they appear to threaten the dynamic equilibrium.

- Change occurs through a diffusion process involving several groups of adopters who engage each other in a sequence mainly driven by interpersonal influence.

- *Stakeholders* are expected to adopt new, ongoing behaviors.

- A change program that does not embedded incentives and structure to encourage ongoing behaviors of the stakeholders is not finished.

To create change in the target system, you need to organize a change system that will generate the influence needed. This book proposes a change system based on the Generating Change Model. The model comprises four basic functions, each intended to achieve a critical success factor needed to create a change.

- *Align* a core group of key formal and informal leaders.

- Use a core group to develop the *design* of what changes.

- *Involve* earlier adopters to use the design and support them in scaling their influence to others.

- *Evolve* the framework that provides the support for large-scale adoption.

If you can bring these together, then you can wield your personal influence to create waves that ultimately change communities, corporations, and even society.

PART II: Align

The Align function is the activity of aligning key leaders and influencers on the intended outcomes and organizing the leadership community to guide and steward the change.

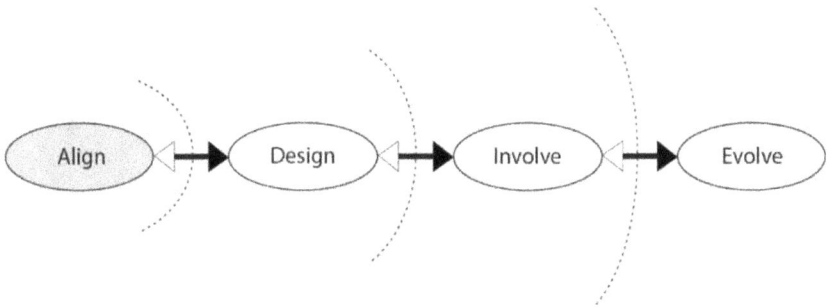

Align ◁━▶ Design ◁━▶ Involve ◁━▶ Evolve

2

What Changes?

Everyone thinks of changing the world, but no one thinks of changing himself.

—Leo Tolstoy

Since you are the primary driver of the change effort, getting started means getting clear yourself on what you plan to accomplish. That is, what is the ultimate outcome? When you want to change something, you might be quite excited about it. Others might also be excited. Emotion is high, and there is a desire to get moving. But research and experience have shown that spending the time to conduct an appropriate amount of upfront planning generally leads to better results.

This chapter covers some questions you can use first with yourself and then later with others when building a core group. Like many aspects of organizational change, this method is executed recursively with expanding communities of people. Review the key questions in this chapter, and then you can use them as a guiding framework to fall back on if things get chaotic or mired down, as they often do.

It is important to think about these questions yourself and work out your initial understanding. Your understanding may change, but the process provides a key learning for you in how to talk to others, as discussed in subsequent chapters.

Why Change Now?

The first question is simply "Why is the change important now?" We are deepening what might start as a feeling or an insight to an idea based on more objective underpinnings. The need for change may seem clear—even obvious—and analyzing the situation further could seem like a waste of time. Yet, before proceeding headlong down the path of implementation, it is critical to turn your feelings about needing a change into a *case for change* that provides a logical and well-considered basis for conducting the change effort.

This is not to say all change efforts must be exhaustively researched before being started. Ideas for change often start as an appealing notion. John Kotter and Dan Cohen are frequently quoted as saying a change initiative is usually launched based on SEE-FEEL-CHANGE rather than ANALYZE-THINK-CHANGE.[1] This is perhaps unavoidable and even necessary, because the passion for the change propels the change initiative forward in the initial stages. If people are not engaged in the change emotionally, the effort goes nowhere, regardless of how logical it is. However, there is also danger that seemingly obvious, exciting ideas will fall apart on closer inspection.

For example, in 2006, an exciting little company named Pure Digital Technologies was founded. The company marketed a line of Flip Video camcorders. These camcorders were easy to use, took great videos, and fit easily in a pocket. One version, the Flip Ultra, became the top-selling camcorder on Amazon. The cameras were marketed extensively, showing people having huge fun sharing videos. In 2009, Cisco Systems, wanting to enter the consumer electronics market, bought this company for $590 million. Yet, roughly two years later, Cisco announced the shutdown of the company. Analysts will debate whether it was Cisco's unfamiliarity with the consumer market or the rise of smartphone-based camcorders that spelled the death knell for Flip Video, but, analysts all agree Cisco got distracted by the excitement of the product and selling it to consumers.[2] A more carefully thought-out case for change would have revealed a more realistic view of the longer-term viability of the product.

In addition to grounding the idea, another reason to create a solid case for change is that while people at first engage emotionally, they will ultimately demand the idea makes sense.[3] People are going to ask "why?" and if they do not get an acceptable answer, their enthusiasm for the change will be diminished. So, while a change might get started based on passion, and the emotional aspects might create compelling communications, there is still the need to create a solid case for change. Thus, it might be more accurate to say a change is launched based on SEE-FEEL-ANA-LYZE-CHANGE.

One way to turn a feeling for a change into a case for change is by analyzing the factors underlying the feeling. Often, the case for change results from, and is grounded on, the partial realization of actual or perceived changes in the operating environment. For example, digitization has dramatically transformed the business models of traditional retail stores, such as booksellers and video renters. Similarly, regulatory changes from Sarbanes-Oxley created costs for companies who had to ensure compliance, but simultaneously created benefits for accounting companies who provided the auditing.

Use the following questions to explore the basic factors more fully:

- **What are the drivers?** A driver is an external force, such as market conditions, regulatory changes, competitor moves, demographic changes, and so on. Rising prices from suppliers could be reducing profitability, driving the need to find a new source. Or, an aging population could increase the demand for pharmaceuticals or single-floor housing.

- **What is the evidence?** What is the supporting evidence for these drivers? What is their projected impact, duration, and magnitude?

As an example, let us consider the case of trying to reduce green-house gases in the state of California.[4] Below are some bullet points sum-marized from the Nature Conservancy, which provide some key drivers motivating the need for such a program.

- The World Health Organization (WHO) estimates climate change may have caused more than 150,000 deaths in the year 2000 alone, with an increase in deaths likely in the future.

- The five hottest years on record have all occurred since 1997 and the 10 hottest since 1990, including the warmest years on record – 2005 and 2010.

- Deforestation, which produces more carbon than all planes, trains and cars worldwide, is responsible for approximately 15% of greenhouse gases emitted into the atmosphere each year. Over 25,000 acres of redwood, pine and oak forests are lost each year in California alone.

- Sea levels have risen between 4 and 8 inches in the past 100 years. Current projections suggest that sea levels could continue to rise between 4 inches and 36 inches over the next 100 years.

- Experts project that by the year 2050, San Francisco's climate will feel much like Los Angeles' and Los Angeles' climate will feel much like Bakersfield's.

From this list, you can see data points about external factors (not controlled by the proposed program) are provided. These data points reference studies that could be obtained for more depth or even to critique the points. This grounds feelings about the need for change in facts and rationale, creating a true case for change.

Note that using this approach helps us avoid a common pitfall. It is very common for people to respond to the question, "Why change?" with a phrase such as "lack of standardization" or "no alignment on vision." But, these kinds of phrases are about the lack of intended solution, not the actual problem or opportunity. That is, "standardization" is a solution to a problem like rising costs or quality problems, and "establishing a vision" is a solution to people being confused about the company direction. Using a "lack of" statement as the problem or opportunity gives a canned solution up front and thus tends to circumvent discussion about innovative options to solve the real issue.

What Outcome Do *We* Want?

Once we have identified an opportunity for change, the next question is, "What outcome do we want?" or "What good or benefit will be created?" This question is about the result. Without a compelling outcome in mind, it is difficult to maintain momentum and direction.

An outcome is different than just a description of a change, because the outcome implies the benefit or value. For example, suppose you plan to build an organization to manufacture robots. The robots would be the product, but they are not an outcome without being tied to the value. The outcome might be winning robot fights, providing transportation, or exploring Mars.

This leads us to the corollary question "Who benefits from the outcome?" Understanding who benefits from a change illuminates the challenges likely to be encountered. For instance, many internal changes are started essentially to produce reports for executives. Arguably, these reports improve the operation of the company for everyone. However, they are often seen as additional work for employees without any visible benefit. This makes the adoption difficult. Conversely, efforts benefitting employees, such as making it easier to submit routine reports, are often adopted much more easily. While there are bona fide needs in organizations for one group to benefit at the expense of another, the situation where only one group wins creates real obstacles to the change process. Being aware of this dynamic up front enables better decision-making about how to develop the design and mobilization strategies, as discussed in later chapters.

In the Nature Conservancy example given previously, the organization said, "Together with public and private partners we are developing comprehensive, nature-based programs to minimize greenhouse gas emissions and manage the statewide effects of climate-related changes." Presumably the beneficiary then is the inhabitants of the state and the world, while those impacted negatively — who must pay for the change — might be producers of greenhouse emissions.

What Are the Changes for the Stakeholders?

The outcome must be translated into tangible actions a person can perform. In project management or technology design, we determine the deliverables, such as aircraft or a house. But in organizational we are concerned with "What do we want people to do differently?"

As discussed in the previous chapter, the people who are affected by a change in an ongoing way are the *stakeholders*. The stakeholders in this definition are not the project team or the partners, who work on designing and delivering the change. Rather, the stakeholders are the people who adopt and perform the change indefinitely.

The stakeholders are expected to adopt new behaviors, where a behavior is an action attributed to a person. The behavior might be clicking buttons on an interface, asking new kinds of questions, or responding to a client in a more consultative fashion. Whenever there are people involved, we are ultimately looking for actions an individual can take.

Note that we are not talking about states of mind, like a "collaborative mindset." This kind of label is often given for change initiatives but must be translated into observable action to be tangible. While the new behaviors might require a shift of mind, we never know if a person has changed their mental models, we only know if they change their observable behavior. So, the essence of design in organizational change (as will be discussed in later chapters) is determining the behaviors that change or the conditions under which those behaviors are most likely to change.

At times, these behaviors are obvious from the start. When you are a parent, you can assign ongoing responsibilities to your children to cut the grass, do the dishes, and clean their rooms. But, in companies, especially those undergoing profound change, the ultimate core behaviors are often not knowable up front. For example, when a company wants to implement a new business model that has never been done before, the way it works must be figured out through an evolutionary process. An initial idea can be outlined, but its actual operation is only discovered when it is tried. It must be *designed* by participatively engaging stakeholders, leaders, and subject matter experts. (There is more about this in Chapter 5.)

Even if the behaviors are not fully knowable up front, it is a good practice to try to imagine them early on. Although some people may initially object, complaining the answer is too granular or not known, the activity will ground you in what the change effort will ultimately take. Many times, people want to focus only at the level of vision, strategy, and deliverables. But this hides the key issue in organizational change in that if the change is not adoptable, then it will fail.

There are numerous examples of this. For one, the United States has officially adopted and welcomed the metric system, used by most of the countries in the world, as a standard for arguably over 100 years. Yet, adoption of the metric system in United States remains low. There are many reasons, some related to poor execution of the adoption effort, but primarily it is low because it would take considerable resources to convert over and few people or businesses want to commit to such an investment. Up to now, the metric system has been largely unadoptable, despite the underlying logic, government support, and good intentions.

So, asking the question, "What will people do differently?" or "What changes for the stakeholders?" helps you think more deeply about the planned change. The question asks you to think from the stakeholder's perspective and get a sense of whether the proposed change is going to be welcomed or rejected.

Who Else Is Playing?

Often, an idea for change does not come up in isolation, and you are not the only one who has decided to act. Possibly, there are other people who are interested or working on the same opportunity or problem. Their approaches could be completely different or highly overlapping with yours; you might find they are further along and they can be good partners. Whichever is the case, it is a good practice to establish constructive relationships with others with similar intentions. This avoids conflicts, unwanted competition, and surprises down the road.

In this kind of analysis, you seek to determine, "Who else is playing?" What is their relationship to you and the intended solution? For example, I was recently involved in an effort seeking to establish a mentoring program for organizational change management practitioners. The intention was to have senior practitioners be available, if requested, to engage in a mentoring relationship with more junior practitioners. On researching the context, our change team discovered there was already a company-wide mentoring program that had an established structure and web-based database. While this corporate system did not have mentors or topics set up in the database for organizational change management, our change team quickly realized that adding to the existing system would be far easier than creating another solution from scratch.

The situation can be usefully illustrated using a context diagram. This facilitates creating a solid, shared understanding because the context diagram clearly shows your own effort and its relationships to others. As an example, a context drawing of the mentoring program is shown below.

The diagram clearly delineates the change team role as defining the topic area in the mentoring program and then encouraging mentors to sign up by submitting their mentor profile and mentees to find a mentor and make a request. The system then notifies the mentor, and a relationship is begun. In the diagram, the mentoring relationship is shown as bi-directional, recognizing that mentors often learn as much as mentees!

Figure 2-1. Example Context Map for Change Practitioner Mentoring Program

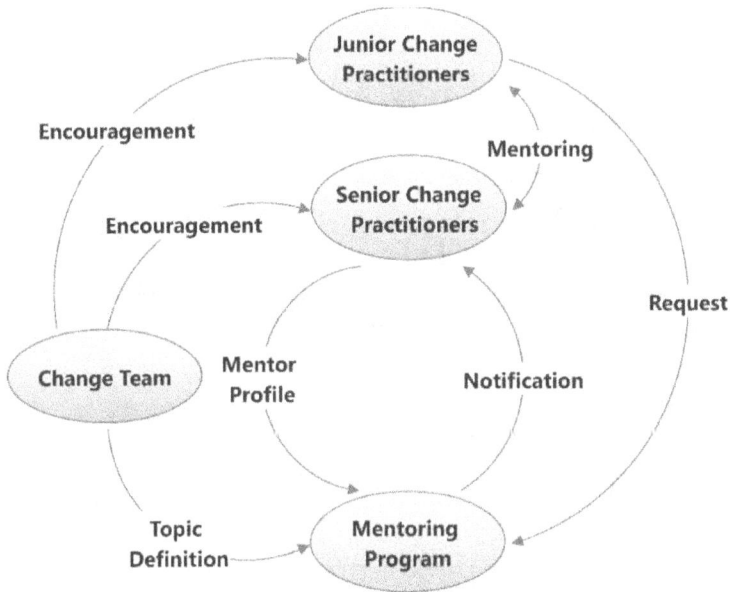

What Is the Failure Scenario?

For good planning, we should also ensure we are being realistic about what is required to accomplish the change. The difficulty, as organizational and social change practitioners often say, is that

> *Every system is perfectly designed to get the results it gets.*

This quote, reportedly coined by Paul Batalden,[5] has, to me, always cleverly insinuated how the intended change will likely be subverted by well-meaning people. While this will be explored much more fully in later stages, it is valuable to get a concept of it up front. One approach to doing so is to ask the question "What is the failure scenario?"

The failure scenario is a sequence of events that will cancel out the change, as our director did in Chapter 1. This pattern may have already derailed any previous attempts to implement the intended change, so we are seeking to learn from the past and not repeat previous mistakes. Asking for the sequence of events is important because it makes it much more real than just asking "what is the problem?"

In the climate controls example discussed above, the problem could be called "global warming," but this does not give us a way to know why it has not been yet addressed. The pattern is perhaps a sequence such as a) advocates try to influence greater regulation, and b) this is opposed by manufacturers and other business who are concerned about rising costs. It is worth keeping the nature of this counter-balancing loop in mind, because any change approach that cannot address this reaction will likely not succeed.

Cheat Sheet

In this section, we covered a series of questions to clarify what the change is about. These questions are listed below.

- **Why change now?** What is the rationale for changing? What makes this change important now?

- **What outcome do we want?** What is the ultimate benefit and who will receive it?

- **What are the changes for the stakeholders?** Will stakeholders consider the change a benefit or a threat? What actual behaviors will they do differently, and will this be easy or hard to accomplish?

- **Who else is playing?** Who are possible partners? Is someone already doing what you plan to do? What are the differences between what they are doing and what you plan to accomplish?

- **What is the failure scenario?** What is likely to go wrong? How might people react to the change?

Use these questions on yourself first to get clear on the change and your intentions. Later, use them to help form shared understanding with your core group, as discussed in the next chapter. The responses to the questions provide the foundation of future planning, messaging, and interactions with stakeholders.

3

Galvanizing the Core Group

Never doubt that a small group of thoughtful, committed citizens can change the world. Indeed, it is the only thing that ever has.

—*Margaret Mead*

All change starts with the change initiator reaching out to others. While a major change might ultimately involve thousands of people, usually this is the result of the initiator galvanizing a small group who then engages a wider group in an expanding circle, much like ripples emanating out from a stone falling into a lake.

Many people imagine the mechanism of change is primarily via the creation and dissemination of powerful messaging. For instance, this assumption was embodied in a Verizon advertisement a few years ago, where a young woman says, "So it stands to reason, my ideas will be powerful, if they are wise, infectious, if they are worthy, and if my thoughts have flawless delivery, I can lead the army that will follow." While certainly some people have had powerful ideas that sparked profound change, at the same time many great ideas have sputtered and died.

History is replete with these examples. In 2011, the world saw hugely inspiring messages that mobilized thousands, even millions, of people for the Arab Spring movements, yet little real change was established as of 5 years later.[1] This is because a great movement based on emotion will eventually be absorbed back into the prevailing system unless there is change to the structure of the people system. That is, many people must change the way they interact with each other, not just replace the person at the top.

So, when Steve Jobs stood alone on the big platform in his black shirt and jeans at Macworld 2007, we were awed by the presence of such a brilliant man introducing such an incredible product as the iPhone. We had the impression Jobs had yet again shaken the world with another groundbreaking invention. Yet, it was not really Jobs alone who did this; rather, it was Jobs and a cast of thousands. In particular, Apple senior vice-president Sir Jonathan Paul "Jony" Ive was the lead designer and conceptual mind for the iPhone. Additionally, as disclosed in recent court testimony, Apple Senior Vice President of IOS Scott Forstall built a team of 2,000 people who designed or redesigned almost every component of the iPhone.[a]

The bottom line is that, while visionary people are important, the change is much more likely to be adopted when the idea is backed by comprehensive organizing that spreads, shapes, refines, builds, and diffuses the change effort across a community of stakeholders. Thus, to initiate this wave of influence, you need to galvanize a *Core Group*. Your Core Group is a primary driver of change effort. This group is the central planning team and brain trust of the change effort; its members perform critical key functions to not only inspire and guide the change but also to involve others in the expanding circle of influence. The Core Group becomes a set of trusted advisors, collaborators — even co-conspirators — from whom you gather ideas, get feedback, and coordinate spreading influence.

Forming a Core Group has many benefits over trying to "go it alone." A cohesive Core Group can pull together skills you might not personally have, and it can harness a diversity of ideas for better decision-making and greater innovation. A well-chosen Core Group can also span organizational boundaries that might otherwise create functional silos. It is much harder to ignore a handful of voices speaking together than a single voice speaking alone. Thus, the well-executed establishment of the Core Group lays a groundwork for influencing the managers and key opinion leaders in the stakeholder community.

Convening

The Core Group members should be well chosen to execute their roles. Therefore, understanding how to select the best members is important even if you have a team assigned to you. The quality and set up of the membership have a critical effect on the results produced and being aware of the ideal qualities of members enables you to focus on finding and retaining the best group membership possible.

In forming your Core Group, you are building a coalition comprising usually two to ten people, although it could start as just yourself and grow. If the group grows beyond ten people, the level of commitment and participation needed often wanes. More time will be needed to coordinate the team, while more of the team members tend to "ride" along and let others do the work. This does not mean the team members are lazy: It just becomes more difficult to productively organize the work of everyone such that they are fully engaged. Then, some people on the team might feel less needed by the group and allow tasks they have outside the group to take priority. So, three to ten persons is a good rule of thumb. In large efforts, more people can be mobilized by breaking them into sub teams.

Review the steps below for guidance in assembling your Core Group. The quality of the group membership is a crucial factor contributing to success, so careful selection is important. Just because people are available does not mean they are the ideal team member. So, periodically reviewing and refining the membership of the Core Group is a valuable exercise. Note the initial selection is not necessarily the final selection: The Core Group membership might change over the duration of the change effort.

1. Create the Invitation

You enroll the Core Group members by inspiring them with your intention. All purposeful change begins with an intention to create a new future. This intention could be one you originated, or it could be one you were assigned from your manager. At the outset, the intention might be vague. It might already have broad-based acceptance by many people, or you might be the only one who believes in it. Regardless of the starting position, your intention must be fanned from a spark to a blaze, and this is accomplished by focusing your intention enough to marshal an increasing sphere of influence. In this way, the intention becomes stronger, clearer, and more appealing to all the potential adopters.

To accomplish this, the intention is formed into an initial *Invitation* that brings others into your sphere of influence. Creating the invitation starts with ensuring your own intention is clear, as you learned in the previous chapter. If people cannot understand your intention or why it is important, they will not support it. They may go along with you for a while out of friendship or because they are your employees, but if the invitation does not keep them engaged, their commitment to the change effort will fade.

Achieving clarity does not mean you must create a finalized or even detailed solution. It simply means being able to communicate clearly and effectively what you intend to change and why in a few sentences or paragraphs. The concept is like what is often called an "elevator pitch," but the invitation is less about selling and more about inviting.

The need for an invitation seems obvious but creating a good one takes practice. You need to craft your intention into a coherent explanation, at least at a high level, so people can latch on and begin to understand it. To do this, you should be able to answer the following questions:

- **What is the pain or opportunity?** All change results from some dissatisfaction with the status quo, either to avoid current pain or to pursue a better outcome. What is the benefit to be obtained? What is the intended outcome?

- **What might the solution look like?** In the initial stages, you might have a clear idea what change is needed. Or you may have little idea. Having only a limited idea of the change can be okay and even an advantage: That is, inviting more people to contribute to designing the solution can harness the power of multiple perspectives, whereas having a detailed solution might discourage their contributions. Nonetheless, to elicit the contributions of others, it is often helpful to have some rough, provisional ideas about how the outcome might be achieved to get them thinking — then let them add to it.

- **Who is likely affected?** Similarly, at the outset, it may be unclear who is exactly affected by the change. But, "guesstimating" who are the impacted stakeholders helps clarify the intention. For example, if the intention is to dramatically streamline the product ordering process, you can conjecture this will significantly make life easier for the people in this process and perhaps for your customers' buying agents.

- **What are you bringing to the table?** People will want to know your role in the effort. Are you the leader? How did you become involved? Why are you passionate about the change? What skills, experience, or resources are you contributing? When people know this about you, it will build your credibility and, consequently, their interest in proceeding.

- **What are you asking from them?** What do you want from others? How are you asking them to engage? What will be their role? Why will this be good for them? Consider adding language to assure them of the following:

  o   Their perspectives will be valued, and you invite them to jointly forge a shared intention for change.

  o   Once hearing the details of your intentions, you will be looking for commitment, not just attendance.

  o   Diverse and open conversation is desired. Dissenting opinions and honest feedback are welcome.

If you can answer the items above reasonably well, you have the rudiments of an invitation you can use to invite the Core Group. You do not need a detailed or fully researched response to these questions, just enough to explain your thinking to others. In this way, you turn your intention into an invitation to participate in exploring a change idea. Spending time crafting your message this way is highly worthwhile as it reduces time up front for people to understand the idea and makes your offer more likely to be accepted.

Your invitation could be spoken, or it could be written in an email, a meeting invite, or a website. Figure 3-1 shows an example from Indiana University with callouts for the key elements.

Figure 3-1. Example Invitation with Callouts

2. Identify Candidates

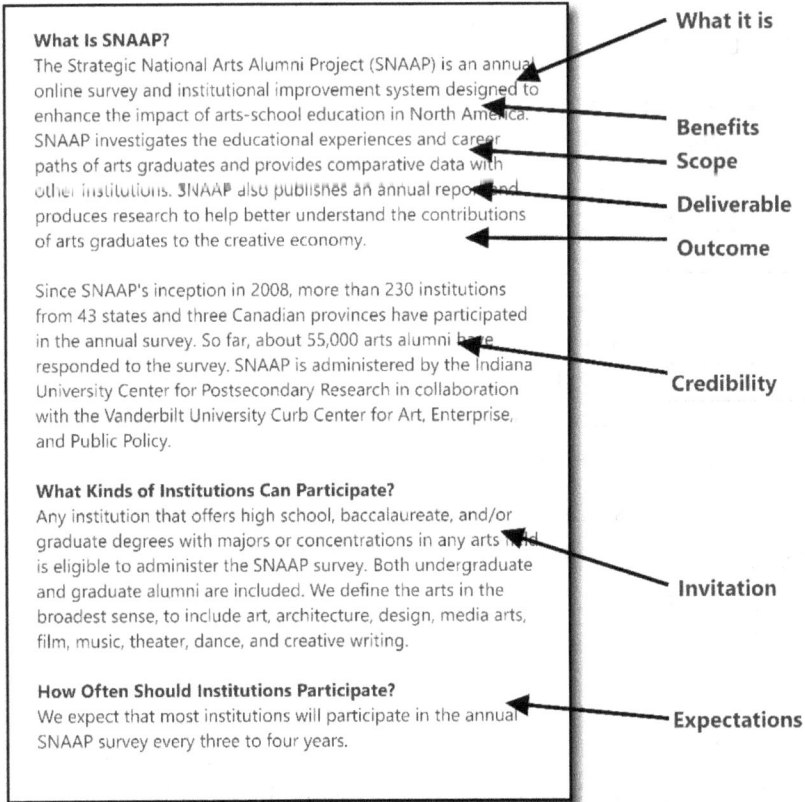

To identify potential members, consider the people who you know who might resonate with what you have in mind. From the group of leaders that you could potentially recruit, consider which have the following qualities:

- Passion for the change
- Connections and access to other stakeholders
- Different perspectives about the change
- Expertise in the change itself or in organizational change
- Wisdom
- Experience in the situations faced by the stakeholders
- Ability to have deep insights about the change effort
- Ability to influence others
- Position power over key stakeholder groups or the ability to secure resources

Mainly, identify the people who are most interested in working together and who can bring the most value to the group. In the beginning, you must rely on their personal passion to keep the team together, and research has found this is best accomplished by starting with members who are already predisposed toward the change and able to bring existing skills and resources to the effort. This keeps planning for the next steps positive and demonstrates to others outside the group that there is support from more than one person.

Core groups can take several forms. Review the following for key considerations with some of the more common forms.

Grass Roots Teams. If you are passionate about a change, you could start a grass roots effort to influence it. In this case, you enroll a mix of people who are also committed to the change. This could include members of various management levels even though they have no formal relationship to you, either as a program team or direct reports. Frequently, large-scale transformations are initially inspired by grass roots efforts that create enough momentum to capture the attention of upper management. For example, I have seen vibrant grass-roots communities formed around Six Sigma, organizational change management, and IT service management ultimately grow to such influence that they became approved as departmental and corporate initiatives.

Program Team. Change efforts are sometimes established as formal tracks or programs. When the team is comprised of direct reports to you or another person in the Core Group, this involves special considerations. On one hand, it is easier to convene the team and get their participation. But on the other hand, people are inclined to shut off their thinking and let the managers make the decisions instead of thinking for themselves. There can be extreme power differentials between managers and workers, and this tends to affect the quality of decision-making, as discussed later in this chapter.

I have often heard managers say, "my people have no fear of speaking up," but it is worth bearing in mind that when people of higher and lower levels in the hierarchy are mixed in a discussion, lower grade employees *are always more subdued to some degree*. Research has shown that, for assorted reasons, people will not speak up even if they know their manager's plans will be detrimental to the company.[3] Those people believe dissenters will be punished, not rewarded, so the truth never gets out.

Senior Leadership Team. Changes might be initiated by a leadership team who intends to change the organization they lead. This creates an inherently top-down situation, which is common. For example, in many re-organizations, the leadership team decides how to restructure and then delegates the responsibility for changing the affected processes, metrics, technology, and culture to lower-level managers.

Note traditional change approaches described in many books often equate the Core Group with an executive team or at least a manager and the manager's direct reports. In such a model, one would expect the initial steps of a change effort to be a) creating a vision, b) communicating the vision, and c) mobilizing the organization to enact the vision. However, although the Core Group could be a formal leadership team, it is a mistake to equate the Core Group strictly to people with positions of power. This incorrectly assumes that change is propagated mainly by the power relationships conveyed in a management hierarchy, which is simply not the case. While those relationships are influential, they are not typically the only — or even the most — influential relationships that exist across an employee population.[4] So, while the Core Group could be a leadership team, it is better to think of identifying the right people to guide the effort and forming them into a Gore Group. These could be the members of a single leadership team, but they could also be a set of people who have a high conviction to making change happen.

3. Enroll the Core Group Members

Once you have determined whom to enroll, you are ready to use the invitation you created earlier. Although you could simply invite your prospective members to a kickoff meeting, it is usually preferable to first meet with each prospective member personally, one-on-one, unless you already know them well. This facilitates forming a personal bond with each team member, and it enables you to listen to their perspective about the proposed change without them being influenced by the opinions of others.

Starting with personal interviews is particularly important if there are sensitive issues. During the interview, discuss the issues and your intentions openly. Solicit their feedback. Recommended guidelines for these meetings are as follows:

- Schedule 30 to 60 minutes, depending on the complexity of the proposal.

- Ensure the meeting is scheduled at a time convenient for the prospective member, when they are not distracted by other priorities.

- Spend perhaps 5 to 15 minutes at the beginning of the meeting to understand a little about them and make a personal connection. Understand their role, current things on their mind, and what they like to do. Find some areas of similarity with them. This will facilitate openness to your ideas.

- Once you have found things in common and the atmosphere is comfortable, outline your proposal. Relate it to their interests, as identified in the previous step. Be brief and invite the other person's questions. Handle the questions and suggestions calmly and clearly, explaining how the proposal works.

Listen and adjust as needed to sharpen the message. Avoid defensiveness or arguing why the proposal is good.

- If the other person seems agreeable on the concept of the proposal, invite them to join the team. Tell them you will be inviting them soon to a kickoff meeting and get their agreement to attend.

This invitation is the first exposure potential members of the Core Group will have to your intention, so taking care to set it up properly will pay off. The activity of thinking it through not only helps you clarify it for yourself but enables the Core Group to make a strong start.

Building the Strategic Framework

Once the Core Group members have been enrolled, you begin building them into a high-performing team. The Core Group is the heart of the change framework, so forging their capability to work together effectively is a critical investment in the success of the program. The first step in making this investment is establishing the strategic framework for the change program. The *strategic framework* is the set of basic agreements about what the change is and the Core Group's role in forwarding the change.

This establishment of the strategic framework is imperative because the Core Group is a unique kind of team. Traditional project management approaches call for common project management steps such as nailing down objectives concretely, defining deliverables, and then backtracking the steps needed to produce them. But, the Core Group should be a sense-and-respond team. A sense-and-respond team sets a direction, then evaluates the emerging conditions to determine the most effective strategy. Over time, this strategy may evolve, and the Core Group must be able to adapt the strategy appropriately. This is not to say project management methods are not valuable to the Core Group, but the group's operation is usually more like coaching a football game than managing a construction project.

A firmly established strategic framework provides the compass and organizing structure for the Core Group to recognize the emerging conditions and respond in a way that keeps the change progress moving forward. To establish the strategic framework, you will hold some initial sessions with the team to explore key aspects of the change model. After these sessions, the Core Group will be well positioned to effectively use the strategic framework to guide the change effort.

Discussion Format

An effective way to reach agreement quickly on the strategic framework is to first discuss the questions you explored for yourself in Chapter 2 as a group. This transforms the group member's independent perspectives into a shared understanding. This can form the basis for both the group's ongoing action and for the change story that will be used to communicate the change outward.

As a rule of thumb, plan for between 4 and 15 hours of discussion to forge the team's understanding. But note, "the time it takes is the time it takes." That is, there is nothing necessarily wrong if it takes 15 hours or more. The exact time needed is variable and depends on the nature of the change, the personalities involved, competing priorities, and myriad other factors.

This discussion can be conducted in a variety of formats, such as a single multi-hour session or even a multiday kickoff session. It can also be done in a series of shorter sessions over several weeks, depending on the availability and willingness of the team members. There are facilitators who advocate building the strategic framework intensively at one time, and this is probably ideal. However, the nature of the change effort and the schedules of the Core Group members may lead to other formats.

A sample agenda based on a one-day format for a modest change effort is shown om Table 2-1. For further discussion about how to construct and run this kind of workshop, see Chapter 6, "Architecting Collaboration."

What Can We Do Differently Now?

Once the key questions have been discussed, and the group is in alignment such that the fundamentals of the change effort are understood, the Core Group begins the motion of the change. Specific actions to be addressed include the following:

Table 3-1. Sample Agenda for 1-Day Core Group Meeting

Time	Activity
8:00 am	**Continental breakfast.** Warm drinks and food.
8:30 am	**Opening.** The overview of agenda, logistics, goals, change journey, and your perspootive about how to approach the collaboration.
8:45 am	**Introductions.** Team members introduce each other and their backgrounds.
10:00 am	Break
10:15 am	**Starting perspectives.** Team members share what interested them in the change effort and what they want to see happen.
11:00 am	**Why change now?** This focusing question is used to explore the impetus for change.
11:30 am	**Discussion.** Use the other focusing questions to discuss the group perspectives.
12:00 pm	Group lunch
1:00 pm	**Discussion.** Continue to discuss the questions, as a long as there are different perspectives from the group.
2:45 pm	Break

Time	Activity
3:00 pm	**Group roles and responsibilities.** After some of the basic perspectives are established, the Core Group should also review and agree on its roles and responsibilities.
3:45 pm	**Discussion of next steps.** Take stock of the conversation and outline the next steps.
4:30 pm	End

Next Steps

Commonly, further investigation and discussion is needed. During the initial session, you should have noted actions that need follow up. These might include gathering further research, consulting potential partners and stakeholders, or holding follow-up sessions on specific aspects. These steps, the responsible parties, and the schedule should be planned.

Cadence

After the kickoff meetings, the Core Group must establish a working cadence. This normally involves a series of regular meetings. Depending on who is available in the beginning, you might wish to simply hold a one- or two-hour meeting on a specific day of the week. These meetings can be used to track action items and continue the discussion. As needed, the Core Group will convene other sessions or alignment workshops, as discussed in Chapter 6, "Architecting Collaboration."

One note worth considering: Some people feel "if there is nothing to talk about, we should cancel the meeting." This is misguided thinking. If the change effort has merit, there is plenty to talk about, and the lack of things to talk about, at least in a weekly meeting, is a failure to do the work needed to keep the change effort going. Commitment is built by participation, so if the group does not meet, commitment fades. Moreover, the reason why there is seemingly nothing to talk about is at times because the group is avoiding difficult issues. If people do not have time to resolve action items, discuss options, and make agreements, then these problems need to be dealt with before the project loses traction.

Change Roles

Depending on the size of the change effort and the Core Group, it might be useful to organize roles for individuals, such as those below. You certainly do not necessarily need a different person in each role, but you should consider how the key activities embodied in these roles are being met.

- **Core Group Leader.** The Core Group leader is the person who is ultimately responsible for ensuring the Core Group meets and moves in the proper direction.

- **Core Group Member.** The members of the Core Group are part of the brain trust, and they have the responsibility to both be involved in the dialogue and decision-making as well as use their influence to further the change system.

- **Change Project Manager.** A project manager organizes and drives the tasks needed to accomplish the Core Group responsibilities. This could involve creating plans, running meetings, and managing action items.

- **Change Consultant or Strategist.** While this book offers basic change management knowledge for all members of a change effort, a large or highly impactful change effort could require team members with deep levels of expertise to augment the team.

- **Metrics Lead.** Tracking of success indicators and other metrics takes time and focused effort. Having a person assigned to define, collect, and post metrics ensures it gets accomplished and communicated to others.

- **Communications Lead.** A big responsibility of the Core Group will be communicating with others. In large change efforts, creating professional communications is important, but it takes time and expertise. Having one or more people assigned to do this helps provide the necessary focus and subject matter expertise.

The Knowledge Base

Documenting the team's decisions, plans, and other content is extremely important. The human mind has limited ability to consider or remember the tremendous complexity that can be inherent in organizational change programs. Moreover, ambiguity is pervasive, and it is easy to waste a lot of time going down paths that seem clear but are based on misunderstandings. Much of this can be cleared up by creating and maintaining an appropriate amount of documentation. Documentation records the team's shared agreements.

When documentation of the team's shared understanding is created, its usage is facilitated by developing a central knowledge base where all relevant information is stored. While documents could be emailed back and forth, a more efficient method is to establish a repository that everyone can access. These days, there are many fine tools such as Dropbox, Box, Google Drive, and OneDrive that can be used.

Commitment

After spending some time together, the Core Group members should, within a few meetings, reach a point where they are willing to commit to working together. This will likely involve dedicating a certain amount of time and energy to the change effort, as well as making it a priority. You may want to spend some time discussing what their commitment will be. Should it be limited to a certain number of months? Until completion? Ensure the members of the Core Group talk explicitly about what expectations they have for each other.

While attendance and participation imply commitment, it is also valuable early on to have members publicly commit to be an active member of the Core Group. You may want to take a few minutes at a Core Group meeting to go around the room individually and ask each person to answer the question, "Are you committed to seeing this through?" Studies outline by Robert Cialdini[5] have shown that people are more likely to follow through on public commitments. It increases peer pressure, surfaces any latent concerns, invokes their self-perception of themselves as a doer, and creates the self-perception of being part of the team.

Guiding the Change Effort

Once the strategic framework is established, the Core Group begins performing its ongoing role in stewarding the overall change effort. This includes the set of activities, agreements, roles, and structures needed by the Core Group to guide change. The primary responsibilities of the team are the following:

- Shaping the Basic Change Story
- Aligning the Leadership Community
- Leading the Change Strategy

These are summarized in the following subsections. Each responsibility corresponds to topics discussed in detail later in this book.

Creating the Basic Change Story

Much of the success of a change program depends on how stakeholders interpret the change actions. If they are surprised, confused, or do not resonate with what is happening, they may assume the worst or attribute negative motivations to leadership. Stakeholders then express these interpretations to others around them, catalyzing a discourse that cancels out the change. When increasing numbers of people express negative attitudes, they further convince each other to hold negative attitudes toward the change. The stakeholders then ignore or subvert the change process.

While it is not possible to control how stakeholders interpret what happens to them, it is possible to influence or shape the discourse through a well-constructed communications campaign. In this way, the Core Group can influence how the change is talked about and the perception of it by communicating focused messaging through stories introduced into the organizational discourse on the change effort. We will call the coherent structure of these intentionally introduced stories the *change narrative*, and the heart of this narrative is the *change story*, as discussed in the next chapter.

Aligning the Leadership Community

Although the Core Group could be comprised of key leaders in the organization, the membership often does not include all the top informal and formal leaders. So, there could be other leaders who are essential to the change effort and need to be bought in to the change if it is to occur. They are often senior managers or executives of affected organizations who will later become sponsors or high-level champions for the change. They could also be other opinion leaders in the organization who are widely followed by others.

Once the Core Group is aligned on the basic change story, it is a good practice to socialize the story to other key leaders. Socializing in this sense means meeting with them and discussing the change story, much as you used the invitation to enroll the Core Group members. Engaging other influential actors in the social network early in the effort has multiple advantages. These leaders can help shape the message, and this will enable you to surface their disagreements before it derails the effort. Further, engaging the other leaders involves them and thus builds their commitment to the program.

At preliminary stages, care should be taken about sharing the story too widely. In the formative stages, the goal is to engage others who can provide feedback to strengthen the story and may be influential in shaping the change effort. Seek out those who are encouraging and constructive to the change effort. While generally it is advisable to seek out diverse perspectives, airing contrary perspectives at the beginning of the effort can also trigger attempts — albeit well-meaning and subconscious — to maintain the status quo, quashing the momentum of the new change. The time for challenging those attempts comes later.

Leading the Change Strategy

The change strategy describes the overall approach to creating the change. It specifies the appropriate sequence of activities for the type of change and the change goals. The Core Group must be responsible for devising the change strategy and leading its implementation, although many other people could be involved in the actual activities. The Core Group's primary responsibilities are as follows:

- **Determine the appropriate design approach,** as discussed in Chapter 5.

- **Ensure adequate resourcing.** Resources are essential to getting things done, and lack of resources is one of the most common pitfalls of a change effort.

- **Enroll the extended team.** Building on the approach you used to assemble the Core Group, engage a wider, extended team. Look for people who will be influential in providing subject matter expertise, change management skills, and leadership influence.

Cheat Sheet

This chapter has covered guidelines for establishing the Core Group that will guide the change effort. The Core Group should be committed, with a clear sense of direction and a strong understanding of its responsibilities. This activity is needed whenever a cohesive and well-functioning Core Group is not in place.

The basic steps to forming the Core Group are as follows:

1. **Create an invitation.** The invitation is the expression of your intention that will attract potential members to the Core Group.

2. **Identify candidates.** Identify leaders who you can approach and who will make a strong contribution to the Core Group. Start with members who are already predisposed toward the change and able to bring existing skills and resources to the effort.

3. **Enroll the members to participate.** It is often advisable to reach out to each member individually, establish a relationship, and determine if there is a commonality of interests before bringing the whole group together.

4. **Organize a series of kickoff sessions to develop the strategic framework for the change.** This framework consists of the shared alignment on the direction of the change effort and the Core Group's responsibilities to guide it. Construct the sessions to explore the focusing questions.

   o   Why change *now*?

   o   Who else is playing?

   o   What outcome do *we* want?

   o   What are the changes for the stakeholders?

   o   What is the *failure* scenario?

   o   What can we do differently now?

      Use these questions as a collaboration framework to ensure a holistic coverage of the key topics. This will keep the Core Group focused on what is important.

5. **Ensure the sessions reach agreements** on the following items:

   o   A cadence for meeting as a team

   o   The next steps for building shared agreement

   o   A clear and publicly stated commitment to the effort by each member

   o   The definition of roles on the team

   o   A common place to store documentation

6. **Guide the change.** To accomplish this, the Core Group must be staffed with committed, capable individuals. The Core Group must also execute its key responsibilities well. The responsibilities are

   o   Creating the basic change story (see Chapter 4)

   o   Aligning the leadership community

   o   Leading the change design strategy (see Chapter 5)

4

The Change Story

It is not what you say that matters, it is what they hear.

—Frank Luntz

Much of the acceptance of a change depends on the perception of it, and this can have positive or detrimental effects regardless of how beneficial the change is. Howard Gardner states,

> *One way to capture the attention of a disparate population: by creating a compelling story, embodying that story in one's own life, and presenting the story in many different formats so that it can eventually topple the counter stories in one's culture. Yet, any old story will not do; it must exhibit certain characteristics.[1]*

In this chapter, we will talk about what this kind of story is and how it is created. But first, we look at an example of how things can go wrong.

Would it be valuable to accurately predict the future economic health of a country? Or the probability of civil unrest in Saudi Arabia? Of course, it would. In fact, a program to do just that, called FutureMAP, was conceived, funded, and approved by United States Defense Advanced Research Projects Agency (DARPA) in 2002.[2] But, days after the program became public knowledge in 2003, it was cancelled. This outcome had nothing to do with the value, effectiveness, cost, or feasibility of the program, which research in the last decade has consistently proven out. Rather, the cancellation of FutureMAP had everything to do with public perception.

FutureMAP sought to forecast various social events in the Middle East using predictive markets. A *predictive market* is a mechanism where investors can buy futures, or place bets, on the likelihood of future events occurring. Studies have shown these markets can be very accurate: For example, presidential elections, box-office results, and even the fall of Saddam Hussein[3] have all been accurately predicted using prediction markets. Hoping to capitalize on this technology, DARPA created FutureMAP.

Then, on July 28, 2003, U.S. Senators Byron Dorgan and Ron Wyden held a news conference lambasting FutureMAP and its prototype website, the Policy Analysis Market (PAM). Based on the senators' interpretation of some mocked up screens suggesting the possibility of investor speculation on events such as the assassination of Yassar Arafat or the overthrow of the king of Jordan, the senators derided the program. Senator Wyden said, "The idea of a federal betting parlor on atrocities and terrorism is ridiculous and it's grotesque." Senator Dorgan called PAM "useless, offensive and unbelievably stupid." Other media pundits and politicians piled on, and soon a viral-like effect was created that put people across the nation in an uproar. "I can't believe that anybody would seriously propose that we trade in death," said Senate Minority Leader Tom Daschle, the Democratic senator from South Dakota.

Within a day, the Pentagon announced the cancellation of the program, and, by the end of the week, the head of the DARPA's Information Awareness Office (IAO), which was responsible for developing FutureMAP, had offered his resignation. A year later, the IAO itself was disbanded. While on the surface, it might seem a grievous misuse of public funds had been averted, some additional details about this story offer a different view.

First, PAM was not really intended to predict assassinations. Professor Robin Hanson of George Mason University, a key participant in the

program, noted that while some of the mock-up screens mentioned inci-
dents regarding the deaths of specific individuals, this was not the purpose
of PAM. The purpose was to predict geopolitical trends such as military
spending by a given country or the world trade balance. Whether for political reasons or lack of understanding the system, the senators high-
lighted the mock-up information which did not accurately represent the
use of the system. According to Dr. Hanson, "The PAM webpages con-
sisted of text describing PAM, shown over faint backgrounds of sample
PAM interface screens. In addition to large sections on geopolitical trends,
two of these sample screens contained a small (less than 2%) miscellaneous
section, with short phrases about a possible Arafat assassination, North
Korean missile attack, and the king of Jordan being overthrown." At any
rate, PAM was not focused on those kinds of "death market" events.[4]

Secondly, attitudes against PAM may have been severely biased
because the program driving it, the Information Awareness Office (IAO),
had already run afoul of public opinion. It has been started about a year
earlier to develop better terrorist information awareness capabilities, in
hopes of better thwarting events like the 9/11 World Trade Center attack.
Since then, the IAO had floated the Total Information Awareness program,
which focused on detecting possible terrorist activity through data mining
records such as cell phone activity. That program, to many people,
sounded like mass, government-sponsored surveillance. Senator Wyden
had also been critical of that effort, which, as most of us now realize, was
continued underground until being ultimately exposed by Edward Snow-
den.

Thirdly, IAO leader, Admiral John Poindexter, the former National Security Advisor under President Ronald Reagan, had a checkered
past arising from his conviction for lying to Congress and destroying documents in the Iran-Contra scandal. Thus, many people viewed his return
to government unfavorably and wanted him gone. Ironically, Dr. Hanson,
in a follow up study, wrote that Admiral Poindexter "actually had little
involvement with PAM."

In the end, the fate of PAM and the IAO had little to do with their
actual merit. Later research conducted by Dr. Hanson showed that news

organizations, once they did their own research, became progressively more favorable toward PAM.

The travails of FutureMAP were set in motion by people who misinterpreted snippets they found on a mock website against the context of their personal experience and biases. This case highlights the fact that human communication is based on a set of signals—whether transmitted by voice, text, or gestures—which people interpret. Sociologist Paul Ricouer called the system of signals and how people interpret them a *discourse*.[5] This discourse of human communication is a stream of signals, and these signals do not have a fixed meaning; rather, the meaning is drawn from the context, just as the meaning of a word in a sentence is drawn from the other words in the sentence, or even the paragraph or book in which it resides. So, as selected information about PAM was introduced out of context, the discourse turned negative because the selected information was correlated with other unfavorable interpretations about Admiral Poindexter and his work, as well as pre-existing fears of government intrusion.

The same situation happens in corporations. For example, an identical change effort can be interpreted as a process improvement leading to greater performance and rising stock price or as a cost-cutting measure intended to reduce jobs and increase the wealth of executives. Which perceptions form can significantly impact the success of a change initiative. This illustrates the importance of Frank Luntz's quote at the beginning of this chapter.[6] While the way people interpret the discourse is not completely controllable, it can be shaped. Political campaigns and advertisers are masters at this, but in corporate change the shaping of the message is often only a casual thought. This leaves the message to be shaped by unpredictable and unmanageable forces.

So, when creating a change story, the Core Group begins purposely shaping how the discourse will unfold. The basic change story is the cornerstone of a connected and coherent narrative for the stakeholders. The change story is needed whenever the questions "Why are we doing this?" or "What is the change about?" cannot be answered concisely in a way that satisfies most stakeholders. When the change story is well established, it provides a guiding beacon for the change initiative, which serves to align the designers and stakeholders in a common direction. While we cannot fully control the discourse about a change, which depends on how stakeholders interpret the communication events they experience, we can shape the narrative by introducing a unified and compelling set of stories.

The Fundamentals

By story, I do not mean a yarn or anecdote for entertainment, even though these could be used to clarify elements of the change story. Fundamentally, people need to know what the change is and why it is important. This has historically been done in business settings by communicating reasons for the change and features of the planned solution, but modern research has shown people are more engaged using a story than logic, because people tend to think in terms of stories. They identify with the protagonist and the challenges faced. The story situates the listener in the context of the challenges faced and the outcome desired, and it engages them emotionally as well as logically. So, while logical arguments or business models may be included in the story, the primary framing is a story.

Your first communication was the invitation to the prospective Core Group, and the next elemental communication of the change narrative is the *basic change story*. The basic change story is the overarching public story we are concerned with regarding the intended organizational change. The basic change story provides the background and context for the change as well as a description of the intended future. The basic change story serves as the appetizer that gets people interested in the meal—it is the lighthouse beacon that keeps the change headed in the right direction.

As we have discussed, it is impossible for any communication to fully convey the change; however, crafting powerful, guiding communications is a critical aspect of mobilizing and framing the change. When the dot-com bust happened in 2000-2001, and major telecommunications companies were forced to quickly shed workers, John Chambers, the CEO of Cisco Systems, stated boldly: "We got surprised so we are going to make a one-time adjustment to compensate. We're still solid, much more so than our competitors, and we are going to begin building our 'breakaway' strategy for the moment the economy turns around." For quite a while afterward, updates were given to employees in the context of where the company was on executing this breakaway story, which ultimately came true.

What Chambers did, which he did skillfully for two decades, was capture the hopes and dreams of the organization with a compelling organizational change story. This provided an explanation for what was happening during trying times and offered a vision of the way out. He inspired confidence by asserting the groundwork for recovery was already laid. In this way, skilled change leaders craft core narratives that resonate with their stakeholders.

For an organizational story like the one told by Chambers to be effective, the stakeholders must be able to relate to the protagonist. That is, the stakeholders must be able to see themselves in the story. This means the story must have broad appeal, and thus organizational change stories are big stories intertwining the many personal aspirations of the stakeholders.

To create this broad appeal, the organizational change stories are usually archetypal. An *archetypal* story is one that embodies the major patterns of human experience, such as the victory of the underdog (David and Goliath), forbidden love (Romeo and Juliette), or rags-to-riches (Horatio Alger stories). In such a story, the surface details might change—for instance, the telling of *A Christmas Carol* has had numerous adaptations over the centuries, including one where a single person played all the roles, and another acted out by Smurfs. But, essentially, the pattern or archetype of the story is the same. As Annette Simmons, author of *Whoever Tells the Best Story Wins*, says, "Borrowing from the language of myth, these bigger stories are archetypal stories that trigger deep personal recognition because they highlight universal patterns of experience/response that draw attention, brings meaning, and creates a sense of belongingness— like kittens attract kids."[7]

Due to the nature of organizations and the global economy, certain archetypal stories are most frequently employed. While all organizational change stories are about being faster, cheaper, or better to employees and customers, these archetypes are common ways the story is framed. Some of the most popular ones are summarized below.

- **Beating the competition.** All organizations, profit or non-profit, must compete for the attention of their customers. Direct and indirect competitors are always maneuvering to acquire the attention of customers and clients. The effects of these actions often show up in declining revenues, charitable donations, or market share.

- **Providing greater benefits to customers.** One way to boost revenues and customer response is to provide more benefits. Products and services can be redesigned to better meet customer needs.

- **Going into new markets.** Companies often expand by offering products or services in new regions, different industries, or in other demographics.

- **New products or services.** Another common way that companies change is to offer new products or services. Older offerings may be declining, and new offerings may be needed to remain viable.

- **Cost cutting.** Organizations are always concerned with minimizing expenses, either to generate greater profits or to provide products at a reduced price to consumers, and many change efforts are launched to reduce costs. However, it should be noted that a cost-cutting message is often threatening to employees, who see it as a pretext for workforce reductions.

- **Agility.** This is a relatively new one, stemming from the increasing pace of change. These days, it is becoming accepted that companies need to be able to change quickly to maintain a competitive advantage.

- **New business architecture.** Restructuring, redesigning processes, and creating new business models are long-standing business change activities. Companies are purchased and integrated with the purchaser; divisions are spun out or sold off. These kinds of changes to the business architecture of the organization are done for a variety of reasons — such as becoming more efficient, reducing costs, or acquiring new products or customers.

- **Employee morale.** Change efforts are often launched to improve employee morale and satisfaction. This may be a reaction to negative results on employee surveys, high attrition rates, or difficulty in attracting top talent.

The themes listed above are among the most frequently used, even though they are not the only ones that could work. Most of the time, a compelling organizational theme will talk about how to make the organization faster, cheaper, or better in a way that is recognizable to people. When developing a core narrative, you should make sure that it fits a broad, recognizable theme, and you can use the list above as a checkpoint.

Creating the Basic Change Story

The change story will be more effective if you create it by following some key guidelines. These guidelines include generating the story concept through a collaborative process, using proven story writing methods to construct the story, and honing the story by testing it and gathering feedback. Following these guidelines will result in a story with maximal impact.

Generating the Story Collaboratively

An effective change story usually does not emerge as a complete finished product from a single individual who works in isolation. While at first it might seem simpler and more efficient to assign a communications expert to come up with the story, creating it collaboratively with the Core Group and other key players of the leadership community or even a wider community is better. Afterward, the story can be refined by communications professionals.

The change story is best forged through of a process of discovery and refinement because the story is not just a document to be posted on a website — rather, the key influencers in the organization must know it, own it, and communicate it concisely and consistently. However, when a program is initiated, those key influencers will have many different conceptions of what the change effort is about, even when they are the direct reports of the CEO. So, the process of creating the change story is also often a process of aligning minds on the outcome.

A divergence of opinion at the outset of the project is natural and usually unavoidable, because everyone has different experiences and learnings that have shaped their perceptions at any point in in time. Reaching a point where those perceptions are more aligned on a complex topic is often directly proportional to the time spent together collaborating on it. Moreover, the community members may be strongly emotionally attached to their initial ideas, and their attachment to those ideas can create conflict and spin cycle. The lack of mental alignment creates a dynamic of pushing and pulling around the story line. As Simmons describes,

> *"The quality of any story chosen to represent a group or agenda inevitably reflects the quality of the decision-making processes and thinking routines used by the group. If the group is disorganized and in conflict, the stories told are likely to be disorganized, conflicted, and weak. When a group is cohesive, deeply committed, open to risk, and disciplined in the face of adversity they have a much better chance of divining a story that pulls from the universal well of meaning."[8]*

So, while the lack of alignment of the Core Group creates the risk of generating a poor story, it simultaneously creates the opportunity to use the story creation process to forge a more cohesive Core Group. By working with the Core Group to surface assumptions and create shared meaning, you will develop both more compelling story and commitment to story.

Answering Basic Questions

A proven way to begin organizing the story is by taking the results of the questions asked while forming the Core Group (Chapter 3) and adding the results of some additional questions. The discussion about the fundamental questions first facilitates the development of a cohesive story by surfacing participants' assumptions. When complete stories are created before discussing assumptions, people become attached to them and get stuck endlessly debating parts of the story that are based on their unexpressed assumptions.

An expanded set of questions is given below (some are the same as when forming the Core Group). You can use these questions by yourself or with a group to get clarity on the core elements of powerful and compelling story. These questions are chosen to elicit and highlight the qualities of stories that are most compelling, as indicated by research. You may also want to use these questions after the story is created to see how many questions are answered in the story.

- Why change now? What research is it based on? What is the reasoning? What is the connection to what is happening in the world?

- What outcome do we want? Who will benefit and how? What is the goal or purpose? What will be the reward or outcome?

- What is it? What are the changes for the stakeholders? How will the outcome look when it is put in place?

- Who is involved? What is their credibility? Do we have enough resources?

- What is the failure scenario? What are we trying to avoid?

- What corporate or departmental strategies or themes should it connect to?

- What corporate or personal values should it connect to? How does it align to common values (efficiency, productivity, profits, life balance) or common interests they have?

- How we are doing it?

- Are expected concerns being addressed? How are we addressing the expected concerns?

- How should the stakeholders be involved?

- How does it connect to what they know and what has been happening? Portray the past as a prologue to a new story. Portray the present as the beginning (or the middle) of a journey toward specific goals and aspirations. Portray the future as a destination where goals are to be realized.

These questions are meant to generate discussion and to surface key issues. It is not necessary to meticulously answer each one, but it is useful to keep in mind these are the kinds of things people often want to know. So being able to answer them is beneficial.

Creating the Story Draft

The responses to the initial questions must be crafted into a coherent story that pits the stakeholder as the protagonist in a relevant challenge. It might not be as dramatic as a Hollywood movie, but the responses should not be simply captured and published.

At the start, the story can be short, the equivalent of a page of information. Try to weave in the responses into a story around one of the archetypal themes discussed earlier. For maximum innovation, it may be useful to create more than one version of the story and test the versions with a supportive audience who can give you constructive feedback.

The story will probably be spoken as well as written, so ultimately you will want to have versions for both. But, you probably want to start by casting it in some tangible form, such as a PowerPoint presentation or web page. This is easier for the group work with during development. Later, there can be more detailed versions in different media.

How much story is needed? That depends on the audience. Some audiences, especially in smaller change efforts, might be satisfied with a concise, pointed core narrative. Other audiences might need a story with more details, more facts, or more examples.

Also, it is more efficient to start the story small. Build agreement by starting with simple basics rather than pitching a fully developed, detailed story, which may have many small controversial points for people to disagree with, thus derailing the entire process. Further, even though the story might ultimately be translated to different audiences, start with the core presentation and then customize it. It is too difficult to develop many versions from the start.

A process for developing the document is below.

1. Have a discussion with the Core Group on the fundamental questions and agree on the outline.

2. Assign someone to develop a draft or assign sections of the draft to different people.

3. Schedule reviews of the draft with the core authors.

4. Socialize the draft with a wider group and gather input.

5. Incorporate the feedback into an updated version of the story. If there was a lot of change, repeat from step 4.

This review process should incorporate the perspectives of the group but still create a meaningful and compelling message. Too often, an uninspiring story results from the people involved trying to find a mutually acceptable, non-provocative wording. The story becomes so watered down and vague it sounds like just more "management-speak."

A vibrant story must have some distinctiveness. As renowned Harvard psychology professor Howard Gardner says,

> "It is not easy for a story to gain a hearing. We have all heard a great many stories before, and several of those stories over and over again. Most stories and most jokes are not remembered for long, because they are too similar to what we have already heard and thus lack distinctiveness. Instead they are assimilated to al-

> *ready-accepted or known stories. (That is why we recall rela-*
> *tively few details of most episodes of television shows that we*
> *have seen.) On the other hand, stories that are too bizarre or ex-*
> *otic may also elude memory. They either are repressed because*
> *they are too alien or too threatening ... or they are distorted so*
> *that they fit comfortably with stories that are already known."* [9]

Gardner adds further, "Optimally, a new story has to have enough familiar elements so that it is not instantly rejected yet be distinctive enough that it compels attention and engages the mind. The audience has to be prepared, in one sense, and yet surprised, in another."

Refining the Story

Once you have drafted the initial story, you must refine it. Like most forms of communication, effective stories do not come out as a single, finished piece. Instead, they are the result of diligent refinement and rewriting. While there is no cookie-cutter template for doing this, and the fundamentals of truly writing a solid story are too much for this book, here are some useful guidelines you can apply as lenses. Follow up on the references to learn the topic more deeply.

Ten Rules of Effective Communication

Stories need to be clear, comprehensive, and compelling. Prominent political pollster and strategist Frank Luntz provides some guidelines for accomplishing this in his book, **Words that Work**.[10] He offers these ten rules of effective communications.

- **Simplicity**. Use small words, particularly with broader and more international audiences.

- **Brevity**. Use short sentences. It's not about saying less. It's about saying the right stuff.

- **Credibility.** The author should have credibility with the audience in the topic area.

- **Consistency.** Repeat the core messages.

- **Novelty.** Offer something new or a twist on something old.

- **Sound.** Sound and texture matter. For example, a string of words with the same first letter or same sound might be more memorable.

- **Aspiration.** People forget what you say but not about how it made them feel. Relate to their life experiences.

- **Visualization.** Paint a vivid picture.

- **Questioning.** A question, even rhetorical, can have a greater impact.

- **Context.** Make sure the benefits are clear and connected to something they care about.

Glove Shrine Story

The basic change story can be reinforced by smaller sub-stories that aid emotional engagement. One type of story is the "glove shrine" story, as famously described by Kotter and Cohen.[11] In the classic telling, an employee of a large manufacturer poignantly illustrated his company's poor purchasing control by piling over 400 pairs of different gloves purchased at a wide range of prices onto a conference room table.

Other examples of this type of story include the following:

- **"This Is Your Brain on Drugs."** In effort to curb adolescent drug use, the Partnership for a Drug-Free America launched a famous ad campaign in 1987, which featured an analogy of scrambled eggs to a brain on drugs. This campaign was not only one of the most successful ad campaigns of all time, it was also effective: Per a 2002 study by the Yale School of Management, the advertising had an impact in reducing drug abuse.[12]

- **The "hockey stick curve" in the film *An Inconvenient Truth*.** When Al Gore showed the sudden rise of global temperature as relatively flat for thousands of years, taking up most of the space on his stage, followed by such a sharp increase in modern times he had to rise on an elevating platform to reach the top. It made quite an impact.

The Springboard Story

Another useful kind of story is the springboard story, as advocated by author Stephen Denning.[13] The **springboard story** is a real story, preferably recent, which paints a compelling picture of the future for the stakeholder. The springboard story does not have to be as rich and compelling as a traditional story, since, generally, people in organizations are busy and have little patience for long stories. So, the springboard story is a quick, relevant example that illustrates the idea in a real setting. Some principles for making one are listed below.

- Must be a "story" with a beginning, middle and end that is relevant to the listeners.

- Must be highly compressed – 35 to 50 words is okay.

- Must have a her — the story must be about a person who accomplished something notable or noteworthy.

- Must include a surprising element — the story should shock the listener out of their complacency. It should shake up their model of reality.

- Must stimulate an "of course!" reaction — once the surprise is delivered, the listener should see the obvious path to the future.

- Embody the change process desired, be relatively recent and "pretty much" true.

- Must have a happy ending.

For example, here is a simple one I used for a while to convince people of the power of social media.

I personally became convinced about the power of Twitter when, during a casual conversation with some friends, one of them mentioned a desire to meet well-known author Geoffrey Moore. None of us knew Mr. Moore, but one of my Tweeting friends pulled out his phone and posted a request for an introduction to his 2,000 followers. Within minutes, we had a phone number and an offer to set up a meeting with the author.

Examples

Finally, some examples may be helpful to understand what a successful change story looks like. See the examples below from ExxonMobil's Math and Science Initiative and from Microsoft's YouthSpark.

Example 1: ExxonMobil's Math and Science Initiative

Let's Solve This

In 2009, the Program for International Students Assessment ranked U.S. students 17th in the world in science and 25th in math. Let's change those numbers. Let's invest in our teachers. Let's inspire our students. Let's solve this.

Let's answer the call. It takes parents, teachers and students working toward a common goal. We support programs that will help secure a better math and science standing in the world and springboard the careers that will follow.

Supporting the National Math & Science Initiative (NMSI). We've committed 125 million dollars in support of this important initiative.

Training elementary teachers through the Mickelson ExxonMobil Teachers Academy. We're in partnership with Phil and Amy Mickelson to train grade school teachers in innovative, hands-on math and science methods.

Example 2: Microsoft's YouthSpark

The world stands at a crossroads. While there are more young people on the planet than ever before, youth unemployment is double that of the adult population. Countries are struggling to develop modern workforces due to the growing gap between the skills of unemployed workers and the skills needed to perform the jobs of today and tomorrow.

Today's young people face an opportunity divide – a gap between those who have the access, skills and opportunities to be successful and those who do not. Closing this opportunity divide is one of the most important actions we can all take to secure the future of our youth and the future of our global economy.

Microsoft YouthSpark is a companywide initiative designed to create opportunities for hundreds of millions of youth around the world. Through partnerships with governments, nonprofits and businesses, we aim to empower youth to imagine and realize their full potential by connecting them with greater education, employment, and entrepreneurship opportunities. We want to empower youth to change their world.

Moving the Story Outward

Once the story is developed, it must be taken outward. This is a key responsibility of the Core Group, as discussed in the previous chapter. This is also the first stage of the change leadership, as outlined in Chapter 11. Getting the feedback and involvement of other key leaders is essential.

Pollster Frank Luntz noted that while people are always asking for specific words with sizzle, the secret sauce is discovering the words through a process of using focus groups and gauging their responses to refine the key words. What works today may not work tomorrow, so finding the right wording and message is always a process. There are several aspects to this, as described below.

- **Optimizing the story.** Messaging may not resonate at first as well as it could. The story should be tested on some audiences and refined based on their feedback.

- **Keeping the leadership community aligned.** The Core
  Group can identify key members of the target people system
  and personally evangelize the basic change story with them.
  During this process, feedback can be gathered and used to
  evolve the story.

- **Deepening.** During the process of socializing the story, it
  may become more evident what kind of more detailed or
  more target stories are needed.

Cheat Sheet

As was illustrated in travails of the Policy Analysis Market, the
prevailing discourse, whether negative or positive, can seriously impact
the viability of a change program. While the Core Group cannot control
the discourse, it can influence it by creating and forwarding a coherent
structure of messaging called the change narrative.

The core narrative provides a guiding, coherent frame for the
change effort to hang on as more and more people are enrolled in the process. The core narrative incorporates ideas that have been formerly called
in organizational development literature of the last few decades as the case
for change, rationale for change, sense of urgency, and vision. But the core
narrative offers a more alive, engaging context for people to understand
the change initiative.

The heart of the change narrative is the basic change story. This
story should be based on one of the primary archetypes and help position
the stakeholders in the change, letting them know the challenge, what will
be done, and how they play in it. Some of the most common archetypes
are as follows:

- Beating the competition

- Providing greater benefits to customers

- Going into new markets

- New products or services

- Cost cutting

- Agility

- New business architecture

- Employee morale

Developing the change story is both an outcome and a group process. Because no small set of people, no matter how expert, know exactly what will resonate with the wider audience, feedback and diverse perspectives are needed to discover what themes and language will resonate broadly with the target population. Using a well-managed development process both refines the story itself and builds the shared understanding and commitment of the leadership community.

The development of the story can be used to galvanize a shared understanding across the Core Group and leadership community. Once this story has solidified, it can be used to communicate to others throughout the target stakeholder population.

Part III: Design

The activity of determining the new behaviors and infra-structure need to support them.

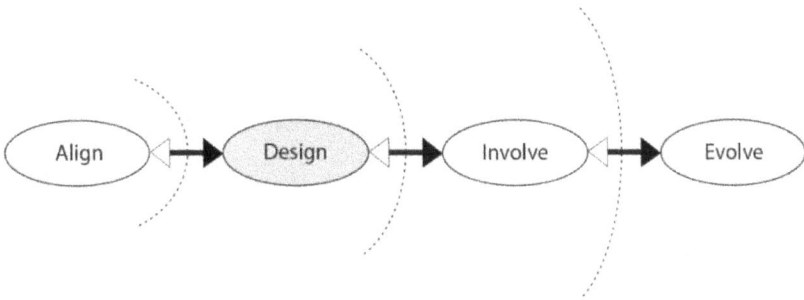

5

The Design of People Systems

The greatness of Picasso was his ability to match his painting style to the type of material he was painting on.[1]

—Norman Mailer

Up to now, we have talked mainly about clarifying and expressing intention. Next, we explore transforming intention into action. This involves *design*, or the application of an appropriate design approach to plan a new or changed people system. While the design of people systems has similarities to the design of tangible things like aircraft or homes, it also differs significantly from the design of objects.

The design of people systems should be a group-creative act. An individual can initiate the process, but a single individual cannot effectively design (or implement) a people system without engaging with others. In fact, the venerable social systems design theorist Dr. Bela H. Banathy asserted to me on many occasions that not only was it necessary for the affected stakeholders to be involved in design, but it was also their right.

Stakeholders have a right to be involved because only they can determine what works or does not work for them. In Agile Software Design, a fundamental tenant is that "running code" is the evidence of a completed task. But while running code is self-evident, the success of a people system, such as the delivery of food services for the poor, is a matter of agreement by the stakeholders. As such, various groups of stakeholders might have different perspectives about what constitutes success. This dynamic was the cause of the dramatic early failures of business process reengineering.[2]

Further complicating the design of people systems is that the stakeholder's perspectives are often, at least initially, divergent. Stakeholders frequently do not know exactly what they want up front. This is not a failure of intelligence, just an inherent quality of people's limited concentration and knowledge. Moreover, what the stakeholders think they want up front changes as they gather more information. Thus, the design of people systems is also a group learning activity.

Designing people systems should also inspire innovation. Design is doing something better than was done before, not just replicating a pattern. The human spirit is engaged by doing new and better things. When people are engaged in such participative design, they are also much more committed to what the design produces.

Organizing a group-creative design effort requires the application of a solid design approach, because group dynamics can quite easily derail a design process and waste considerable time and effort. So, applying solid people systems design principles is the best way to keep the effort on track.

While designing organizations and communities is a topic far too complex to be completely covered in this book, we can learn a useful way to frame our intended result and identify the appropriate pattern of the design. We will look at these fundamental phases of a participative design effort:

1. Understanding the desired outcome

2. Innovating solutions

3. Analyzing the context

4. Applying the appropriate design approach

By understanding the appropriate design pattern for your situation, you can focus on the further guidance and resources that will be needed to conduct the design.

Understanding the Desired Outcome

Creating a truly workable design involves first getting agreement on what it takes to produce the desired outcome. In Chapter 2, we discussed clarifying the desired outcome. Then, in Chapter 4, we developed a story about how to communicate the outcome to others. Our next step is objectively understanding the *critical success factors* (CSFs) that will produce the desired outcome. From there, we can effectively design a solution to meet those factors.

Framing a change initiative in terms of an outcome and its critical success factors has two advantages: a) focusing the planning on activities that are truly needed to sustain the outcome and b) providing the context for more innovative thinking.

We can understand how it inspires innovation through an example. It has been often reported in recent years that turnout in U.S. elections is comparatively low compared with other democracies. Suppose our Core Group wants to improve this situation, not just for a single candidate or election, but for all elections going forward. We might begin designing a Voter Turnout Improvement System (VTIS).

First, we create an *outcome model*. The outcome model consists of the outcome and the critical success factors that cause the outcome to happen. For this example, we can get input from a *Washington Post*[3] article that alleged the factors of getting more people to vote could be categorized as a) registering to vote, b) going to the polls, c) understanding and being interested in the issues, and d) being able to cast votes efficiently and effectively at the polls. These are contributing factors to our outcome, as shown in Figure 5-1.

The figure shows our outcome model. The factors on the bottom row are the critical success factors (CSFs), as given by the article we are using for this example. The concept of critical success factors draws from the seminal work of John Rockart,[4,5,6] who showed how to effectively design by identifying these "sub-outcomes" that must be achieved for the outcome to occur. According to Rockart, the CSFs are loosely defined as a few key ongoing functions that will ensure successful results.

Figure 5-1. Outcome Model for the Voter Turnout Improvement System

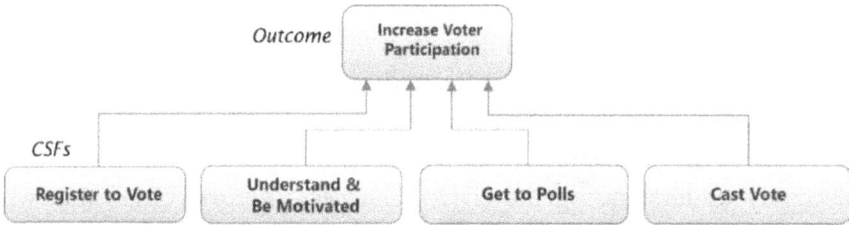

Outcome models can be simple, with just a single outcome and a handful of CSFs, or the outcome model could be highly complex with multiple outcomes and a hierarchy of CSFs. In a real outcome model, work should be done to ensure the CSFs are accurate, causal, and complete. For this example, we simply assume they are correct.

Innovating Solutions

Having framed our intended result as an outcome model enables us to be innovative because it shows objectively what is required to achieve the outcome. With this understanding, we can generate alternative ways to achieve the critical success factors and evaluate which is better. We can ask ourselves, "What actions are needed to enable those CSFs?" To illustrate this, let us take the next step in coming up with a solution for improving voter turnout.

To simulate the process of generating various ideas, we can compare proposals from different writers who have published articles on the subject. Normally, you would generate ideas with your team, but we will use the four writers listed below to demonstrate.

- "5 Ways to Fix America's Dismal Voter Turnout Problem," by Kira Lerner[7]

- "Simple Ways to Increase Voter Turnout," by Lee Drutman[8]
- "Why is turnout so low in U.S. elections," by Eric Black[9]
- "Improving Voter Participation," by Janice Thompson[10]

In the graphic below, the ideas of our four writers are compared against the CSFs they are addressing.

Figure 5-2. Voter Turnout Improvement Outcome Model with Solutions

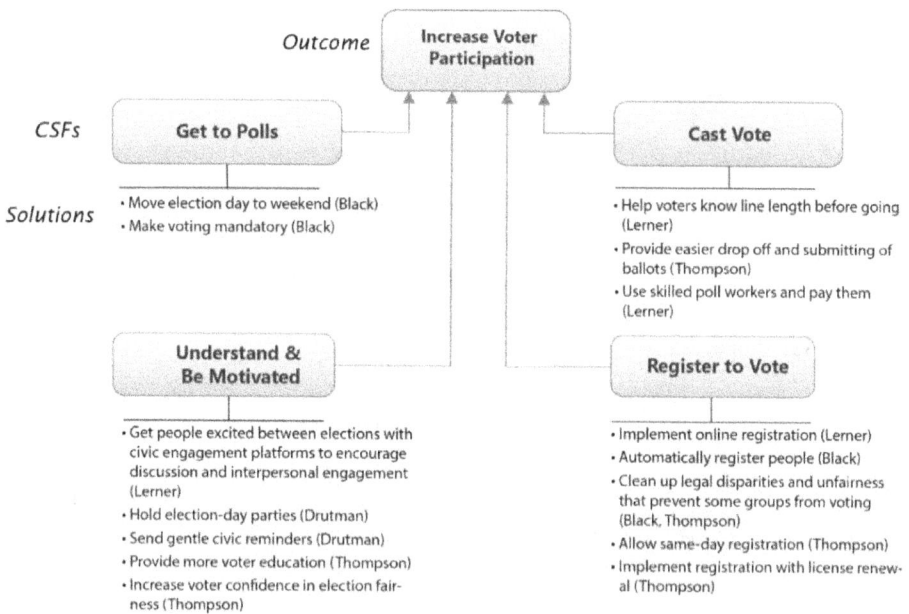

Outcome — **Increase Voter Participation**

CSFs — **Get to Polls**

Solutions —
- Move election day to weekend (Black)
- Make voting mandatory (Black)

Cast Vote
- Help voters know line length before going (Lerner)
- Provide easier drop off and submitting of ballots (Thompson)
- Use skilled poll workers and pay them (Lerner)

Understand & Be Motivated
- Get people excited between elections with civic engagement platforms to encourage discussion and interpersonal engagement (Lerner)
- Hold election-day parties (Drutman)
- Send gentle civic reminders (Drutman)
- Provide more voter education (Thompson)
- Increase voter confidence in election fairness (Thompson)

Register to Vote
- Implement online registration (Lerner)
- Automatically register people (Black)
- Clean up legal disparities and unfairness that prevent some groups from voting (Black, Thompson)
- Allow same-day registration (Thompson)
- Implement registration with license renewal (Thompson)

So, now we have a set of ideas for each of our CSFs, and we can proceed with the next step of design.

Analyzing the Context of the People System

In life, there are things we can affect and things we cannot affect (within reason). As discussed in Chapter 2, other entities external to your effort provide varying levels of support and constraint on what can be designed. For example, our Voter Turnout Improvement System will exist in a larger people system. This larger system includes government agencies, political parties, the court system, the U.S. Constitution, and numerous other civic organizations. In some cases, it might be possible to change these; in other cases, they become constraints that would be very hard to change and must be taken as fixed for our design.

We could decide on influencing this larger system, by pursuing some of the suggested ideas such as

- Moving Election Day to a Saturday

- Auto-registering everyone

- Cleaning up legal disparities that marginalize some groups

Pursuing these ideas might improve the vote-casting process, but these activities would comprise straightforward planning to influence legislation, and our goal for this chapter is to explore designing a new or improved people system. How we accomplish this depends on what we are trying to design and whether the people system is existing, not yet existing, or a system we just want to influence certain behaviors. Approaches for these situations are discussed in the following subsections.

Optimizing Existing Systems

Some of the proposed solutions for improving voter turnout are essentially refinements, or *optimizations*, of existing processes. For example, consider these ideas,

- Making it easier to drop off ballots

- Knowing the line length ahead of time

- Same-day registration

- Online registration

These are ideas about improving the existing voting process. They are ideas about how to make the process faster, cheaper or easier.

Playbook

The essence of the optimization design approach is measuring the output of a given process and then analyzing the constituent steps to see if they can be streamlined or made cheaper. The most popular method for doing this is DMAIC, a core method of Six Sigma, which was developed by Motorola in the 1980s.

The basic steps are summarized below.

1. Define and agree on what outcomes and critical success factors are being sought.

2. Measure the output of the current system.

3. Analyze the current system and determine where improvements can be made.

4. Implement the changes.

5. Control the resulting output. This means measure the output and correct for any variance from the target.

Application

To see how the DMAIC method might work, we can return to our Voter Turnout Improvement System. We have already agreed on the outcome model, so the next step is measuring the current process. Let us say the average voting time for a person in our area is 2 hours and 55 minutes, starting from studying the issues to casting the ballot. We then map out the steps and determine how much time each step takes, as shown in the figure below.

Figure 5-3. Example Vote-Casting Process

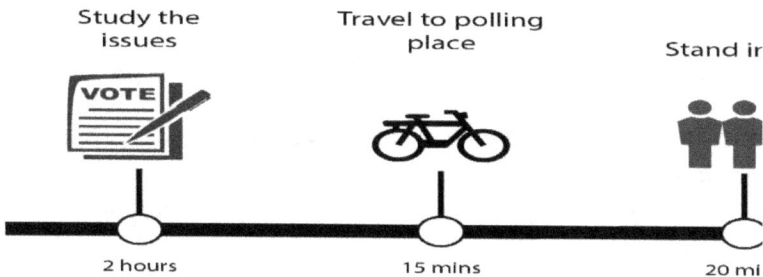

Study the issues	Travel to polling place	Stand ir
2 hours	15 mins	20 mi

From our proposed solutions, we can see if any of them would reduce the time of one of the steps in the process. Several that seem promising are listed in table 5-1, along with an estimate of the time they might save.

To complete our analysis (step 3 of DMAIC), we could look deeper to see which of the solutions are most feasible and if they are truly likely to save the estimated amount of time. Some preliminary analysis has been given in the table. We would then adjust the list to the most fruitful ideas and implement them. Once they were implemented, we would measure the average time again and see if perhaps it had been shortened to 15 minutes or more, which might increase the number of people who decide to vote.

Table 5-1. Estimated Time Savings of Proposed Solutions

Solution	Est. Time Saving
Phone app to determine the line length before showing up. Enables the user to pick times when the line is short, on average only 5 minutes long.	15 minutes
Skilled poll workers. Speeds up the vote-casting process and potentially the line.	5 minutes
Curbside drop off for the ballot. Enables people to avoid waiting in line if they have an absentee ballot. But this solution only affects a subset of the voters.	10 minutes

Other Examples

Some other examples of optimization are given below.

- **Streamlining the financial reporting process.** Examples include streamlining order management processes, automating financial reporting, and making reporting from suppliers more efficient.

- **Cleaning up customer data.** Over time, different systems and processes in the company may have developed diverse ways of capturing customer data. A data clean-up process would connect the disparate processes together using similar ways of describing customers and managing their data. This could require people who use customer data to change how they input, label, and use the data.

- **Making operations reporting more efficient.** Reporting processes are essential elements of running companies, but they add overhead. Sometimes, a lot of time is spent gathering and sanitizing data requested by management. Streamlining this effort so it is as efficient as possible can be a great savings.

Evolving New Systems

The optimization design approach deals with an existing process. But what if we want to design a new process? Designing new people systems differs from a traditional engineering approach because the design cannot be done by a single individual or small group. Instead, a *participative design* is needed where inputs from stakeholders are gathered and organized into a design that has broad agreement across the stakeholder community.

The participatory design process is a learning activity, where enough structure is provided for stakeholders to focus on the outcomes, provide ideas, resolve differences in perspectives, and be engaged in owning the eventual design. Instead of outlining a fully complete future state, the output of design in evolutionary approach is a model that describes a framework for other appropriate groups to experiment and learn. It is a container for an extended design conversation. This container breaks down the elements of the intended future into manageable functions and provides key guidelines, relationships, and nomenclature.

Think of it a little bit like growing a metropolitan area. We are not trying to specify everything everyone does, just establish some guidelines to keep it together. People can still do what they want in their area of responsibility, but they need to coordinate on where their spheres of operation intersect or where there is a need for governance and consistency.

Playbook

By architecting the right collaboration, as will be discussed further in Chapter 6, you can organize many people to generate such a model of a future people system and move toward it in an evolutionary way. Use the steps below for guidance.

1. Determine the outcome model for the initiative.

2. Analyze the context.

3. Participatively envision the future people system.

    o   What is the purpose of the new system?

    o   What services should the new system provide to clients?

    o   What functions, processes, services, and other enabling functions are need for the people system?

4. Participatively envision the organizing framework.

5. Mobilize teams to design in their respective domains.

6. Design ways to close the gaps.

7. Learn and evolve.

Application

To illustrate how this works, we return to one of the solutions proposed for our Voter Turnout Improvement System. For example, Drutman cited research by Yale political scientists Donald P. Green and Alan S. Gerber, who held several Election Day poll parties and found they increased turnout. According to the scientists, turnout was around 90% in the late nineteenth century, possibly because voting was much more of a community event.

So, if our Core Group wanted to influence more Election Day poll parties, we should design a new people system to influence this to happen. Sure, we could organize them ourselves, but this would be difficult to scale

across the country. Or we could try to get the government or political campaigns to organize them, but this might be difficult to sustain. Instead,
we'll assume our general strategy is to create a people system that will
encourage other people to self-organize Election Day poll parties. Our
goals will be to provide them with encouragement and resources to make
it easier.

For this outcome (a sub outcome of the program) we can define the
next level of critical success factors.

- **Best practices.** People might benefit from guidance on how
  to organize and conduct the election parties. This could include an organizer's handbook, lists of fun activities, and
  patriotic recipes.

- **Tools.** Tools automate the process and make it easier. For
  this initiative, we might have a website to distribute the best
  practices, provide community calendars of when events are
  occurring, and provide a subscription service so people
  could sign up to be notified.

- **Hooks.** People need to know about the program. Ideally, the
  information on how to act should be in front of people when
  they are interested in seeing it. This might take the form of
  email sent at election time, posters near voter registration
  and voting sites, or advertisements in voting materials.

- **Adoption metrics.** Metrics should be gathered to begin the
  improvement process and self-correct if there are problems.
  These metrics might include

  o   Number of events held

  o   Number of subscribers

  o   Number of participants

  o   Percent of members who make it to the polls

- **Incentives.** People need to be motivated to hold the parties
  and get a form of payoff. So, attention should be placed on
  making the activity rewarding in some fashion. There are

numerous human motivations that could be compelling (as discussed in Chapter 7), but for this example perhaps fun, camaraderie, and the potential of being on the evening news if the party was large enough would suffice.

Next, we analyze the context or environment of our system to see our assumptions or constraints. For example, how many people are in the local area? Where are polling stations? Could events be held on the grounds of the polling place, as Green and Gerber did? Are there public areas where signage or ads could be placed? What civic-minded organizations might be interested in contributing resources or money as Working Assets did in the Yale research?

Table 5-2. Functions for Election Day Polling Party Program

Function	Description
Website	• Content • Scheduling app • Subscriber profiles and database • Discussion board
Best practices	• Gather feedback from subscribers • Develop handbooks, tips and tricks, and other collateral to provide best practices
Community relations	• Send messages to subscribers • Put out ads for the program • Solicit donations to fund it • Public relations – media contacts • Collect metrics and reach out to the subscribers
Website	• Develop functionality on website • Maintain website

Now that we know our constraints and opportunities, we need to establish how these critical success factors will be accomplished. We can organize them into *functions*, or sets of ongoing activities, that we will eventually have people and machines do. There are probably numerous ways to conceptualize this, but one straightforward way is shown in Table 5-2. These functions could have a relationship with each other. So, it is often informative to show them in a graphic like Figure 5-4.

Figure 5-4. Functional Diagram of the Election Day Polling Party System

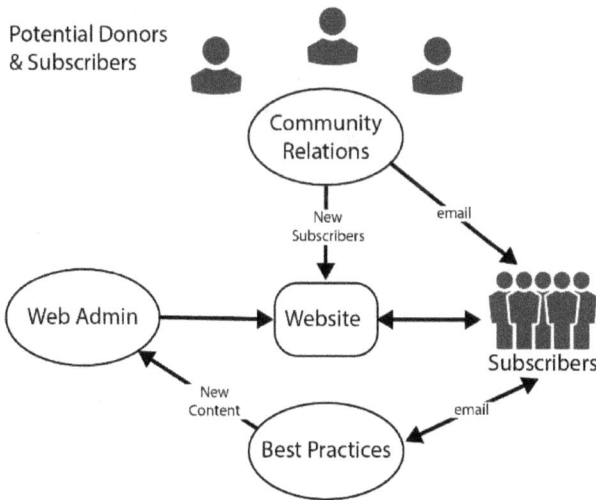

To better understand how the system would work, we can also create some processes. Recall from our discussion about optimizing a process that a process is a sequence of steps that transforms inputs to outputs. So, for example, our people system might have four key processes as summarized in the Table 5-3. These functional and process models do not have to be meticulously detailed. With a basic understanding of the system from these models, we can begin to plan our implementation. This includes tasks such as the following:

- How many people are needed to operate this system?

- What technology and resources are required?

- What finances are needed and where can they come from?

With this knowledge, we can then organize a set of tasks and create a plan for creating the system.

Table 5-3. Key Processes for the Election Day Polling Party System

Subscription	Content Development	Ad Process	Evangelizing
1. Access website. 2. Fill out form to subscribe. 3. Verify email address.	1. Collect feedback from successful party-throwers. 2. Create documents. 3. Have documents reviewed by a few subscribers. 4. Update documents. 5. Post to website.	1. Three months before election, identify key places for ads. 2. Buy the ads. 3. Monitor performance of ads.	1. Three months before election, start sending tips and tricks to subscribers. 2. Solicit feedback, ideas and stories to be shared on website. 3. Curate the feedback and send out in next newsletter. 4. Ask for pictures to be submitted of subscribers' events.

Other Examples

Besides the Voter Turnout Improvement System, some major examples of designing people systems over the last couple of decades have included the following.

- **E-commerce.** A wide number of businesses have moved from live purchase transactions to selling online, where no live person is needed. In many cases, the dollar volume of transactions over an e-commerce site exceed those in live settings, such as a retail location.

- **Digital delivery.** Many industries, such as book publishing and movie rentals, have moved or are moving from a model where the physical product is stocked in retail outlets to one where the product is delivered digitally on demand.

- **Crowd-sourcing.** Numerous services are now provided by individuals who connect to each other through a crowd-sourcing site, such as TaskRabbit or Uber. These sites provide a platform where others, who are not direct employees of the company, can coordinate their services through the platform. That is, they respond to requests for service directly from clients via websites and mobile phones.

- **Software as a service.** In the old days, you purchased a product and that was it. You got a CD or downloaded it to your system. If you needed to upgrade, you bought a new CD or download. Now we are moving to models where you subscribe to the software and pay by time, such as by the month. Microsoft and Adobe are now using this model for common consumer software.

These examples are getting to be well-known systems now, but in the beginning, they were frontiers to be explored.

Cheat Sheet

This chapter has introduced basic concepts of designing people systems. The concepts were introduced using examples for improving voter turnout in the United States. The basic steps of design are the following.

1. Understand the desired outcome

2. Innovate solutions

3. Analyze the context

4. Apply the appropriate design approach

We then discussed two common design approaches, one for optimizing existing systems and the other for designing new systems. The basic steps of each are given below.

Optimization

In an optimization design, we have an existing system that we are trying to improve. The most common process is as follows:

1. Define and agree on the outcomes and critical success factors.

2. Measure the output of the current system.

3. Analyze the current system and determine where improvements can be made.

4. Implement the changes.

5. Control the resulting output. This means measure the output and correct for any variance from the target.

Evolving New Systems

When creating a new system, it often must be designed using an iterative process, such as this:

1. Determine the outcome model for the initiative.

2. Analyze the context.

3. Participatively envision the future people system.

   o What is the purpose of the new system?

   o What services should the new system provide to clients?

   o What functions, processes, services, and other enabling functions are need for the people system?

4. Participatively envision the organizing framework.

5. Mobilize teams to design in their respective domains.

6. Design ways to close the gaps.

7. Learn and evolve.

Involvement

Both design methods should be done by involving affected stakeholders. In existing systems, it may be possible to involve fewer people because the process is well known to the stakeholders. However, participative design requires the facilitation of agreement across many people by eliciting their input, structuring it, and socializing it back with them. Approaches for doing this will be discussed in the next chapter.

6

Architecting Collaboration

To change the organization, change the conversation.[1]

—Peter Block

The design of organizational change requires the collaboration of many people. Their diverse perspectives must be melded together into an implementable design. This collaboration could have a wide range of design goals, including developing strategies, processes, or technologies. These must fit well together and support the intended behavior changes. This form of design requires the interaction of many people. But, when humans interact on complex issues, the resulting design effort can often be waylaid or fall short of expectations due to the subtle dynamics of organizations. Thus, architecting an effective collaboration is a key activity of the Core Group.

When designing physical deliverables like computers, we use the principles of engineering. Requirements are gathered, end states are defined, and the engineering discipline is applied to create an outcome as close to the requirements as physically possible. This is based on physical laws that are largely invariant. However, when we are designing how people will collaborate, an important outcome is the shared mental concepts about how people will work together in the future. There are few fixed laws that govern what will work, and many solutions may work equally well. What is needed to reach a beneficial outcome is a design process that engages the designers in learning together what they want and how to express ideas in similar language.

The situation is often described as "herding cats" because of the many divergent opinions that surface about how the intended change should be accomplished. These opinions often create a great milieu of ideas requiring many interrelated decisions. When there is no architecture for facilitating this conversation, it can fall into a "spin cycle" where the conversation seems to go on indefinitely. This causes anxiety in many people, who fear an unending vortex of meaningless and boring conversation that wastes valuable time.

One common response to a spin cycle experience is to declare "all this talk is going nowhere. We just need to make a decision and move on." The frustrated people then call for an executive decision that will put the matter to rest. However, while this relieves the immediate anxiety, it often simply pushes the problems down the road. Having no additional access to better information or judgment, the managers who are tasked with making the decision will resort to going with "gut" or "intuition" even if everyone is not happy with it. The problem is, as we saw with our director in Chapter 1, that this can produce not only counterintuitive or surprising results, but also results that instead perpetuate the original issue. It was exactly unawareness of the downstream impacts that produced the situation in the first place.

The solution is a middle ground between allowing a free-for-all and locking diverse voices out of the process. This is accomplished by architecting an effective collaboration process that will both engage diverse voices and keep the progression of ideas moving forward. The essentials of this approach are a) establishing and maintaining the conditions for authentic dialogue, b) facilitating a forward flow of ideas, and c) getting the appropriate people to the table so the collaboration will occur.

Authentic Collaboration

Effective collaboration is underpinned by an open, honest, assumption-checking form of conversation we will call *authentic collabo-*

ration. Often, people use the term "collaboration" to simply mean "working together without fighting" or "sharing information with each other." But, authentic collaboration is more than sharing information: It is about working together as a team to make better decisions and create more effective action than any of the members would have been able to do on their own.

To collaborate authentically involves understanding that how a group reaches a decision affects the quality of the decision. Often, little attention is paid to how the group reaches a decision, and this means the quality of the resulting decision varies unpredictably. That is, while groups can make good decisions even if they are unaware of their group process, they can also make very bad decisions. This happens even if the members are all smart and competent individuals. As an example, Professor Roberto, in his book *Don't Take Yes for Answer*, discusses how both the Challenger and Columbia shuttle disasters may have been precipitated by a culture of **groupthink** at NASA.[2] This groupthink is a phenomenon where individuals become hyper-focused and self-confident about their decisions on certain flawed solutions while discouraging voices that would expose the flaws.

The phenomenon of smart individuals making dumb group decisions results from how the decision is approached. Regardless of intelligence, natural human tendencies create dynamics where poor collective decisions are made. This can result in the status quo being subtly reaffirmed rather than changed. Or it can result in risky decisions that imperil the success of the program.

To avoid this, our first task is to establish a style of interaction—authentic collaboration—that is more conducive to reliably good decision-making. Groups often make poor decisions because more forceful members speak first and prevail over the diversity of voices. This may be particularly prevalent in Western cultures where we are trained as children to focus on debate and winning. In the lore of Western management, effective leaders are expected to be decisive and forceful. We are trained to take a position and argue for it. Having one's initial position prevail is considered winning and other competing ideas are considered losing or being a weak leader. However, this is not conducive to innovative change programs for three reasons, as follows:

Better decisions are made by integrating diversity. When forceful and opinionated voices are introduced early in the group process, they tend to shape the discussion toward those opinions, meaning the tone and direction set by those forceful opinions becomes a group norm. This is called *information cascading*. In information cascading, members conform by contributing ideas like, and not radically different from, what has already been said for fear of being viewed as unusual or out of step by the other members. Further, group members then want to contribute, so they add to the direction already set, creating a snowball effect where the initial position becomes more strongly affirmed by the group than it was at the outset of the discussion. For example, if locations for a leadership workshop are discussed, and the first options that are proposed all entail using low-budget facilities or onsite conference rooms, others in the group may interpret that suggesting travel to an offsite conference facility would be viewed as too lavish or not fiscally responsible.

To see how this works in a humorous way, consider this sketch by Muppets Statler and Waldorf. The two Muppets play theater critics sitting on a balcony overlooking the theater.

```
Statler: That was wonderful!
Waldorf: Bravo!
Statler: I loved it!
Waldorf: Ah, it was great!
Statler: Well, it was pretty good.
Waldorf: Well, it wasn't bad...
Statler: Uh, there were parts of it that weren't
very good though.
Waldorf: It could have been a lot better.
Statler: I didn't really like it.
Waldorf: It was pretty terrible.
Statler: It was bad.
Waldorf: It was awful!
Statler: It was terrible!
Waldorf: Take 'em away!
Statler: Bah, boo!
Waldorf: Boo! It was awful.
```

Statler and Waldorf's views progressed from the show being wonderful to being awful in a few lines of dialogue. This conversation comically illustrates the information cascade, which happens in teams (with less drama and humor) all the time. Each speaker cues off what was said by the previous speaker, until the initial assessment is completely abandoned. Along with this comes an emotional high and a belief the group is right.[3]

Research on group decision-making has shown that better decisions are usually made by incorporating a wide range of viewpoints. This counteracts the phenomenon known as groupthink, and, in complex cases of organizational change, fully understanding the implications and the truth lie in the synthesis of the many views. So, skillfully integrating many perspectives tends to create a much richer, more accurate understanding of the situation.

Mental engagement is needed for deeper understanding. A second issue with allowing only the most active voices to speak is others tend to become passive and not engaged mentally. This leads to less active mental engagement, which in turn results in many discrepancies in understanding what the idea really means, ultimately resulting in miscommunications and missteps down the road.

Around 2010, I was part of an initiative to align the IT department of a major telecommunications company to a services model. The initiative was originally broached to the entire department by the CIO via a few PowerPoint slides at an all-hands presentation. The vision was to conceptualize the entire work of the organization as a service. However, for some time after the initiative began, I conducted leadership off-sites to get senior-level teams going on the initiative and even these high-level managers understood the intention quite differently. Some managers thought the initiative meant more focus on serving customers (customer orientation), while others thought it meant organizing technical services at different layers of the technology stack (service-oriented architecture), and still others thought it meant providing more services to customers (being a service provider). The truth was really all those views, and it often took live workshops held with the executives and their staffs—where they could ask questions and relate the intention to work situations — to meld these diverse perspectives into a complete and shared understanding.

So, for a group to truly understand the strategic framework, they need to be engaged in thinking about it, which is usually through asking questions and testing the responses against their own experience. This enables them to align their understanding more accurately.

Involvement builds commitment. Not only does discussing the ideas openly build greater understanding, it also deepens commitment. When people invest their own time and energy into the idea, they are more committed to it. Numerous studies have shown that once people engage even a little in doing something, they are more likely to accept the next task, even if it increases their involvement. This is often called the "foot in the door" technique.[4]

These three factors — incorporating diversity, engaging people mentally, and deepening their commitment — can be maximized by nurturing authentic collaboration. This term describes the style of collaboration needed to harness the collective decision-making power of the group.

Authentic collaboration means relating to each other in a way that draws from the form of dialogue advocated by writers such as Martin Buber, William Isaacs, and Daniel Yankelovich.[5] This form of interaction shifts the communication objective from winning the debate to using conversation to jointly inquiring and finding a deeper truth. Authentic collaboration is thus a joint inquiry into exploring, discovering, and building new knowledge. As an example, consider the two versions of a conversation between a service manager and a technical writer about changing a service manual, shown in Table 6-1.

Notice how the conversation in Version 1 and Version 2 start with the same statement by the Service Manager but from there the conversations reach quite different end results. Specifically, Version 2 leads to a much more productive and less contentious result because the comments made by the Service Manager are not taken at face value. Rather, the Tech Writer asks questions about the assumptions being made and discovers that the assumption of a "major change" is not nearly as significant as the Service Manager imagines.

Authentic collaboration seeks to reach a greater, shared under-standing of the topic than either participant had at the beginning of the conversation. To accomplish this requires the space for the following things to happen:

Table 6-1. Debate vs. Dialogue

Version 1	Version 2
SERVICE MANAGER: The field guys want major changes to the service guide.	SERVICE MANAGER: The field guys want major changes to the service guide.
TECH WRITER: Our writers have looked at it exten-sively and think it's good the way it is. We have no time or resources for a big revision. Budgets are tight.	TECH WRITER: What kind of changes?
	SERVICE MANAGER: We need to change the service guide, so the installation chapter is second not first.
SERVICE MANAGER: It has to be done. We'll have to take it to our VP to get a prior-itization.	TECH WRITER: Why second?
	SERVICE MANAGER: The service guys want it second.
TECH WRITER: Fine, go ahead but I doubt there will be any change.	TECH WRITER: I would think they would want it first be-cause that is what they do first. Why do they want it second?
	SERVICE MANAGER: All the other guides out there have a system description first and installation second, so that is more familiar to them. They want to be able to refer to common sections when they talk to people over the phone regardless of which book.
	TECH WRITER: So just switch the System Description Appen-dix to Chapter 1? We could do that.

- **Ask questions.** Rather than seeking to always talk and win the point, we ask questions to understand why others see things the way they do. We ask about their assumptions and what led them to their conclusions. The Tech Writer asks questions in an impartial way and does not leap to the assumption that the change will involve significant resources.

- **Vulnerability.** People must be willing to share their assumptions and be wrong. This means an environment of psychological safety must be maintained so group members can share ideas without having to be "right."[6] In Version 2, both the Tech Writer and Service Manager enter the conversation with a willingness to find additional information that might inspire them to modify their initial beliefs about the causes or solutions to the situation. The Service Manager willingly explains the reasoning without trying to hide it or still be "right" about the significance of the change.

- **Listening.** We should listen to what other people are saying and use that information to question our own assumptions. This is often difficult because we are so used to thinking about what we are going to say while the other person is talking, rather than truly listening to what they are saying.

- **Empathy.** To act with empathy requires taking the view of others and trying to see through their eyes. The Tech Writer is willing to see the situation through the perspective of the Field Engineer, rather than maintaining a sense of purity to the original manual design.

- **Skillful advocating.** Of course, everyone cannot listen all the time. Someone must talk and advocate. But this should be done in a skillful way that maintains the psychological safety while making our own assumptions known to better facilitate the collaborative inquiry.

The above was just a summary of the desired interactive modes. Of course, these modes take practice and need not be done perfectly. We do not have time to cover it in more detail here but see the referenced material for further study.

Collaborative Idea Flow

Another dimension of architecting collaboration is managing the flow of idea development. Groups can engage in several modes of interaction, including relationship building, exploring, idea generating, evaluating, and action planning. Usually, groups are accustomed to simply conducting these modes in somewhat random order, with a mode being initiated ad hoc, without attention regarding how the modes fit together. But, as we shall see, managing the flow of ideas through the appropriate modes of interaction produces better results.

The effective management of interaction modes is demonstrated in a creative workflow once observed at the Walt Disney Company. The Walt Disney Company is often an inspiration for excellent group creativity, and so it is insightful to look at how they produced cartoons. Per author Robert Dilts,[7]

> [Disney] had one room that was a dreamer room which had pictures and inspirational drawings and sayings all over the walls. Everything was chaotic and colorful in this room, and criticisms were not allowed – only dreams. For their Realist space, the animators had their own drawing tables, stocked with all kinds of modern equipment, tools and instruments they needed to manifest the dreams. The tables were arranged in a large room in which all of the animators could see and talk to other animators. For the critics, Disney had a little room that was underneath the stairs where they could look at the prototype pencil sketches and evaluate them. The room always seemed cramped and hot, so they called it the 'sweatbox.'

Walt Disney recognized key aspects of the creative process. First was the importance of setting. The setting provides physical cues and associations for people about how they should act. Being in different settings affects their moods and assumptions about what is appropriate behavior. It provides triggers and emotional associations to let people know how they are to interact. In a similar vein, well-known management consultant and writer Peter Block advised me that even the arrangement of chairs and tables makes a difference to the quality of discussion.

Second, Disney recognized the value of separating the idea-generating mode from the critiquing or evaluating mode. Moving to critiquing ideas and creating solutions too fast can kill innovation. This accords with findings by creativity researcher Edward de Bono, who found people often dismiss or accept ideas too quickly based on prevailing assumptions. To collaborate more effectively requires developing a process flow where ideas are generated and explored while suspending the assumptions about why the idea will not work. This is beneficial, because occasionally we need to review if perhaps changes in technology or the operating environment might have enabled a previously unfeasible idea to now be feasible. Moreover, the full advantages and disadvantages of an ideas are often easy to overlook. De Bono found that people who considered the pros and cons of ideas often made different decisions than when they just considered the idea from one side.[8]

We can employ these ideas with the Core Group by organizing the flow of collaboration to emphasize distinct modes of knowledge building. Keeping the modes separate aids in keeping the flow moving. These modes are described below and can be remembered using the acronym BUILDER.

- **B**uild Community
- **U**nderstand Perspectives
- **I**nquire and Organize into Collaboration Frameworks
- **L**earn Together
- **D**ecide on Action
- **E**xecute
- **R**eflect

The importance in these phases is keeping them distinct from each other. The development of ideas also moves roughly in the order given, even though there can be some back and forth movement between the modes. Building community is done throughout the process but should be started first so there is a basis of trust to support the discussion. Putting specific attention on it is important or it will get lost in the hurry to get things done. Generating options, criticizing ideas, or planning action steps too early leads to suboptimal decisions, as we have discussed.

Build Community

Although you may be excited to get action going, it is valuable to invest time early on for building relationships of the Core Group. People who know each other better tend to work better together: They learn each other's communication styles and begin to recognize how they are similar. This builds trust, and people are more readily influenced by people they like and trust.[9]

So, it is preferable to start off with some activities to get people to know each other better and feel more comfortable. This can involve things like

- **Simple introductions.** Have the team members introduce themselves and share a little about their background and interests.

- **In-depth introductions.** Get to know each other's history. Discuss backgrounds, career histories, and how members came to be in their job roles. Talk about hobbies, families, greatest achievements, and other outside interests.

- **Icebreakers.** An icebreaker is an activity designed to get people talking. Sometimes, these are fun ways to get to know a little about each other. Other times, the icebreaker teaches teamwork skills or develops agreements about how to work best together.

- **Have some fun.** Adding some fun can help people know each other better. Laughing together is bonding. People let down their guard, come out of their scripted ways of acting. These kinds of things can be interspersed in the agenda to keep people's attention. For example, Doni Tamblyn's *Laugh and Learn* provides many activities for fun but serious learning.[10]

- **Social media.** Additionally, the team may want to connect to each other on social networking applications like Facebook and Twitter or on an enterprise collaboration platform like Jive. These can help build relationships by giving the team members insight into what each other is doing without spending live meeting time on it.

- **Ground rules.** Norms of accountability, punctuality, and respectful communication should be explicitly identified. Both the consistency to the norms and the avoidance of hurtful communication help build and maintain trust.

- **Physical space.** Try to ensure the physical space is conducive to meeting. Temperature and outside noise should be controlled. Serve food, hot beverages. In fact, it is probably best, even though we live in an increasingly virtual teaming environment, to strive for at least a few face-to-face meetings or even a lunch or dinner together in the beginning. This provides an opportunity to develop comfort and trust as well as a history of enjoyable interaction.

Of course, this kind of community building is not a one-time event. Rather, it should be regularly built into the ongoing work of the team. This facilitates reaching agreement on all issues.

Understand Perspectives

In this mode, the Core Group searches for common ground by considering each person's orientation to the change effort. The essential activity is giving everyone a chance to share their perspectives and for everyone else to genuinely listen to what is said. Some specific methods for accomplishing this are listed below.

- **Establish core values to show how we are similar.** Go

around the room and have everyone offer core values that they would like to see maintained in the group dialogue or in the future state. Write these on a flip chart or shared file where everyone can see them. Look for and point out core values that are the same. My dissertation committee chairman, Dr. Bela Banathy, often said that all agreements are built on a base of common core values. So, the broader the base of shared values, the better.

- **Clarify terminology.** Part of the knowledge base can be definitions of commonly used terms. But this should be limited to essential key terms that are regularly used — it is very easy to waste a lot of time defining many terms that are ultimately not used or changed as time goes on. The same dynamic of meaning formation is always at play. Moreover, the definition of the terms mainly resonates with the group that works on defining the term and getting a wider group to accept the terms then in turn requires an investment in discussion with them.

- **List expectations.** Have everyone provide their expectations for the outcome of the collaborative process and list those expectations in a visible place (e.g., flip chart or digital file.)

- **State your case.** Ask them each participant to state their perspective on the situation at hand. What are its causes? What are the key factors? Everyone else listens but does not critique or debate it.

It is not necessary to use them all. Just pick ones that seem to fit. As people respond to the questions, instruct others to listen and not critique or hijack the conversation to their own agenda. By uncritically surfacing issues in a safe environment, the tendency toward spin cycle is lessened.

Inquire about Data

Ideally, decision-making should be evidence based. Determine what evidence can be gathered to support decision-making. This will add to the case for change information gathered in Chapter 2.

- **Establish core information.** What basic knowledge do people need? Review company strategies, industry trends, and historical background.

- **Assess the current state.** What is the current state? Are we behind competitors? Is our technology or infrastructure out of date? Is there a turnover or morale problem? The classic management technique of Strengths-Weaknesses-Threats-Opportunities (SWOT) analysis has been used effectively for many years for this.

- **Identify linkages.** A linkage analysis looks at who else is working on elements of the same issue. What are others working on and what do they have to offer?

Learn Together

Up to this point, more information and data has been taken in with an emphasis on listening and sweeping in information. Now, the focus turns to converging and making that information into knowledge by collaborating as a group to decisions and narrowing. Dr. Bela Banathy proposed a cycle comprising three parts that iteratively worked on building a knowledge base of the idea.[11]

- **Identify Success Criteria.** The group determines the essential characteristics of a successful option. This summarizes the learning from the collaboration framework.

- **Generate Options.** Generate multiple solutions, as was shown in Chapter 5. This improves innovation. De Bono also found that the first idea to be mentioned is often not the best idea.[12] In fact, it is sometimes the worst idea from an innovation perspective, because it is the knee-jerk reaction that affirms the status quo.[13] Then, as discussed previously, the utterance tends to limit true exploration and development of innovative ideas. Groups generated more innovative outcomes if they are allowed many options to emerge before deciding.

- **Evaluate Options.** Select the best option based on the group's agreement about the success criteria. A solution is settled on, decisions are made, and actions are planned. The action of strategic dialogue is the determination of the appropriate framework action.

The result of this would be an agreed on and committed to concept of something to be done together that could be turned into action, as will be discussed in future chapters.

Decide on Action

Although solutions may be chosen, the work in an initial workshop will likely be just beginning. Probably, the solution will be directional and need further action. The actions that need to be included are the following:

- Continued discussion of the issues and work on aligning the group.

- Delegation of some parts to sub-teams who come back and report, so the group can reach a consensus.

- Establishment of a governing structure going forward (steering and operating committees).

- Giving tasks to design teams to continue the design at the next level.

- Giving tasks to mobilization teams to mobilize agreed-on design elements.

Execute

A team, such as the Core Group, should set up a cadence to track and manage the next steps. Even if the agreed upon actions are to be executed by the Core Group, they still require scheduling and tracking. Obstacles need to be addressed and course adjustments or refinements to the decisions may be needed. A matrix like the one shown in Table 6-2 is often useful.

Table 6-2. Example Tracking Matrix

Team	Goals	Milestones	Success Measures

The columns are defined as follows:

- **Team.** This is the sub-team assigned to the effort.

- **Goals.** This is the goal of the effort. What constitutes success? When is the work complete?

- **Milestones.** These are the major milestones for steps on the way to completion—what key accomplishments will let us know it is progressing?

- **Success Measures.** These are the success measures of what is to be achieved. See Chapter 8.

This kind of a matrix is useful because it provides essential information for the assigned team to proceed while at the same time providing the right level of information for the Core Group to track progress.

Review

Periodically, as things progress, time should be dedicated for assessing if there are ways to improve the process. This promotes learning for future projects. There are many ways to conduct this kind of activity, often called a retrospective or after-action review.

One popular method is the "plus-delta" exercise.

1. Create a two-column chart. One column is labeled "Plus", and the other column is labeled "Delta." The two columns could be cre-

ated on a flip chart (in a face-to-face setting) or on a shared electronic document such as a PowerPoint file or Word document (in a virtual setting).

2. Go around the room one-by-one and have the team members offer ideas about things that went well or aspects that need improvement. Comments about things that went well are listed in the Plus column and suggestions for improvement are listed in the Delta column. Give hash marks to ideas that are mentioned multiple times.

3. Take volunteers for people to work on implementing the popular and promising improvements.

Alignment Workshops

Even though people know how to collaborate and are willing to do so, they often avoid it. It is just human nature to avoid difficult discussion. So, it is often necessary for the Core Group to organize sessions, or workshops, for the collaboration to occur.

Workshops not only create a venue for the collaboration, but they are frequently more efficient than other approaches. While you could try to continuously meet with key designers in small groups, this can be very inefficient. With each meeting, ideas change, and those changes then must be coordinated with other affected designers. This can create a confusing mess of information that leaves everyone with different ideas about what is going on. Thus, aligning the key designers is often best accomplished by organizing one or more collaborative workshops, which are working sessions, where the major emphasis is on facilitating how the participants generate new ideas, new agreements, and new plans for working together. In the workshop, they take the intentions in the basic change story and make them more implementable, according to relevant change design strategy adopters. Properly designed and conducted workshops speed up the work for many reasons.

- Everyone hears the same messages at once.

- Communications blockages are reduced.

- Workshops enable peer learning, role modeling, and peer commitments.

- Workshops build on the advantages of aggregating multiple and diverse perspectives.

The intended outcome of the workshop is thus mental alignment across a community. This means the community holds shared agreements about the design objectives, a design itself, or a plan of action. This method of architecting collaboration can be used for countless types of issues, although we will discuss it here using the example of collaborating to design what is to change.

Historically, leadership workshops were usually done for top management and team building situations. However, the advent of complex and continuous change makes the workshop a much more valuable tool at all levels of the organization. As the change maker, you must learn to design and facilitate these sessions.

When I first started proposing workshops, there was a lot of concern from managers who worried about the time workers spent away from "real" work. But, a properly designed workshops are a way to speed up the work. Let us see how it is applied.

Planning

The key to effective collaboration is planning. While the act of facilitation often seems to outsiders like a spontaneous, free-flowing conversation, it is usually the result of planning. The planning aligns divergent viewpoints ahead of time, prepares the ground, and creates boundaries and contingencies to keep things from going haywire during the session. Proper planning is especially important if many people will be involved, because 5 minutes of 60 people's time being wasted is five hours of time! This could cost thousands of dollars.

The planning process can take many forms, depending on who is available and the size of the program. In my experience, successful large workshops (30+ people) usually involve establishing an event team of two to five people that prepare and coordinate the event. Roles on the planning team include:

- **Sponsor/Lead.** There is often a senior-level person who pulls the event together. This is not required, of course, but it can help get people to attend and keeps the management communication channels open.

- **Event Coordinator.** Event planning involves some basic project management. There are many tasks to be tracked that must be completed on time. The event coordinator calls the planning sessions, runs the agenda, maintains the task list, and ensures action items are completed.

- **Facilitator(s).** Facilitation and meeting design are skills developed from training and experience. Although the entire team does not have to be facilitation experts, having at least one person with strong facilitation skills is valuable. This person may also be the facilitator during the event.

- **Logistics Coordinator.** In addition to managing the task list and design activities, it is helpful to offload many logistical tasks to the logistics coordinator. This coordinator can find the meeting rooms, arrange for catering, find and buy props, and send out agendas.

For an event that is more than a few hours for 15 or so people, the team should start planning several weeks ahead of time. In the weeks leading up to the event, they should meet regularly, perhaps 1 or 2 times a week for an hour and work out the design and plan. This preparation involves the following activities.

Establish the context. The first discussion should be determining the following key parameters of the event.

- What is the goal? What do you want to achieve?

- Who will be the participants? Will they be in-person, virtual, or mixed?

- Are there any emotional issues to be aware of?

- What other guiding ideas should be adhered to? The guiding ideas are things like "be inclusive" or "be as innovative as possible" or any other principles that the team wants to introduce that should underpin and guide the design.

- How much time is available?

- When and where will the event be held?

Outline the high-level design. Determine the big blocks of the conversation that will lead to the goal. Each block needs to only have a basic goal, a concept, and a time allotment. The goals and order of these blocks should be guided by the BUILDER methodology.

You should outline the big blocks first and refrain from delving into specifically how they will be conducted until later. This keeps a focus on the end-to-end event and avoids getting bogged down debating the details of the initial activities, which can waste a lot of time in the preparation. Blocking the agenda into high-level modules enables you to then delegate those modules to others to be more fully developed.

Schedule the room, send invitations, and manage the invitee list. This activity should be started as soon as possible, and the effort required should not be underestimated. People are busy, often especially the key people needed to make good decisions. So, getting a placeholder on their calendar as far ahead as possible is critical to maximize the attendance of key people. Also, when you are trying to build alignment across several organizations, the list can take some negotiation to manage. Replacements must be found for people who are unavailable; some of the invitees or their managers will want to add others to the session. Cancellations will happen. The scheduling and working with the attendees can be surprisingly time consuming.

Establish a Repository. Common documents should be stored in a central location. Documents such as a) a detailed design document, b) an action list, c) an attendee list, and d) a public agenda are needed and should be kept centrally so the latest documents are available to the event team and can be modified appropriately.

Socialization. Most of the time, it is best to socialize the goals and high-level agenda with key people as soon as possible. You should not only make key people aware of what is being planned but get their feedback on how to improve the agenda. In some cases, it might also be valuable to inquire about their perspectives on any politicized issues that might come up. This could also be done in the form of a stakeholder analysis — that is, understanding the key issues, concerns, issues, and expectations of the attendees as input to building out the detailed agenda and facilitation plan. (See Chapter 7.)

Design the detailed agenda. For each module on the agenda, a specific facilitation plan should be worked out. The detailed agenda can be used to refine the breakdown by time of the events in the workshop. of these are described later in this book. If possible, these modules can be delegated to members of your event team or even invitees. It is often a wise idea to have different people involved in making presentations or facilitating sections of the agenda because the many voices adds to the sense of widespread support.

Send out pre-work and agenda reminders. If there is pre-work, this should be sent out as soon as possible. Reminders for both the agenda and the pre-work should also be sent.

Prepare presenters and facilitators. It is a best practice to meet with presenters and facilitators. You might want to give presenters a template in PowerPoint so that they have an idea of what to present. It is very common for presenters who do not have direction to bring far too much material for their time slot, causing the time to run way over. Facilitators of small groups may need to be trained.

Dry runs. If the workshop involves many people, it can be wise to schedule one or more walk-throughs to ensure everyone knows their part and that all the gaps are covered. Also, check out the room to see its configuration. Confirm with presenters.

Constructing an Agenda

With the BUILDER method in mind, there is a useful approach to building an agenda by thinking of it in terms of almost always having certain key blocks in a certain order, as shown in the table below. Almost all workshops should have these blocks, but the time allocated will vary. The rough percentage of the total time to be allocated to that block is given.

Table 6-3. Standard Agenda Blocks

Block	Contents
Intro (10%)	The start of the meeting gives the purpose, overview of the agenda, ground rules for interaction, and logistical information attendees may need to feel comfortable. Icebreakers and introductions should be used to get the attendees familiar with each other.
Context Setting (20%)	Attendees need to know why they are there. This block of the agenda includes history leading up the meeting, the change story, supportive and directional comments by key leaders, as well as key information and research that will facilitate the conversation.
Exploration (35%)	The attendees are there to collaborate, so the cornerstone of the workshop is the activity of learning together. It might include group discussions, breakouts, and other facilitation methods designed to work with data and generate new insights and ideas.
Decision-Making (20%)	Once the key issues and perspectives of the attendees have been explored, decisions need to be made.
Decide on Action (10%)	Once decisions are made, then action planning should be done.
Closing (5%)	Finally, the meeting should close by summarizing what has been done, how it connects to the original purpose and expectations, and the next steps.

The meeting designer can use these blocks to construct how the facilitation of the meeting will go. For example, a typical organizational design meeting for a one-day workshop to kick off a design effort involving 20 participants might look as follows.

Time	Event	Presenter
8 am to 8:30 am	Opening • Purpose • Ground rules • Logistics • Introduction of each participant • Icebreaker: "What's your favorite movie and why?"	Facilitator
8:30 am to 8:45 am	View from the top. Remarks by vice president of marketing on importance of this effort and support of senior management	VP of Marketing
8:45 am to 9:15 am	Key trends in the industry	Outside speaker
9:15 am to 9:30 am	Current performance numbers	VP of Finance
Break		
9:45 am to 10:45 am	Group SWOT activity	Facilitator
10:45 am to 12 pm	Operating model options. Small groups break out and discuss operating models that would address the SWOT analysis	Small groups
12 pm to 1 pm	Lunch	
1 pm to 2:30 pm	Read out and discussion of proposed operating models	Facilitator

Time	Event	Presenter
2:30 pm to 2:45 pm	Break	
2:45 pm to 4 pm	Integration of models, decision-making on a mutually agreed model	Facilitator
4 pm to 4:30 pm	Next steps planning	Facilitator
4:30 pm to 5 pm	Closing	CEO

While this agenda is focused on a senior leadership activity such as might be held at an offsite location, numerous variations are possible for distinct types of groups, time commitments, and settings. Workshops could be set up, for example, in weekly 2-hour segments. How the implementation occurs depends on your analysis of the situation and application of BUILDER to achieve an important level of collaboration that advances the design and change effort.

Facilitation Guidelines

Experienced and knowledgeable change makers know that good decision-making results from a good decision-making process. Without this, the group dynamics easily lead to either the most opinionated or powerful people telling others what to do or to a decision-making deadlock that is hard to get out of. For this reason, especially when using online collaboration technology, the course of a discussion is planned and managed by experienced facilitators. They do not determine the content, but they provide a framework and keep decision-making moving forward within that framework.

Using facilitation methods in groups can be daunting at first. Participants feel they have things that they want to say, and for various personality and perceptual reasons may feel restricted at first by methods that ultimately will help them achieve their goals. As the change maker, you must learn to guide the group in a flexible way. Give them just enough theory and terminology to get them going. Be aware of which situation would benefit from a more structured facilitation approach and try to work it in. Not all situations require them, and some group decisions can be guided very lightly while others require more structure. Eager change makers often try to put too much rigor on to groups, so it is important to remember that you should connect with them at the level they can accept. One of my favorite maxims is

Make the connection with them where they are at.

If you are serious about creating change, you should invest in a facilitation class and in mastering the methods. However, here are some tips and guidelines that skilled facilitators use.

- **Build agreement in small steps.** Rather than tossing out big, complex questions for discussion and hoping for the best, organize the discussion to build up to major decisions by structuring it as a series of small steps. The first steps will often be broad agreements on very general structures, which are then used to contain the conversation and build on it. Group indecision arises because too many people have too many different ideas about what is being discussed and time is not taken to methodically sort them out and clarify them.

- **Build agreement by using organizing frameworks and artifacts.** Write things down, even if they will be changed later. Create tables, graphs, and drawings of key concepts. They do not have to be the final answers, but seeing things written down removes some of the vagueness and ambiguity and ensures clear communications. It also lets people know that their point is captured because they can see it "on paper."

- **Use parking lots.** A parking lot is a visible document showing the items held, or "parked," for later. Capture key points that are not ready for prime time by saying, "that's a great point, but can we put that in the parking lot to discuss later?"

- **Mixing modes of interaction.** People get restless and bored if the work is too tedious. Research shows that physical activity and changing mental modes — such as switching from lectures, to individual writing, to small group conversation, to puzzle solving — helps. Additionally, using different modes allows different personality types to show their strengths. For example, some people are stronger thinking on their own, while others thrive in vigorous conversation.

- **Dealing with action items.** A lot of action items might be suggested during the workshop. Due to the way workshops operate, these items might be simply the output of brainstorming, not vetted action items. Resist the temptation to assign owners to all of them. Instead, discuss setting up a team or two to review and follow up on them. The teams can then comb through them and determine which are most appropriate to do and manage the work going forward.

- **Avoid presenting too much complex information at once.** Focus on relevant information that is used to build agreement. Do not try to cram in too much just because you have that much material. People can only process so much at once. Focus more on them learning and using relevant content.

- **Maintain ground rules.** The ability of the group to have an authentic conversation rests substantially on being able to trust each other. Having open and honest conversations requires vulnerability to critique, and for this to happen requires psychological safety. The facilitator must ensure people treat each other respectfully and productively while avoiding personal attacks.[14]

Cheat Sheet

Many situations in organizational change require collaboration across of a community of people and the alignment on shared ideas. This is particularly true when executing the change design strategy, which requires the Core Group to engage the designers in a collaborative conversation that will transform the change ideas into something implementable. Achieving an authentic collaboration is done by managing both the intellectual and human components of the change process in a way that keeps the conversation from being mired in irresolvable complexity. A useful approach to designing this collaboration is based on the acronym BUILDER.

- Build Community
- Understand Perspectives
- Inquire and Organize into Collaboration Frameworks
- Learn Together
- Decide on Action
- Execute
- Reflect

The BUILDER method is often used in workshops, whether they are short or take up several days. This sort of collaboration is an essential play for the change maker. It is used throughout the change effort to organize and maintain alignment with the Core Group and to take vague ideas and transform them into further action. A successful collaboration is itself an influencing method, because it involves people in co-creating together and thus develops ownership over the outcome. A well-structured collaboration also incorporates methods to improve group creativity and the quality and speed of decision-making.

7

Engaging Stakeholders

People don't resist change—they resist being changed.

—Peter Senge

Changing organizations and communities at first seems daunting when we have made assumptions about the beliefs and interests of the stakeholders. A common pitfall in change planning is treating everyone as having the same interests. But, getting to accurately know the various constituencies and their interests enables us to see the stakeholders much more richly, and from this we can see strategies that will enable change. We must place a high priority on understanding what motivates them and on keeping their perspective at the forefront of planning.

For example, the phrase "people always resist change" is commonly said. But do people always resist change? Not really. People welcome being promoted at work, buying new houses, and getting married. As the Peter Senge's quote above suggests, people only resist certain kinds of change: They resist change that is forced on them and is perceived as counter to their interests. It turns out that in most change efforts there are aspects of it that appeal to some people and not to others, so understanding how the change will be perceived by different stakeholders provides leverage for the change strategy.

I used to organize a small annual conference for academics and students on social systems change theory. It was held in beautiful, seaside Pacific Grove, California, and it brought together small research teams to study various aspects of systems theory together for several days. The planning team and I originally assumed everyone came because of their interest in the topic. But, we wanted to increase attendance, so we decided to poll everyone about why they came. Their reasons were quite diverse. While interest in the topic was a motivator, other reasons included:

- A work get-away to beautiful location

- Meeting luminaries in the field that attended the conference

- Reconnecting with colleagues

- An opportunity for face-to-face collaboration with colleagues on projects only peripherally related to the conference

For some attendees, these reasons were more important than the official conference topics. The last bullet was a particularly shocking in that some teams were bringing their own outside work and simply using the conference as a convenient and comfortable venue to do it!

So, understanding the stakeholders and their interests enables us to create change strategies that engage the motivations of the stakeholders. In this chapter, we will discuss how to identify, prioritize, and understand the stakeholders in a way that will increase our chance of success.

Who Are the Stakeholders?

Our first task is to identify the stakeholders. When we formed the Core Group, a vague understanding of the stakeholders and communities was enough. But, for ensuring an adequate design of the change and for adoption planning, a more fine-grained understanding of the stakeholders and the impact on them is necessary.

So, as early in the Design function as possible, you should try to map out who are the stakeholders. There are multiple reasons for doing this early on, including the following:

- Getting their input on designs.

- Better understanding pf potential adoption issues.

- Engagement of the stakeholders in the design process increases their commitment to the change.

- Improved targeting of communications and influencing activities.

- Enrolling champions to help widen the adoption, as discussed later.

- Assessing the readiness of the design for implementation.

- Evaluating the readiness of the stakeholders for the change.

Use the steps below to properly identify and assess the stakeholders and impact.

1. Creating the Behavioral Future State

It is common in organizational design to define a future state and contrast it with the current state. This future state often describes technologies, policies, staffing levels, organizational structure and so on. In this section, I introduce a tool called the *behavioral future state*, which is a view of the future based strictly on core behaviors, or what stakeholders should do differently. I have used this successfully for over a decade, and it provides a valuable way to get critical focus on the human change aspects that are often overlooked. It thus provides a foundation for planning activities we will discuss later in this book.

The essence of creating the behavioral future state is to relate the core behaviors identified in the design process to the stakeholder who must perform them. For this, it is useful to create a matrix of stakeholder groups and their core behaviors. Initially, this can just be a rough cut based on your current understanding of the core behaviors and the stakeholders. It will be used to guide further inquiry, as discussed in subsequent material.

For our example, throughout the rest of the chapter, we will use an effort I was involved in at a major computer networking company to improve IT service management. This model had been introduced a few years prior, and it entailed organizing IT work as services (such as video conferencing, laptop support, telephones, and so on.) These services were presumably operated by people filling a set of service roles. After a few years of operation, there were concerns the model was not working as well as planned, and I was asked to conduct stakeholder research.

The future state describes what the system is supposed to look like. A simplified version of the intended future state is shown in the table below.

Table 7-1. Stakeholders and Behaviors for IT Service Roles

Stakeholder Group	Core Behaviors
Service Executives	• Align strategy with business. • Approve service strategy. • Approve changes to service portfolio.
Service Owners	• Be accountable for service operation and adoption. • Evaluate service demand and identify new clients. • Develop and manage service strategy. • Ensure alignment to technology architecture.
Service Offering Managers	• Drive service adoption and use. • Provide a comprehensive business solution.
Service Roadmap Managers	• Facilitate service roadmap development. • Develop overall schedule of projects and programs within the service category.
Service Lifecycle Managers	• Manage service improvement and optimization opportunities. • Identify changes in client usage of service. • Recommend service roadmap and service portfolio changes.

In the matrix, the left column shows the stakeholder or stakeholder group, and the right column gives the core behaviors they were expected to perform. In this example, the behaviors are like a role description, but this not necessarily always the case. Note this list should be limited to only the essential few behaviors that are needed, not an exhaustive list. Further, the groups can be refined, as discussed in the next section when you get more information.

Choosing the stakeholder groups is a kind of art form, meaning that it takes judgement based on experience and there are probably several approaches that would work equally well. Also, this analysis will be iterative, so you improve the accuracy of the analysis as you understand more about the groups and the change. But, the essence is to segment the stakeholders into appropriate groups, so we can design a change strategy that is focused on the unique needs of that group. Fundamentally, the group is determined by one or both of the following:

- **Different change impacts.** If the change asks for different behaviors from one set of people than another, then these are two distinct groups. For example, in a portfolio management process, there could be people who analyze costs of a project (analysts) and people who drive the tasks on a project (project managers).

- **Different perceptions to the change.** In some cases, the impact is the same but the stakeholder's perception to it might be radically different. For example, if the change will create a new department of project managers from people currently in other roles in the organization, some of them might consider it a promotion and others a demotion.

We segment the groups this way because these factors will ultimately lead to different influencing strategies for each group. The idea is to create groups that can be approached with similar messaging and influencing strategies. Here are some guidelines to consider when choosing the groups.

Stakeholder group number and size. Group the stakeholders at the highest level where there is a distinguishable and crucial difference.

Usually, this is the top five to ten most impacted groups. While sometimes a group can be a single key individual, such as the CEO, avoid the temptation to exhaustively list everyone who will be affected. Only do this if you can also identify differences between them that will drive further change planning.

Types of stakeholder groups. The natural first response of many people is to list organizations, such as human resources, sales, and engineering, as stakeholder groups. While this is possible, you should think carefully about whether everyone in the organization is impacted in the same way. Usually there are better breakdowns, such as by geography, role, age, gender, ethnicity, or a variety of other factors. Later, breakdowns by organization are useful for organizing communications because the list gives names of contacts who can help make sure messaging goes to the right people in the organization. See "Contacting Stakeholders."

Holistic. Make sure that all the groups needed to sustain the change are identified, not just the primary target group. Often this means identifying the actions management, external departments, or even customers must take. This points to the need to not only change the relationships and conversations between peers, but also between levels of management. For example, the table from above could be expanded with these groups to show a more complete picture.

Table 7-2. Additional Stakeholders for IT Service Roles

Stakeholder Group	Core Behaviors
Subscribers	• Consume the service.
Technology Developers	• Understand service needs. • Develop technology solutions.
IT Analysts	• Gather information for reporting to management.

2. Assessing Impact

Once you have a draft of the behavioral future state, it is useful to add the columns with following information:

- **Size** estimates the number of people in the group. Prior to finalizing the adoption plan, it is important to know the sizes of groups so that logistics can be managed – number of sessions needed, number of people to be trained and where, etc.

- **Impact Level** estimates the degree of change (high, medium, low) for the stakeholder group in terms of how significantly they must change their behavior or how much they might react emotionally. The degree of significance is estimated based on the stakeholder's perception of change to him or her personally. Higher impact generally indicates higher resistance and thus greater effort needed to bring the stakeholder on board.

- **Influence** indicates the importance of having the stakeholder on board to the program. Make/Break stakeholders are essential — their lack of buy in is a showstopper. Influencing stakeholders can heavily impact the success of the design. Their concerns should be addressed as fully as possible. The buy-in of these stakeholders is very important. "Affected by" stakeholders (none shown) have minimal influence on the project. Usually these stakeholders are informed about changes but their buy-in is not essential.

- **Estimated commitment** is the approximation of the stakeholder's commitment to the change (supportive, neutral, resistant).

This will result in a list that looks something like the example in the table below.

Table 7-3. Example Stakeholder List

Stakeholder Group	Count	Impact	Influence	Orientation
Service Executives	5	Low	Make/ Break	Supportive
Service Owners	20	High	Influence	Supportive
Service Lifecycle Managers	40	High	Inform	Neutral
IT Managers	150	Med	Influence	Resistant
Subscribers	4,000	Low	Inform	Neutral
Technology Developers	300	Low	Inform	Neutral
IT Analysts	20	Med	Influence	Neutral

These estimates give us an initial sizing for focusing efforts. Later, we need to engage with stakeholders and data sources to verify the numbers.

3. Prioritizing

At this point, our analysis enables us to begin prioritizing the stakeholders. There are several levels of this, as will be discussed further in later chapters, but initially the matrix enables prioritization of which stakeholder research should be done first. General guidelines are as follows:

1.   Make/Break stakeholders who are neutral or resistant

2.   Large groups who are resistant

3.   Large groups who are neutral

Contacting Stakeholders

Even though we know who the stakeholders are, we must design effective ways to get their attention. Everyone experiences a barrage of bids for their attention every day. This comes from family, friends, co-workers, advertisers, charity organizations, the government, and employers. We are always receiving messages that try to get our attention and influence us to act, but from which sources do we look for them and accept them?

First, we can explore these questions:

- Are the stakeholders on identifiable email lists?

- Do they read certain publications or attend specific meetings?

- What are their reporting chains?

- Are there online communities or discussion boards that are frequented by the target groups?

It may take a combination of these venues to reach the intended audience. Later, when planning our communications and outreach strategies, we will consider how these venues might be used. But, initially, we must seek to identify them.

Secondly, what kind of approaches are the stakeholders likely to respond to?

- Who are the recognized authorities? There may be people whose opinion is more valuable than others. This often is a different group than the direct manager.

- What are the recognized standards? Does the group adhere to certain professional standards, such as Six Sigma or ISO? These may indicate recognized authorities.

- What is the language of the group? In this sense, we are looking not so much for the cultural language, but the style.

What are the buzz words? Is the focus more on people, finance, law, or technology? What are the key terms and concepts the people use to communicate?

- What are the preferred communications styles? Do they prefer data or inspiration? Are they excited by technology or personal stories?

- What is the history? What has been the history — what have they seen before and what might be a charged topic?

All this information will be used later for shaping plans and communications. This helps understand the best kinds of messaging and influencing methods, but it does not help for determining how to reach them. For this, you must develop a contact list.

The *contact list* gives the specific means for contacting people in stakeholder groups. This could involve having the email address of every member, or a set of mail addresses for each organization that has project managers. It could involve identifying contact people who will relay messages to others they know, or it could involve specific regular meetings or forums where members of the stakeholder group can be contacted.

Building the contact list and its form will depend on the change effort. In the case of the IT Service Roles program, there was a service database listing all the people and their role. In a different company that had many different manufacturing sites, one of the field managers maintained a list of all the sites and their contacts that she was able to provide on request.

Methods of Collecting Stakeholder Information

When properly defined, each stakeholder group has different perspectives about the change. At first, imagining their perspectives is usually satisfactory. But, before fully designing the change approach, research should be done to determine the stakeholder perspectives more accurately.

Many different methods can be used to understand stakeholder perspectives. While the details of these methods are beyond the scope of this book, a summary of these methods and some useful resources for further study are given in the following table. Review the information provided and consider which methods you should study further for the types of change you are creating.

Interviewing

Interviews are usually live, one-on-one conversations with selected stakeholders. They are best conducted in person but can be done using Skype, Zoom, or another communications technology.

Interviews have the advantage of creating a greater connection with the interviewee. A skilled interviewer can help the interviewee feel comfortable to answer sensitive questions. The interviewer can also adapt the format as needed to rephrase questions, drill deeper into topics that emerge during the interview, and keep the interviewee focused on the relevant information.

The downside of interviews is that they are very time consuming to conduct and to process the information gathered. Each person must be individually contacted and scheduled. Notes must be captured during the session or transcribed from recordings and put into a consistent format for analysis.

The overhead-per-person usually limits the amount of people who can be interviewed to a small number. A single person can perhaps interview 30 people in a few weeks, and even if multiple people are available it is hard to get a representative sample of a population bigger than a few hundred people.

Table 7-4. Pros and Cons of Interviewing

Pros	Cons
• Create greater trust for discussing sensitive issues.	• Time consuming. • Usually impractical to get a representative sample.

Pros	Cons
• Get a deeper understanding of the issues. • Have more flexibility to follow up with detailed questions as needed. • Develop rapport with individuals who can later participate as early adopters.	

Focus Groups

Focus groups are conducted with many people at once. The group can give feedback on prototypes, plans, and other issues. Like interviews, focus groups are also best done in a face-to-face setting, but can sometimes be done using online meeting or videoconferencing technology.

Focus groups are also time consuming to prepare, conduct, and analyze. The format should be tested head of time. More care is needed to set up the room. In a corporate setting, the participants tend to cancel at the last minute, show up late, or need to leave early. So, focus group designers must prepare for these variables in the design of the session. Consequently, it is often also difficult to conduct enough focus groups to get a representative sample of population.

Further, a focus group introduces certain group dynamics. Particularly, talkative people can inhibit quieter people from talking and can also set a tone in the focus group that biases what people feel willing to talk about. Skilled facilitation is needed to gather useful data.

Table 7-5. Pros and Cons of Focus Groups

Pros	Cons
• Participants interact and may spur innovative ideas. • More people involved in short period of time.	• Time consuming. • Usually impossible to get a representative sample, • Possibly inhibited by group dynamics around sensitive topics or even the opinions of less assertive people,

Surveys

Surveys are sets of questions that are administered to people in the target population. They could be administered using paper forms, but these days they are almost always implemented using electronic tools like SurveyMonkey. These electronic tools greatly facilitate the delivery, collection, analysis, and reporting.

Surveys have the advantage of being able to collect generalizable data about the total stakeholder population, if you get a big enough response (sample size). For large stakeholder groups (over a few hundred), it would be difficult to contact enough them with methods like focus groups or interviewing.

While the ready availability of survey tools has made it much easier to conduct a survey, it has also reduced the effectiveness of surveys in some ways. People are now bombarded by surveys, so response rates are declining due to survey fatigue. Moreover, more people are making inadequate surveys. *It is very easy to create a survey to generate data, but that data can very easily be bad data.*

Table 7-6. Pros and Cons of Surveys

Pros	Cons
• Can get a representative sample • Easier to compile • Better statistics	• Takes time and expertise to develop • Easy to collect bad data • Effort needed to get a representative sample • Effort needed to get a representative sample

Data

With so much work now being done with interconnected computers, there is much more data available now than there used to be. It is much easier to collect, and there is a lot more of it. This lends itself to many new and innovative ways to profile stakeholders.

In fact, a new field called *data science* as developed around this, and these methods are just beginning to be applied effectively in organizational change. Many companies, like Google and Facebook, are using these approaches to understand how to improve productivity in novel new ways.

Table 7-7. Pros and Cons of Data Methods

Pros	Cons
• Often more objective. • Can be used for a representative sample. • Can be automated to create real-time metrics.	• Still subject to interpretation of what the data means. • May require technical expertise to obtain.

Analyzing the Stakeholder Perspectives

Once we have identified the stakeholders, we can look at how to influence them to make a successful adoption decision. We do this by finding the levers that are available for creating an effective strategy. This is called *stakeholder analysis*.

In stakeholder analysis, we analyze the critical success factors to adoption. Some of the most critical and relevant ones are as follows:[1]

- Is the change an advantage? What about the change will be compelling to the stakeholders? What will be threatening or make adoption difficult?

- Is the change compatible with the way they work and their environment?

- How complex is the change to learn and understand? Will it require special training?

The critical success factors explored by these questions are further discussed in the material that follows. The results of this analysis are used then to design and improve both the mobilization and planning and the design of the change and its supporting framework.

Is the Change an Advantage?

Clearly, from the stakeholders' perspective, there is no point in adopting a change that is not beneficial. The change should somehow make their life better than before. While this is obvious, it is easy to overlook. In corporate environments, people assume others will adopt a change because they are told to; in communities and other social organizations, people assume the change will be adopted because it is a moral or social good. But, people ultimately adopt for self-interest, although there could be many tangible and intangible factors in the calculation of self-interest. In organizational change literature, this calculation is called understanding "What's in it for Me" or WIIFM (pronounced wiff-um).

The benefit calculation can include inherent aspects of the change itself as well as the context. For example, the benefits of learning to play golf can involve more than the joy of a well-struck ball. The benefits could also include enjoying the outdoors, time spent with friends, the challenge of self-improvement, the thrill of competition, and even potentially winning money in a tournament.

This holistic view of the benefits is important in creating social change because at times a specific individual might find the core aspects of the change more difficult than what they were doing before. So, it can be useful to design the context to make the change more motivating.

People often ask, "How can I motivate people to change?" They are concerned with motivation, because motivation deals with the desires that people must have to act purposefully. That is, our motivation comprises the emotions, ideals, and perceptions that result in goal-oriented behavior.

Human motivation is covered extensively in psychology, and there are many diverse, contradictory, and overlapping theories covering a wide variety of life situations. But what we are interested in here is that subset of motivation theory which can be applied to creating organizational change. A summary of ten relevant aspects is provided below.

- **Safety.** Of course, people are motivated by physical and psychological safety.

- **Pay.** In organizational change situations, a primary motivation is to keep one's job and the paycheck coming in. This corresponds to the motivation to meet basic needs, identified way back by Abraham Maslow and Frederick Herzberg, including basic needs for food and security for oneself and for one's family.[2,3] However, numerous studies have also shown that pay is not as large an effect as often assumed. Specifically, after people have achieved meeting basic needs, it is even less a factor. Moreover, in organizational change situations, pay is usually a difficult lever because the pay levels and possibilities for increases and promotions are controlled by corporate human resources policy.

- **Greater comfort or less work.** Unsurprisingly, things that are more comfortable or easier are preferred.

- **Community or relatedness.** People naturally seek supportive relationships and acceptance from their social community and family. Psychology researcher Roy Baumeister calls this the need for social worth or justification,[4] and Maslow talked about the need for belonging and love.

- **Purpose.** The desire to have purpose in life is widely felt. It often underlies the search for the "meaning of life"[5] and is noted by Viktor Frankl[6] as well as Baumeister.[7]

- **Efficacy.** This category involves feeling a degree of control over life's events. People want to feel as if they have some control over what is happening to them.

- **Self-worth.** Baumeister[8] and David Myers[9] both noted that people report greater satisfaction with life if they are in some way better off than others. Myers stated, "Happiness is relative not only to our personal past experience, but also to our social experience … and we feel good or bad depending on whom we compare ourselves to" (p. 56). This speaks to the popularity of recognition programs because they single the person out as being special in some way.

- **Learning.** When we learn something or are surprised, our brains release a chemical called dopamine, which generates feelings of pleasure and reward. This is a chemical release that is like the effect of cocaine, albeit much safer and more productive. This biological reaction to learning makes it intrinsically rewarding to learn.[10]

- **Certainty.** We like to be sure about things. Getting information or assurances about the future can reduce anxiety.

- **Fairness and justice.** People often resist change that is not perceived as fair or just. Paterson found resistance to change was greatest when people perceived certain people or groups were being given special consideration.[11]

Considering the Net Effect

In the IT service management research mentioned earlier, I primarily used interviewing and some data collection. By examining a subset of the results, we can see how a *force-field analysis* works. This method was invented back in the early 1900s by Kurt Lewin, one of the key founders of the field organizational development. It is a common and highly useful way of analyzing stakeholder perspectives.

To set the stage, here are a few of the surprising results that were uncovered:

- In contrast to the formal role description, many service owners, particularly those who were executives with large departments, believed they had more important things to do than operationally running a service. So, they delegated the responsibility to someone else.

- The delegated person did not appear on official lists, so the services were often overlooked in cross-service communications.

- The service owner did not want to give up the title, because it was viewed as prestigious and having direct access to the CIO. They also enjoyed the strategy development aspects.

- Much of the operational work on the service was not done by a single person. Rather, the responsibilities for certain task, such as compiling service metrics, had been assigned to a person who collected metrics for many services.

The impact of these findings on adoption of the intended service owner role can be examined with a force-field analysis. The basic idea is that the stakeholder adoption decision is heavily influenced both by factors that compel the change and those that discourage the change. The driving forces are the aspects of the change that compel adoption — the relative benefits and other influencing factors. The restraining forces are those that answer the question "Why wouldn't the stakeholder adopt the change?"

An example of a force field analysis for getting the IT service owner to adopt their role as designed is shown Figure 7-1.

Figure 7-1. Example Force-Field Analysis for Service Owner Role Adoption

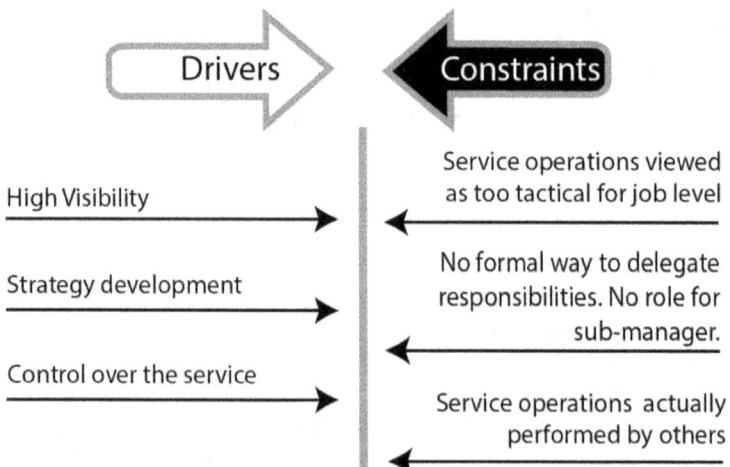

The force field analysis expresses the stakeholder situation as a contest between the driving forces and constraining forces for the stakeholder to adopt; the driving forces must be significantly stronger than the constraining forces. Given a situation that is roughly equal on both sides, the force-field analysis prompts us to study how to strengthen the driving forces or reduce the constraining forces. In the case of the IT service owners, it became clear that the definition of roles needed to be altered to fit reality. Some of the approaches taken to reduce the constraints are shown in the Figure 7-2.

Figure 7-2. Example Interventions

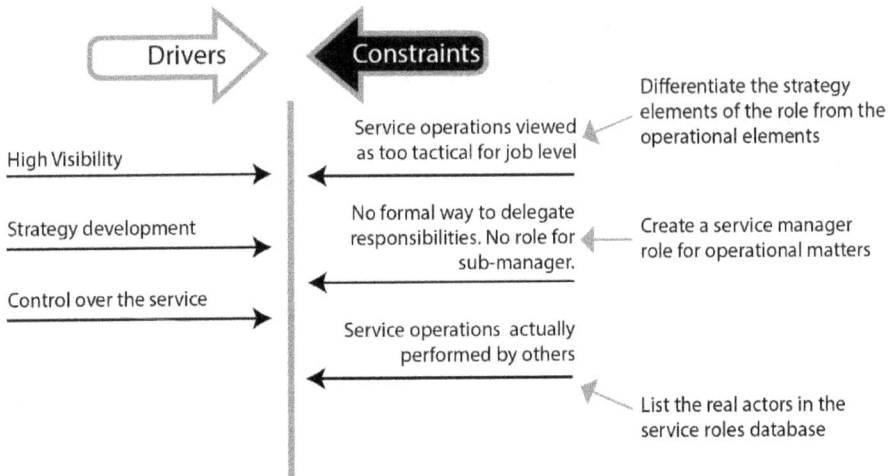

Cheat Sheet

Analyzing the motivations and constraints of stakeholders is critical to understanding the situation well enough to devise a solid change strategy. The results are used for both improving the change design and for developing mobilization plans as will be discussed in upcoming chapters.

The analysis has used the following artifacts:

- **Behavioral future state.** This matrix shows what the primary stakeholder groups are expected to do differently. It also provides some key information, such as the group sizes, impact levels, and commitment levels.

- **The audience/contact list.** This table identifies the channels that are available to reach the stakeholders.

- **Stakeholder analyses.** These are documents that provide insight into the stakeholder perspectives. These would include the results of interviews and associated force-field diagrams.

The basic steps of conducting the analysis as follows:

1. Identify the stakeholder groups and core behaviors.

2. Assess impacts on the stakeholder groups.

3. Prioritize.

4. Develop contact lists.

5. Interview and collect information from stakeholders.

6. Analyze the drivers and constraints.

This information is used to develop the change plan. How to do this is described in the upcoming chapters.

8

Developing Change Success Indicators

There are two possible outcomes: If the result confirms the hypothesis, then you've made a measurement. If the result is contrary to the hypothesis, then you've made a discovery.

—Enrico Fermi

How do you know if you are making progress or not? Without some form of feedback, it is difficult to know. At first, anecdotal feedback may be enough, but ultimately, and with large numbers of people involved, establishing some standardized change success indicators becomes valuable. While it is possible to get a sense of change progress through anecdotes, you risk falling into a groupthink or believing that because all the people you meet understand the change, it is understood by everyone.

The field of organizational performance metrics has blossomed over the last couple of decades. There are rigorous approaches to developing metrics for organizations, and there has been significant study on how to do it well. However, like several of the practices we have discussed previously, a lightweight version is often all we need, at least initially, in the fast-changing modern world. A lightweight version enables us to lay some groundwork and learn from it before a substantial investment is made in institutionalizing it. Moreover, at times only a crude, temporary framework is needed.

In this section, we discuss how to develop basic success indicators. These should be developed soon after the core behaviors are defined. The outcome of this activity is a handful of success indicators that are baselined in preparation for mobilizing a change. To understand how to do this, we will review some basic concepts of indicators and then a lightweight method for developing them.

The Success Indicator

A key challenge is determining what to measure. There are an infinite number of things that can be measured in any community or organization, not all of which are relevant to tracking change progress. Further, many relevant measures might be difficult, expensive, or time consuming to collect. So, we must understand how to select the most appropriate and useful feedback indicators.

We will use the term "success indicator" to refer to a form of metric used to provide the feedback needed to evolve and adjust the change effort. The term indicator is thus better for the ambiguous situations we encounter in organizational change, because the term "metrics" implies something more exact and objective. While specificity and exactness are desirable factors, they are often elusive. We will use metrics also, but as components of success indicators. Efforts to make everything strictly exact and objective are often not effective or worthwhile when considering the marginal utility for a change effort.

What to Measure?

Measuring the actual, intended outcome is certainly preferred. We would like to know the answers to such as questions as "How much was productivity improved for the client?" "Were they more creative?" "Did they save money?" Unfortunately, this outcome measurement is customarily the most difficult to obtain. We can conduct "voice of the client" surveys or gather customer satisfaction ratings, but these methods are often only partially accurate and risk irritating the client if done too frequently or too extensively.

To understand this better, let us revisit the Voter Turnout Improvement example from Chapter 5. In our outcome model, we defined an outcome and the critical success factors (CSFs) to reach it. If our outcome is simply to increase the number of people who cast votes, then it is simple to measure. But, often we also want to measure factors that contribute to the outcome, such as our critical success factors as well.

Moreover, what if the outcome is not easy to measure? Then, we must rely on measuring the CSFs to get an idea if success is being achieved. For example, if our outcome was to increase the number of *informed* people who cast votes, we probably could not ask all voters to pass a test before being allowed to vote. Instead, we would have to extrapolate the general preparedness from attendance at voter information sessions, hits on websites, participation in online forums, and so on.

Navigation Not Measurement

Has our Voter Turnout Improvement program done worse if in the first year there were 57 million voters and in the next year only 56 million? Likely, we do not know. There are too many factors that could affect a small percentage in turn out from year to year. The *variance* between 56 and 57 million might be due to random factors. This demonstrates that exactness, which is often expensive to acquire, is often unnecessary in these kinds of situations.

Exactness is important for measuring materials for construction or for valuing a stock portfolio. But the kind of measuring we use in organizational change is different. It is a *navigational indicator* that lets us know if the change is progressing as expected so we can course-correct if necessary. These indicators also let us know if we have reached a certain point in the change effort or the destination.

These indicators can be proxies. That is, they do not have to be the direct measurement of what we want to measure, but instead can be another more easily measurable phenomenon that moves in the same direction as the measure. For example, it is difficult to measure engagement or commitment to a program, but often meeting attendance suffices as a *proxy indicator* for engagement. While it is not a certain correlation, it might be better than nothing.

Leading, Lagging, and Current

Indicators can have several characteristics. One of them is time-relatedness. Some indicators are active at various times relative to the desired outcome. *Leading indicators* are good predictors of the future event, *current indicators* give the state now, and *lagging indicators* show feedback after an event occurs. For example, employee turnover is probably a lagging indicator of morale, while increasing order bookings may be a good leading indicator of future revenues.

In terms of measuring adoption, success in earlier stages of the adoption cycle may give an indication of future adoption because it is a progression. For example, the adoption cycle starts with awareness of the change and continues into understanding the benefits and then to commitment to try it. (This is discussed further in Chapter 9.) If we know the level of awareness of the change program at a given point, it is a leading indicator of future adoption because it is an essential first step.

Balance

Another characteristic of good success indicators is holistic coverage. That is, a chronic issue of success indicators is that once they are in place for a while, they can drive counter-productive behavior or become sub optimized. The phenomenon of sub-optimization occurs when keeping the indicator at a specific level becomes the focus of the effort rather than generating the desired outcome. For example, a focus on reducing costs to improve profit margins could result in reducing quality, which reduces the value and the price, thus reducing profit margins rather than improving them.

To address this issue in organizational metrics, back in the mid-1990s, Harvard authors Robert Kaplan and David Norton revolutionized the world of corporate measurement when by extending the traditional financial measurements to include additional dimensions such as innovation and learning, operational excellence, and customer value.[1] They asserted such a system would have less tendency to be sub-optimized because the dimensions would counterbalance. So, they created the Balanced Scorecard, which held that measures affect each other, and we need to understand the combined state or pattern of the measures rather than any single measure.

Anatomy of a Success Indicator

A success indicator thus has a certain anatomy that you should know to construct one properly. We will treat the success indicator as an index or composite of one or more measurements, each of which might be proxies for specific CSFs. How these are combined may involve some judgement by the practitioner, based on evaluation of the situation. The basic structure of this is shown in the figure below.

Figure 8-1. Anatomy of a Success Indicator

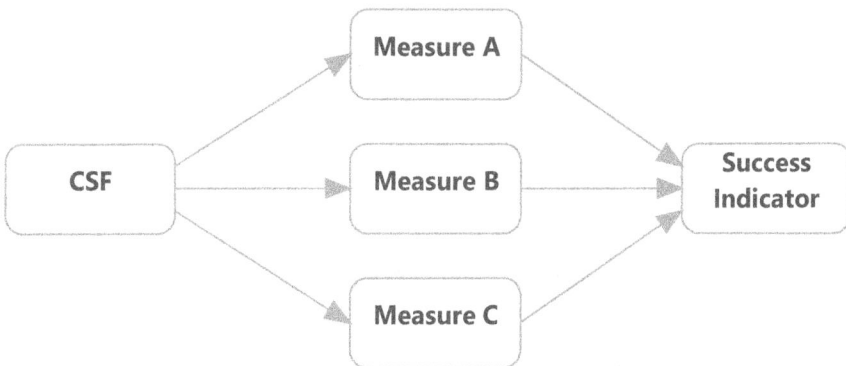

The definitions shown in the graphic are given below.

- **Critical success factor (CSF).** This is the condition that will likely result in the outcome being achieved.

- **Measurement.** The measurement is "what is measured?" This includes measures like hits on a web page, accesses to a building, or the percent of project plans filed.

- **Success indicator.** This is an overarching gauge of what the underlying measurements mean. It is the navigational indicator we will look at to feel comfortable that we are headed in the right direction. The connection can be loose: It gives an indication of whether the critical success factor is being met. Success indicators can pull together other metrics and indicators. In this usage, they do not have to be strictly mathematically related, although that is often desirable if it is feasible. So, for example, speedy delivery is often a critical success factor for the success of a pizza restaurant. The speediness of the delivery (say within 30 minutes of the order within 10 miles of the restaurant) could be the success indicator.

To see how this works in an example, we can build out the success indicators of our Voter Turnout Improvement program a little more.

Table 8-1. Translation of Critical Success Factors to Success Indicators

Critical Success Factors	Measures	Success Indicators
Register to Vote	# number of people registered	Registered Voters
Understand & Be Motivated	# subscribers to political news # social media conversations # attendees at political rallies and events	Citizen Engagement
Get to the Polls	# people who arrive at the polls who intended to vote	**Poll Arrival.** Calculated from number of people who show up divided by numbered registered

Critical Success Factors	Measures	Success Indicators
	# number of people registered	
Cast Vote	# votes cast	Votes Cast
	# of people who leave without voting # of people who cast invalid votes	**Vote Rejection.** Calculated from % who show up but don't vote

As you can see from the table, the CSF can require a couple of measures to get a sense of it, as shown in the middle column. Only a couple of measures are shown for simplicity, but more could be used. Separate measures can be grouped together to give a single indicator for reporting purposes.

In addition to measures, which are the class of things measured, we have metrics, which are the actual numbers the measurement gives. So, if the measurement is "clicks to reach desired web page," then "3" might be the metric. In looking at metrics, we often have two kinds, as below.

- **Target metric.** The target metric is the desired number we want to result from the measurement. For example, if the measurement is hits on a website per days, the target metric might be 10,000.

- **Current metric.** The current metric is the current result of the measurement.

Lightweight Development Process

In this section, we discuss a lightweight methodology for developing the indicators, as well as some guidelines and examples.

Methodology

Developing change success indicators does not have to be a long and arduous process. The key is twofold: First, remember that the indicators can and should be changed as you experiment with them. Do not try to decide on a fixed, final set and codify them forever. Try them on paper first and adapt to what seems to work. It is a learning process. Second, make sure to focus on what is important and what will be used, not everything that is nice to know.

A lightweight process for developing change success indicators is shown in Figure 8-2. The process is shown in step-wise format, below. This could be conducted in a workshop, as discussed in "Architecting Collaboration" in Chapter 6.

1. Review the outcome model and your critical success factors and behaviors. List these in a table.

2. Assemble a group of people knowledgeable about the organization and brainstorm possible measures for the CSFs and behaviors. Use the guidelines in the next section to refine the list. Associate the measures with success indicators.

3. Socialize the success indicators with others. Incorporate the feedback from the socialization.

4. Figure out how to operationalize the metrics by determining where, when, and how they will be collected.

Figure 8-2. Basic Success Indicator Development Methodology

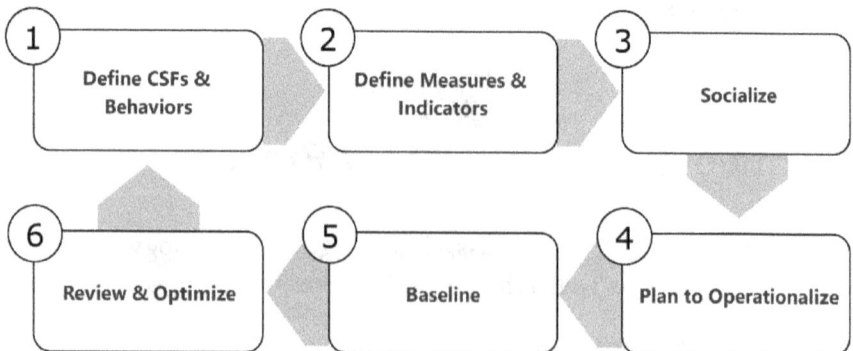

1 Define CSFs & Behaviors	2 Define Measures & Indicators	3 Socialize
6 Review & Optimize	5 Baseline	4 Plan to Operationalize

5.   Baseline metrics. Review the baseline and adjust if needed.

6.   Establish a schedule and start collecting the metrics regularly. Review them with the operating committee and determine at which point there is a need for further inquiry. Conduct the inquiry and determine if corrective action is needed or the measure should be adjusted.

Guidelines

When selecting the indicators bear in mind the following guidelines:

- **Choose a small number of indicators.** The top-level indicators should ideally be around 5 but less than 12. The indicators should provide a navigational view of the people system in terms of pointing to where problems are emerging as an impetus for further exploration.

- **Align from top to bottom.** Avoid conflicting measures. Cascade metrics down from the top. Then, align them among interdependent roles at each level. Only use what is necessary, as cost and the potential for error is increased with each additional metric that is tracked.

- **Ensure criticality.** Measure what's most important. Measure the drivers that make a significant difference if they change.

- **Watch for unintended consequences.** Consider what will happened if people do try to accomplish the measure. What side effects could happen? Check that measures do not drive undesirable behaviors.

- **Balance the measures.** Go beyond financial measures. Balance financial measures with corresponding measures, such as efficiency, client value/satisfaction, and operational efficiency so that a holistic picture is created. For example, monitoring operating expenses and customer value enables you to know that if expenses decrease and customer value also decreases, something is wrong; whereas, if expenses decrease and customer value increases, productivity has improved.

- **Use leading and lagging indicators appropriately.** Use lagging indicators for accuracy; use leading indicators to predict future trends.

- **Set challenging but reachable targets.** Set targets to be challenging but not impossible.

- **"Pick pockets."** A consultant once told me this at a dinner once. His point was to simplify collecting metrics by finding easily available measures that could serve as proxy indicators. Since everything is connected in a people system, sometimes it is easier to measure a proxy, or a metric that is good indicator of something else that is hard to measure. This notion is like the maxim, "Where there's smoke, there's fire." For example, number of messages in an email inbox might be a good proxy for manager workload.

Using Success Indicators

As mentioned earlier, success indicators are for navigation, or informing you if the change process is on track. They should be reviewed regularly, but they should not necessarily be taken strictly at face value. Rather, they are indicators to flag unexpected conditions so that further inquiry can be made.

A colleague of mine once told me about a consulting assignment where she was asked to investigate why there had been an increasing number of calls to a credit card support center asking for balance information. Her inquiry discovered that the person who was responsible for clicking a button to send out statements had been let go during a recent reorganization. The responsibility of making that one small but consequential action had been overlooked, leaving thousands of people wondering what happened to their statement.

Inquiry into what the success indicators are telling you could lead to changes in the indicators themselves. Indicators that are always the same can be dropped and replaced by indicators that will flag other conditions that need to be tracked.

Cheat Sheet

In this section, we covered the basics of a lightweight methodology for developing change success indicators for a program. Change success indicators are important to knowing if we are achieving the critical success factors for the desired outcome. Some key features to remember are listed below.

Table 8-2. Success Indicators Is and Is Not

Is	Is Not
• Lightweight—easy to collect. • Drives decision-making and action. • Disposable—throw away when not useful. • Useful for shorter term directional applications.	• Permanent. • A rigorous definition for enterprise implementations.

The basic process was as follows:

1. Define the critical success factors.

2. Define the change success indicators that would suggest the critical success factors are being met. Determine what the measurement structure is and the metrics.

3. Socialize the success indicators with others.

4. Figure out how to operationalize the metrics.

5. Baseline them.

6. Start collecting them, review and optimize.

    Use the following guidelines when selecting:

- Keep the set to around 5 and less than 12.

- Align from top to bottom and keep the total set to less than 150.

- Ensure the measures are truly critical.

- Watch for unintended consequences.

- Balance the measures.

- Use leading and lagging indicators appropriately.

- Set challenging but reachable targets.

Part IV: Involve

The activity of engaging the first adopters and providing the framework for them to use their influence to scale the change.

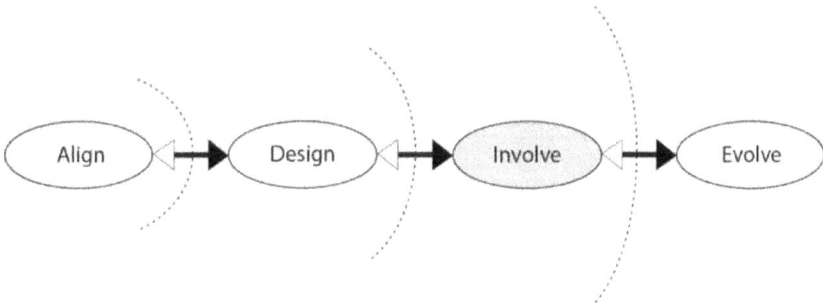

Align → Design → Involve → Evolve

9

Mobilization Strategy

Vision without execution is hallucination.

—Thomas Edison

Once the change is identified, it must be taken out to the target population, adopted, and embedded in the way people work or interact together. Otherwise, the change effort will be wasted. In a large stakeholder population, this will entail a significant effort to diffuse the change across the population. So, *adoption* is where "the rubber meets the road"—that is, when stakeholders are influenced to implement a new behavior and to sustain it.

Making sure this happens requires a *mobilization strategy.* This strategy details how to get stakeholder groups to adopt a specified change in behavior during a focused time frame. The success of the mobilization strategy is underpinned by optimization of the design because it is going to be much harder to influence adoption if the change has limited benefits to stakeholders or is otherwise inconvenient. While this seems obvious, in practice it is easy to rationalize away the difficulty of getting adoption by making statements like, "It is a mandate, so they have to."

To develop the mobilization strategy, we will first look at the conditions for a change to be ready for mobilization. Then, we will look at how people adopt a change. Finally, we look at how to frame a strategy to create a mobilization strategy.

Ensuring Change Readiness

To mobilize the change, the change should be as adoption-ready as possible. This means optimizing the appeal to adopters—interfaces are easy to use, instructions are clear, training is in place, and so on. Certainly, these change-readiness factors will never be perfect, but we can focus at least on doing what can be done and being realistic about the chances of success. Too many unrealistic changes are launched because someone powerful wants them without genuine consideration of whether those changes have a real chance of being adopted, regardless of the effort applied.

Thus, a best practice is holding a readiness review with the Core Group and other key team members to determine if the change is ready for launch. This ought to be an explicit decision by the group because although the design approach should produce an adoptable change, this is not always the case due to various complications and pressures that exist in real situations.

How People Adopt a Change

To effectively plan for a change, it is important to understand how people adopt a change. A well-designed change program facilitates each stakeholder going through the option cycle individually. Thus, for every change situation that you encounter, you should ask yourself,

"How is this change going to work at the individual level?"

Then, creating change across a population is a matter of organizing how to create an adoption experience that will work for each stakeholder.

Research on diffusion theory has given, over many years in diverse situations, numerous insights on this issue. This research has shown peo-

Figure 9-1. Personal Adoption Process

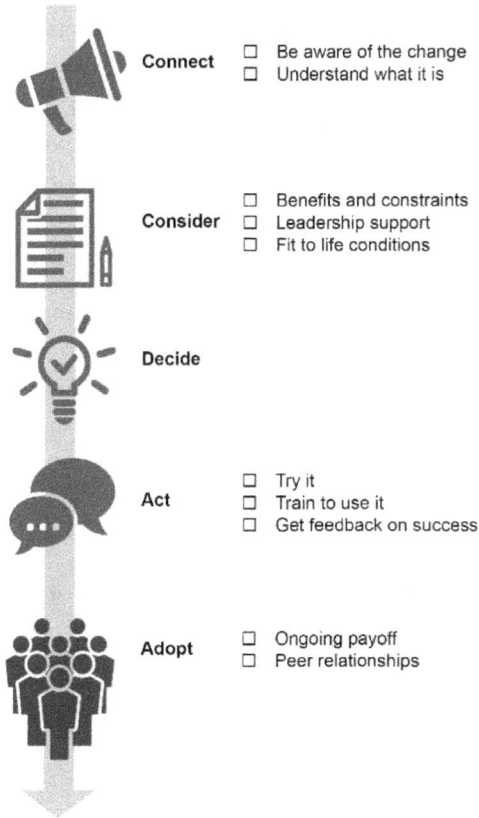

	Connect	☐ Be aware of the change ☐ Understand what it is
	Consider	☐ Benefits and constraints ☐ Leadership support ☐ Fit to life conditions
	Decide	
	Act	☐ Try it ☐ Train to use it ☐ Get feedback on success
	Adopt	☐ Ongoing payoff ☐ Peer relationships

ple go through a sequence of stages to adopt a change. One way to represent those stages is shown in Figure 9-1. This is a rough approximation: People go through the process in diverse ways, but it does serve as a handy guide for planning.

We will briefly review the stages shown in the figure in the next few sub-sections.

Connect

The Connect phase pertains to establishing positive awareness of the change. If stakeholders are not aware of the change, of course they will not adopt it. Similarly, if their attitude toward the change is not initially positive, they will not continue the change adoption process.

Establishing a connection with stakeholders is more difficult than it seems. There are two key challenges in this phase. First, people are busy, and it is often hard to get their attention. They have pressing meetings, deadlines, and demands from coworkers and relatives. This situation is compounded when you cannot interact with them personally, such as in large populations. Connecting with a large population can require many messages delivered in multiple formats over an extended period.

A second challenge occurs when the change is not intuitively appealing. That is, while the benefits of a new iPhone are readily understood, the benefits of conserving water or reducing one's carbon footprint are often viewed skeptically.

Consider

The Consider stage is when the stakeholder gathers any information needed to decide whether to adopt. The stakeholders must not only understand change and its potential benefits, but they also need to know how to perform the change and if it will work for them. This is the difference between understanding what a motorcycle does versus knowing how to drive one and being able to use it for one's needs.

In an organizational or social change setting, this consideration can include several key factors such as:

- **What's in it for Me? (WIIFM).** A primary consideration for stakeholders will be whether there is a benefit to them. Does it make their work or life easier?

- **Leadership Support.** In an organization, usually, stakeholders will need to know the change is supported by their management.

- **Peer Support.** As we saw in the discussion of diffusion theory in Chapter 1, a relatively small percentage of stakeholders will adopt the change on their own research. But, most people will look for varying levels of adoption from trusted peers before they do it themselves.

- **Supportive Environment.** The environment must also be supportive (e.g., the effort does not try to introduce Macs into a mainly PC environment, or metric equipment where English measurement units are used.)

- **Skills.** Does the stakeholder have the skills to use the change? Or, do they have confidence they can acquire them?

Decide

The crux of the change effort is the decision to act. In this stage, the stakeholder might consciously deliberate, even to the point of making detailed analysis. Or, they may simply choose by gut feeling. Whichever method is used depends on the person and the situation.

Act

The Act stage involves experimenting with the change and evaluating it. This could involve developing skills or adjusting configurations. While success can be limited initially, the stakeholder must soon experience a benefit from the change or they will drop it.

Adopt

Once the stakeholder has determined the change can be done successfully, there must be sufficient support for it to be maintained. Even though the stakeholder performs the new behavior a few times, it is not guaranteed that they will continue doing it indefinitely. The following are some of the factors that contribute to sustained adoption.

- **Critical mass.** If enough people have adopted, often called *critical mass*, then the system of peer expectations helps reinforce the change.

- **Adaptation.** Simple changes may be adoptable in the same way by everyone, but more complex changes usually need to be customizable or adaptable to the specific situation. This makes the change a better fit for different stakeholder situations.

- **Governance.** A skillful change practitioner should strive to create situations where stakeholders are motivated intrinsically to adopt and maintain the change. But sometimes this is not possible, and oversight must be applied. This is often only marginally effective and costly, so it is usually not the preferred approach if other motivations are feasible. But, for some kinds of change, oversight, or governance, is essential to ensuring the change sticks. This could be metrics, policies, and laws. The need for this is found in such things as speed limits, disaster recovery preparedness, and ethics policies where there is not enough intrinsic motivation. Also, governance can provide a systematic way to periodically check and refine things to keep up to date with changing conditions.

- **Incentives.** The incentives in the people system might need alteration. This is especially valuable when the benefits of the change accrue more to the organization as whole than to the direct stakeholder who is impacted. Then, it can be useful to design in new incentives to make the change more appealing. might be needed to keep the new direction on track. These incentives could take many forms, such as awards, bonuses, special parking spaces, or even personal "thank you" calls from senior executives.

Building the Mobilization Strategy

Now, using our understanding of how adoption occurs, and the analysis of the stakeholders discussed in earlier chapters, we can explore how to put together a change strategy.

1. Determine the Type of Change Effort

To plan the change effort, you first develop an idea of the basic activities that will be needed. This enables estimating the resources and the major activities. While it is often difficult to be precise upfront, due to the vagueness of initial information, there are four broad approaches that are common.

Icons from the preceding personal adoption process indicate how these activities influence stakeholders to make the adoption decision.

Basic Influencing

The most basic change situation is influencing a small group of people (1 to approximately 40) to adopt a change that is largely beneficial to them. This is a low-impact change: it is largely welcomed and easy to understand. These kinds of changes come about regularly in normal life.

In this situation, a personal connection can be made. The group can be convened relatively easily. They can discuss the change and get to know the people who are encouraging it. This method relies mainly on developing a Core Group, crafting a strong change story, and engaging other people. So, use the methods that have been used in earlier chapters.

Resistance in this type of change mainly stems from lack of awareness or clarity on what the change is. So, invest in crafting clear messaging, whether it is email, presentations, or websites. Depending on the circumstances, written communications alone may be enough. Or, the change initiator may have to spend time personally reaching out to the affected people to ensure they understand the messaging clearly.

Communications Outreach

When the change affects a large group that mostly welcomes it, the challenge is to get everyone in the target population aware of it. These kinds of minimal impact, high-scale changes occur frequently, and the change approach is fundamentally a mass communications effort. Thus, acceptance of the change is highly dependent on the quality of the messaging and the organization of a communications campaign.

Examples of this category of change include the following:

- Upgrading the company phone system or providing employees with new personal computer software

- Rolling out a new code of conduct

- New procurement applications

While this type of change calls for mass communications like email, you should keep in mind that a single email is probably not enough. A single email will likely be discarded by over half the recipients. So, it will undoubtedly take several communications to get most of the people aware of the change. This becomes even more complicated if the communication channels are not reliable.

For this kind of approach, you will need to study the upcoming chapter on Change Communications. Depending on the type of change, it could also be important to create a training plan and mobilize change leadership, which are also discussed in upcoming chapters.

High-Touch Engagement

When the change has a high impact, it is going to require a high-touch approach, which means people talking to people. The high impact might be due to an emotional reaction, the complexity of the change, the need to adapt, or the need to co-design the change with stakeholders. Or it could be several of these aspects together. In these cases, stakeholders will need live engagement and discussion to understand the change, ask questions, and collaborate on how to move forward.

Examples include the following:

- Reorganizations of small departments

- New group leadership

- Process change involving small numbers of people

Because the group is small, a mass communications campaign is not needed. This kind of engagement might be accomplished by holding one or more meetings and working through it. The structure can be relatively loose, since the stakeholders can ask questions, and decisions can be made as a group. For this kind of change, the upcoming chapters on Training and Change Leadership will be most useful.

Scaled High-Touch Engagement

The final change type we will discuss is when the change both affects many people and has high impact. This combines all the previous change approaches into a comprehensive system. These kinds of changes require extensive planning and skillful change approaches.

Examples of this category include

- Significant changes to benefits plans

- Significant movement of operations offshore

- Creating new project planning processes in a large organization

- Changing the leadership style of a large company

To accomplish this, you must mobilize many communications along with in-person meetings. This requires structure and planning, as well as resources. If you are conducting this kind of change, you will need to understand the material in all the remaining chapters, including how to organization change agent networks and put in place appropriate incentives and governance.

2. Evaluate Strategic Considerations

With the basic change type in mind, there are several overarching considerations that can help optimize the strategy. While these are often determined by circumstances, it is advisable to give them some thought.

What Is the Current State of Adoption?

After defining success indicators, as discussed in Chapter 8, "Developing Change Success Indicators," a baseline of the success indicators should be made. This will enable you to track the adoption progress and thus adjust where necessary.

In many cases, the indicators may be zero when the change effort is starting out, but this should be checked. Sometimes there is a partial adoption of sorts by some stakeholder groups, and this might affect choices in the mobilization strategy. You should review the state of the stakeholder groups on your stakeholder list and determine who are the priority groups. For example, if some constituents are already favorable, it may not be necessary to spend as much time with them. Or, groups that are holdouts may merit further inquiry to understand their concerns.

What Is the Intended Adoption Rate?

Often, release schedules are given based on the completion of documentation, decisions, or technology, and the program is anticipated to end at that point. There is a hidden assumption that 100% adoption occurs then. The expected rate of adoption should be made explicit, as this greatly affects the resources and methods needed.

Remember that in general, all changes happen on an S-curve, and a 100% adoption rate on the day of launch generally does not happen. The steepness of the S curve depends on many factors discussed throughout this book. Although you can make the S curve steeper through better change approaches, it also depends heavily on factors like the adoptability of the change and the resources applied to planning and conducting the change effort.

Are there Timing Constraints?

As it is popularly said, "Timing is everything." The best laid plans and most well-crafted communications are useless or severely diminished if not done at an appropriate time. Change efforts need momentum in terms of the effort needed to get attention and get commitment to adoption. A change launched when other priorities are taking precedence will have a weakened effect and potentially be a wasted effort. The following factors should be considered.

Change capacity. People can only absorb so many changes at once. When there are other efforts going on at the same time, the confluence of change efforts becomes confusing and disorienting. Moreover, key players might be tied up elsewhere and unable to participate fully in the change effort.

Dependencies. Other programs may need to be released first to support the change, or other major activities might be occurring, such as major restructurings, that may need to settle before your change effort can be done properly.

Time windows. There often are certain time windows that must be accounted for, such as blackout periods, end-of-quarter financial closes, and mergers.

Can It Be Rolled Out in Pilots?

The natural decision process in many organizations is biased toward "big bang" launches or going out to all stakeholders at once. Managers tend to think that because the change is good and needed, it should go out to everyone as soon as possible. Although a big bang is sometimes necessary, it is usually preferable to roll out changes as a pilot and then move in stages to the rest of the target population.

Piloting a change effort has several advantages. First, smaller efforts are easier to manage and organize well. They take less people and do not require the same level of preparation.

Second, a pilot enables you to learn and evolve. It is very difficult to get the communications and other support elements correct for a rollout, so a pilot launch enables you to test the launch itself, get feedback, and evolve it for the next group.

Third, the pilots build a base of peer pressure and modeling that is important to influencing other stakeholders. The big bang style of release often incorrectly assumes everyone will just jump on board on command. But most of the population will be not adopt until they see others (the first adopters) doing it. So, the piloting method enables a more realistic and controlled way of showing success and building on it.

3. Assemble the Critical Moves into a Strategy

Your high-level strategy consists of a set of critical moves. It probably actually has many more but focusing on a small set of key moves keeps focus on what is important. I have known colleagues who printed the critical moves of a program and taped the list on the wall to keep them at the forefront. Situations are varied, so it will just depend on your analysis. See Figure 9-2 for an example.

Figure 9-2. Example Critical Moves for Portfolio Management

1. Have selected groups use a manual spreadsheet-based process to rationalize their data to the new model and do it on paper first. Realize from the stakeholder analysis that the groups have divergent methods already and the process is going to shift and adjust as they figure it out. Establish some loose standards from this.

2. Move the paper activity outward to other groups to get them used to it so they don't put bogus data in the tool.

3. Start with just the budget module (or another one).

4. Put projects with greater $50M budget in the tool. This will be the biggest bang for buck. They can be tied to a value assessment earlier.

5. Create a top layer of common data and have everyone provide it. Get them in the habit of using data to make decisions.

4. Develop Mobilization Indicators

Using the same approach outlined previously in Chapter 8, "Developing Change Success Indicators," we can now develop indicators for the mobilization effort itself. An example using the portfolio management case is given in Table 9-1.

Table 9-1. Example Mobilization Indicators

Mobilization CSF	Specific CSF	Measures	Target
Awareness and positive perception	Awareness of process changes and new policies Knowledge of where to find the tool	Effective reach	70%
Develop requisite skills	All program and project managers are trained on process All program and project managers are trained on tool	Training completion	80%
Clear direction and prioritization from management	Prioritization of programs and projects is clearly available	Current prioritization list	Monthly update
Incentives	Compliance with prioritization and updates	Regular incentive applied	Monthly
Establish governance	Governance systems are operating	Occurrence of meetings of operating committee	Monthly meeting with at least 80% attendance

The table is just an example. Every situation will be different, so you will have to analyze the conditions and apply good judgment. Use the material in the subsequent chapters to get a better idea of which indicators will work best for your initiative.

Note that some items, like awareness or positive perception, cannot be easily determined in a definitive way. However, the occurrence of certain activity, such as "effective reach," may give a suitable proxy indicator.

5. Construct the Rollout Sequences

The critical moves will give a map for how to involve the stake-holders. From there, the stakeholders are engaged using rollout sequence. This comprises putting together a sequence of change actions that influ-ence the stakeholders to go through the adoption cycle as efficiently, reso-lutely, and quickly as possible.

As described above in "Determine the Type of Change Effort," there are four general types of change. Each type calls for one or more of five sub-strategies that are explained in the following chapters: Communi-cations, Change Leadership, Training, Ground Campaign, and Embed-ding.

These strategies are meant to approach the organization as a sys-tem, holistically, by initiating the change at all levels: top, middle, and bot-tom. The strategies facilitate the stakeholders' movement through the de-cision cycle toward making a sustained adoption decision.

When scaling the change effort to a large population, the process is maximized and most efficient when these strategies are done in a se-quence that focuses on mass media first but then gives way to engaging groups and interpersonal communications later. The sequence of the strat-egies is shown below.

The broad communications are usually the first strategy to start. Ideally, these communications could influence Early Adopters—who are more attuned to mass communications—to trial the change. But, for the other stakeholder types, the broad communications serve to address early parts of the decision loop for stakeholders by gaining awareness and basic understanding. So, the early start serves to 1) notify stakeholders that changes are coming and minimize the surprise, 2) get a leg up on and the awareness building, which takes time to accomplish, while other aspects of the adoption and change are being more worked out.

A simplified plan for rolling out portfolio management has the basic structure shown in the table below. Note there are main primary

Figure 9-3. Five Basic Adoption Strategies

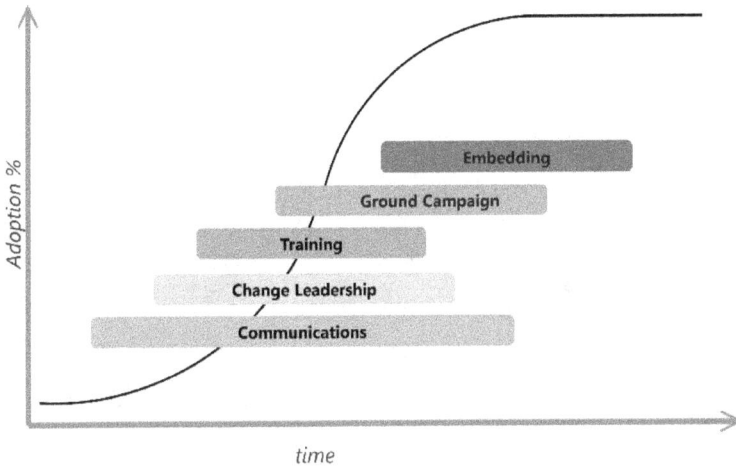

rollout packages: an overall one and then a focused set of influencing activities toward managers and then toward project managers. These are targeted toward one group of project managers and their management chain. Later plans using a similar structure could be used to roll it out to other groups.

Table 9-2. Example Summary of Change Plan for Portfolio Management

ID	Activity	Timing
1.0	**Overall**	
1.1	Awareness communication (email)	1 month before launch
1.2	Informational sessions	1 month before launch
2.0	**Managers**	
2.1	Core Group gets buy in of managers. Program is adjusted based on feedback. Managers discuss with their staff in subsequent meetings.	1.5 months before launch
2.2	2-hour training on new process and using reports	2 weeks before launch

ID	Activity	Timing
2.3	Review of reports in staff meeting	Weekly starting a week before launch First meeting before launch used to discuss expectations
2.4	Cross-organization portfolio review	Monthly starting after several groups are brought on board
2.5	Process evaluation and refinement, plus award given to top project managers	Every 6 months after launch
2.6	Periodic feedback to project managers on performance	Monthly after launch
3.0	**Project Managers**	
3.1	1-day portfolio process training	1 week before launch
3.2	4-hour portfolio tool training	1 week before launch
3.3	Community of practice meeting	Monthly starting after launch
3.4	Periodic feedback sessions with process owners and developers to adapt and improve the process and tool.	Weekly for the first few weeks after launch, then extending to monthly and then to annually

Of course, this plan is just a starting point and should evolve along the way.

6. Determine the Teams/Resources Needed

An adoption effort takes resources, and this is sometimes surprising to people. In Scaled High Touch types of change plans, it could take as many people to create adoption as it does to design the change. People are needed to create communications, give presentations, conduct trainings, hold brown bag seminars, answer questions, and drive project plans, as defined by the mobilization strategy. More specifics about who is needed are discussed later in this chapter, but if these are not in place, no amount of wishing will make the adoption happen. Author Robert Miles states it clearly:

> *Individuals' resistance to change builds in direct proportion to the magnitude of the gap that is perceived between the level of effort required and the resources available.*[1]

One benefit of using the five adoption strategies is that they are packaged in a sequence. The other benefit is that they are focused on teams that employ certain skill sets and communities, much like the phases of the framework.

There are many ways to break down responsibilities for change management across individual roles. An example is given in the table below, which is in the form of a classic Responsible-Accountable-Consulted-Informed (RACI) matrix. From these analyses, the needed resources can be identified and acquired.

Table 9-3. Role-Based Change Management RACI

Ongoing Activity	Program PM	Analyst	Engineer	Training PM	Sponsor	Consult
Charter change team: ensure resources available for team, clear structure and roles, purpose, case for change, clarity on end state.	R				A	R
Conduct stakeholder analysis and gather feedback.	A	R	C			C
Create and drive change management plan.	A		C			C
Sponsoring to affected leaders: ensure resources are available, resolve conflicts, use personal influence to get them on board.	R				A	C

Ongoing Activity	Program PM	Analyst	Engineer	Training PM	Sponsor	Consult
Define and collect success indicators. Implement ongoing reporting to leadership team about change progress.	A	R	C			C
Develop and execute general communications plan.	R		C			C
Develop and execute training on changes.	R	R	C	A		C
Manage stakeholder engagement: set up ambassador groups, forums, trainings, information sessions, problem resolution; set up incentives.	A	R				C

Cheat Sheet

This chapter has discussed the challenge of creating a mobilization strategy that will have the best chances of getting an organizational change diffused as quickly as possible within a target population. Extensive research on diffusion theory has shown that the diffusion of change requires a combination of methods that take advantage of the ways that different adopter categories are influenced. The characteristically low performance of adoption initiatives can be tied back to ineffective strategies that do not account for the real dynamics of change diffusion, and so change makers, conversely, devise strategies that capitalize on those dynamics.

Our mobilization strategy assumes the design CSFs have been maximized to the extent possible. We then must devise a strategy to meet the following involvement CSFs that will facilitate stakeholders going through the adoption process:

- Connect

- Consider

- Decide

- Act

- Adopt

We have covered a process for developing a mobilization strategy that involves the following primary steps:

1. Determine the type of change effort and the kind of strategies it will probably need.

   o Basic Influencing

   o Communications Outreach

   o High Touch Engagement

   o Scaled High Touch Engagement

   See Table 9-4 below for guidance on which strategies to use with a certain change type.

Table 9-4. Change Types and Strategies

Strategy	Chapter	Basic	Out-reach	High-Touch	Scaled
Strategic framework	2 to 9	Yes	No	No	No
Communications plan	10	Yes	Yes	No	No
Training plan	11	Yes	Maybe	Maybe	Maybe
Leadership engage-ment Plan	12	Yes	No	Yes	Yes
Ground campaign	13	Yes	No	Yes	Yes
Embedding	14	Yes	No	Yes	Yes

2. Evaluate the strategic considerations.

   o **Current state.** What is the current state of adoption? Was there a partial or failed adoption effort before? How did this current state come about?

   o **Timing.** Are there finance closing, mergers, re-organizations, natural disasters, socio-economic events, or other considerations that would affect the plan?

   o **Pilots.** Can the change be started with a pilot and expanded from there in an evolutionary fashion?

   o **Intended adoption rate.** What is the targeted adoption rate? Is it realistic? Does the plan make sense for achieving this rate?

   o **Decision type.** Are people adopting by mandate? Is it voluntary?

3. Assemble the critical moves.

4. Develop mobilization indicators.

5. Analyze the rollout packages.

   o Communications (Chapter 11)

   o Training (Chapter 12)

   o Change Leadership (Chapter 13)

   o Learning Communities (Chapter 14)

   o Governance and Incentives (Chapter 15)

6. Construct rollout sequences.

7. Determine the teams and resources needed.

In the following chapters, we will discuss how to build out the key change activities.

10

Change Communications

The single biggest problem in communication is the illusion that it has taken place.

—George Bernard Shaw

A change effort is wasted if stakeholders are not aware of it or do not believe it is real. In perhaps the most dramatic example in history, on August 15, 1945, Emperor Hirohito broadcast a radio message to the Japanese people informing them of Japan's surrender to the Allies, thus officially ending World War II. But this simple, authoritative announcement was not immediately realized by everyone. Japan still had a far-flung military who did not get the message immediately, and many military units continued fighting on. In fact, the last soldier, Lt. Hiroo Onoda, did not stop fighting until 1974 — thirty years later![1]

While communicating the Japanese surrender is an extreme case, many of the same human dynamics are present in any large-scale communication within any large population. The dynamics that arose from communicating the end of the Pacific War paint in high-relief the challenges faced in any change situations.

In this chapter, we will look at the basic principles for communicating information about change to a large audience. We'll look first at the challenges of reaching people, getting attention, and relevancy. Then, we will look at how to construct a robust plan based on this knowledge. Finally, we will look at how to develop the content specified by the plan and optimize it.

Reaching People

The first challenge in announcing the end of the war was simply reaching people. In the Pacific Theater, this was especially difficult due to the technology of the day and the geographic dispersion of the forces. Moreover, some units had been cut off from their command chains by advancing American forces and were left in remote parts of isolated Pacific Islands. This was the case for Lt. Onoda and other Japanese holdouts who did not hear of the war's end for months and years afterward. These holdouts often had to be reached by dropping leaflets or by sending search parties with loudspeakers into the jungle.

These days, we usually do not have to resort to dropping leaflets: We have email, mobile phones, text messages, and streaming Internet media. It is much easier technically to get a message to a recipient anywhere in the world. But just because we can technically reach them does not guarantee they are conscious or accepting of the message.

For example, if you want to reach all stakeholders in sales in an organization and you have an email alias "sales-all," does it really cover the intended audience? Are the names on the sales list that same as the actual intended users? Or, if you are giving a webinar, will the potential attendees cover the stakeholder group?

The *effective reach* is how well the communications channel reaches the intended audience. This has technical aspects, such as whether the audience has the right device or software to receive the message. But, it also has cognitive aspects. For example, an email about the change might have to contend with hundreds of other emails received by the stakeholder in the same time.

So, just reaching the inbox does not mean it gets read. I once worked on a program that invited people to contact technical support and

get a new laptop, which generally appeals to everyone. However, after repeated emails and communications, there were still some people who did
not show up. An investigation revealed some of the reasons: Many holdouts were on maternity leave or other extended absence. Some simply believed their existing machine was so customized to them that it could not
be improved on.

So, people being on vacation or receiving too many messages are
some of the many reasons the message does not reach them. Like the end-
of-the war communications, just physically getting the communication to
people can be difficult. Moreover, there are still many environments that
cannot be effectively accessed via email, often for security reasons.

Getting Attention

The second challenge was getting the attention of the far-flung soldiers. In fact, Lt. Onoda had seen the leaflets and short-wave radio messages from time to time, starting from a few months after the war. But for
30 years, he assumed it was all a trick. In an interview, he explained the
messages had errors in them that led him to believe they were created by
U.S. operatives. He would not even believe his own brother, who showed
up in person, because he suspected him of being a traitor. Lt. Onoda's con-
victions that Japan would never surrender simply convinced him to fight
on regardless. He finally surrendered only because his former commander
appeared in person and relieved him of duty.

In modern situations, similar suspicion of messages happens. A
major consumer products company where I worked recently had many
different sites around the world. People at those sites viewed email from
corporate suspiciously, suspecting it of being spam. In many cases, they
would first confirm the validity of the email with their trusted site representative before acting on it.

People habitually believe that business-as-usual will continue.
Thus, change communications must be a little like advertising — they need
to get attention — but they also need to get attention by sticking out from

what is usual. For this, a little attention to making a catchy message can help.

Consider this list:

- The Goodyear Blimp
- LIVESTRONG wristbands
- "Got Milk?"
- Smokey the Bear
- "What happens in Vegas stays in Vegas"
- "Where's the Beef?"
- "Plop, plop, fizz, fizz"
- Breakfast of Champions

These are examples of sticky messages. They got our attention. They stuck with us, often for decades. "Breakfast of Champions" was invented in the 1930s. Notice they weren't all print ads. The Goodyear Blimp is an aircraft. Smokey the Bear is a fictitious icon. LIVESTRONG wristbands are neon-colored plastic strips.

Besides sticky messages, another way to break into the stakeholder consciousness is *effective frequency*. This concerns the optimal number of times the stakeholder is exposed to the change messaging, which could be through any combination of media — emails, webinars, live conversations, and so on. Effective frequency is important because if the messaging is not seen enough, it may not even register in the consciousness of the stakeholders.

How many times a stakeholder must see a message for it to be effective is an old conversation. Thomas Smith, a nineteenth century, London businessman (1885) famously said it took 20 times for a message to be converted into a sale.

The first-time people look at any given ad, they don't even see it.
The second time, they don't notice it.

The third time, they are aware that it is there.
The fourth time, they have a fleeting sense that they've seen it somewhere before.
The fifth time, they actually read the ad.
The sixth time they thumb their nose at it.
The seventh time, they start to get a little irritated with it.
The eighth time, they start to think, "Here's that confounded ad again."
The ninth time, they start to wonder if they're missing out on something.
The tenth time, they ask their friends and neighbors if they've tried it.
The eleventh time, they wonder how the company is paying for all these ads.
The twelfth time, they start to think that it must be a good product.
The thirteenth time, they start to feel the product has value.
The fourteenth time, they start to remember wanting a product exactly like this for a long time.
The fifteenth time, they start to yearn for it because they can't afford to buy it.
The sixteenth time, they accept the fact that they will buy it sometime in the future.
The seventeenth time, they make a note to buy the product.
The eighteenth time, they curse their poverty for not allowing them to buy this terrific product.
The nineteenth time, they count their money very carefully.
The twentieth time prospects see the ad, they buy what is offered.

Mr. Smith may have been being facetious, but the point is clear even if 20 is not the number. The question of how many contacts equal an effective frequency is not definitively settled, but several perspectives have arisen over the years. The most well-known maxim, deriving from research in the 1960s and 1970, is the "three-plus rule," which says the target audience must see the message at least three times.[2] More recent findings have suggested the number is closer to seven. Guerilla marketing guru Jay Levinson asserts the number is up to 30 times.[3]

But these mere guidelines. The exact number needed depends on the situation. Probably 3 to 12 contacts is a good rule of thumb for planning change communications activities, as will be discussed later. But, it also depends on if you are addressing the relevant audience with the relevant content.

Part of the reason this works may be that repetition has positive effects in terms of building familiarity, which in turn builds positive perception. In psychology, this is called the ***mere-exposure effect***, which asserts the more people are familiar with something, the more they tend to like it. The mere-exposure effect has been shown to have the most effect for unknown companies and for more complex changes — repetition in those stages tends to improve perception.

Often, people are worried that too much messaging will make the stakeholders negative about the change. This is called ***message fatigue.*** While there are some studies supporting the notion that excessive messaging can eventually turn people negative toward a brand, this effect seems to only occur at high numbers of contacts that are characteristically hard to achieve without significant funds. In fact, some studies have shown that the message fatigue and commensurate negative perception has more to do with people getting irrelevant messages than too many messages.[4]

In practice, the concern about too much messaging or negativity is frequently a gut reaction by people who are more in contact with the change effort and who have seen the message and are tired of it, not realizing that the message is going to a broad audience who may not have not noticed it yet.

Relevancy

In terms of what we explored in Chapter 4, Emperor Hirohito had set out the basic change story in his concession speech. He said: "*Although the Japanese government had set out to protect Japan's interests, the tide had turned against them. The enemy had new and devastating weapons, so now it was in Japan's best interests to concede."*

For this basic change story to go from Emperor Hirohito's radio address and be enacted across the far-flung empire, it had to be translated into messages relevant to different stakeholders. The military had to be told how to stand down and surrender. Government officials had to be told how to receive the conquering administration. The populace had to be told what this meant to them, their lives, and their beliefs about Japan's destiny and righteousness.

In short, for the message to be absorbed and to be useful to the stakeholder, it must be relevant. Relevancy in organizational change involves targeting and segmenting stakeholders rather than just sending the same messages to everyone. This is important for a couple of reasons. Of course, as mentioned, getting non-relevant messages can create negative perceptions and waste people's time. Furthermore, using non-relevant lists can skew feedback numbers, because the lower percentage of response may not mean the message is poor but only that the wrong people received it.

In Chapter 7, we covered how to identify and segment the stakeholders. That chapter also explained how to analyze what motivates and constrains stakeholders from adopting. In development of your communications strategy, you use this information to determine which core messages can be matched up with the stakeholder groups that need to understand them.

If you try to make a single message appeal to too many different interests at once, it dilutes the impact. The stakeholders will have difficulty discerning what is useful to them. And they may tend to discard the message. This is especially true with busy people. It perhaps bears remembering philosopher Paul Grice's four maxims for effective communications.[5] Summarized, the communication should

- Be true, or at least what you believe to be true

- Have enough content to convey the message, but not more than needed

- Have only relevant content, as much as possible

- Be clearly conveyed

This means that for generating broad messaging, you must high-light what appeals to them and offer evidence to ameliorate their fears and misconceptions about perceived negative effects. This points to the need to translate the basic change story into more relevant terms that deal with the concerns of unique needs.

So, we expand the basic change story into change narrative which we will define as the set of stories we purposely create and tell in a change effort to shape the discourse. This narrative comprises the ongoing telling of the change story in various forms. The narrative can potentially contain many sub stories, depending on the size, type, and complexity of the change effort, as shown in Figure 10-1.

Figure 10-1. Change Narrative Architecture

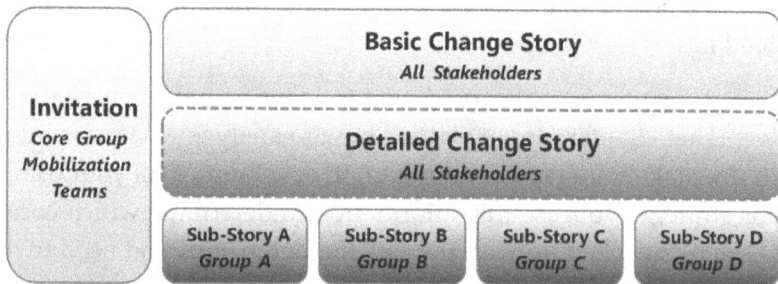

The elements of the narrative architecture are described below.

- **Invitation.** This is the few basic lines summarizing the
  change story enough to attract interested people, such as the
  Core Group and members of the leadership and other communities in participating. One way to look at the invitation
  is, over time, it is the simplest expression of what the change
  story is. It helps maintain focus. The invitation is concise,
  perhaps a few lines or a few paragraphs of information.
  Guidelines for developing the invitation were covered in
  Chapter 3.

- **Basic change story.** This is an overarching or umbrella story that provides common themes applicable to all stakeholders. It casts the organization as the leading characters pitted in a struggle to reach new opportunities, overcome the competition, or survive environmental threats. It is brief enough, perhaps a paragraph or page of content, so it can be used in most opportunities to talk about the change, as discussed in Chapter 4.

- **Detailed change story.** If the story needs more depth, then it may be necessary to create a more detailed change story. This should be enough to answer most questions about the change and might actually be several different documents. Likely, this would only be provided as backup, perhaps in a white paper or on a website.

- **Sub-stories.** It is often important to have modified versions of the change story targeted to the interests and concerns of specific key stakeholder groups. The more they can understand how the change is relevant to them, the more likely they will be inclined to adopt the change.

Whether there are deeper layers of the change narrative, such as detailed stories or targeted sub stories, depends on the nature of the change. For example, in a recent ERP-upgraded I consulted, there was an overall story about why the change was important, and then there were specific versions of how the change affected each function, like Finance and Operations. So, the communications plan included some overview videos for everyone, then separate emails were created for each function. Each email had the same introduction but then had different details about the impacts.

How much detail is needed is based on factors such as the complexity of the change and what is already known. In some cases, the basic level change story could provide only a very thin umbrella, with very deep and distinct sub stories for different stakeholder groups. Or, the change story could be very detailed with minor variations for some stakeholder groups.

The Communications Planning Process

Successful execution of the change communications strategy is more likely when a well-organized and well-conducted communications plan is used. Change communications must catch the stakeholder's attention and sustain it long enough for them to engage in doing the new behaviors.

While the communications plan will likely change a lot along the way, having a plan enables being proactive, which is important to creating and capitalizing on momentum. The basic steps for developing the communications plan are listed below and explained in the following subsections.

1. Translate core messages to stakeholder groups.

2. Create communications plan.

3. Develop core content.

4. Analyze communications effectiveness.

Generally, dedicated focus will be needed to develop and execute such a plan. If the numbers are small, perhaps one person is enough to carry it out. Stakeholders can meet and discuss the changes. But, with large numbers of stakeholders, a team may be required to develop and distribute professional content in a timely fashion.

Translating Core Messages to Stakeholder Groups

In Chapter 4, you learned to develop the basic change story and you enrolled leaders in taking the story outward personally. Now, when it comes to taking it outward to a wider audience, you need to adapt these messages to highlight the needs and concerns of various stakeholder groups. The core message from the basic change story is the same, but terminology and emphasis of certain ideas can be adjusted for the audience.

In the initial phases of the program, you will probably focus on these kinds of topics.

- The support for the initiative at the highest levels

- The overall benefits and intended future state

- The case for change

- The truth about misconceptions

- How to be involved next (call to action)

Consider this list and think about how it might change for the different stakeholder groups.

Create Communications Plan

With your core messages and stakeholder groups established, you can begin to build out the communications planning matrix. This matrix is the foundation of the communications plan. This matrix shows how the core messaging will be implemented through various communications deliverables and channels. While other planning tools, such a Gantt chart, could be used, experience has shown the matrix is usually the easiest to manage because the items are often repeated, and dates often change.

To assemble the matrix, create a table like the one shown below. List the core messages in the leftmost column, and then begin filling out the table by creating a set of communication events that give the best chance for achieving the goals of the program. Pay attention to the phase you are in and plan that out for a few months, assuming you will evaluate and revise the plan as you go.

The columns are described below.

- **Event Name.** A convenient label for the event.

- **Messages.** The core messages to be delivered.

- **Target Audience.** The people who receive the messages.

- **Delivery Date.** The date the messages are to go out. Sometimes it is repetitive, like weekly.

- **Delivery Format.** How it will be delivered, such as email, video, web site, etc.

- **Owner.** The individual responsible for the development and delivery of the message.

Table 10-1. Example Communications Matrix

Event	Messages	Target Audience	Delivery Date	Delivery Format	Owner
Executive Email	The new application is coming Executives support it and believe it to have great benefit We need it to stay competitive	Everyone	Day 0	Email	Carol
Organization meeting	Panel of key leaders Q&A session	Everyone	Day 2	PowerPoint shown live and made available afterward	Pedro
Website	Detailed information FAQ Case studies	Everyone	Day 0	Website with blog	Ravi
Department meeting	Direct manager support Overview of impacts to specific teams	Each team	Week 1	PowerPoint slides delivered by department managers	Shilpa

Event	Messages	Target Audience	Delivery Date	Delivery Format	Owner
Update post	Latest develop-ments Timelines	Everyone	Biweekly	Blog post & email	Susan

There are numerous possible delivery formats for messaging. One must consider both the impact of the type of message as well as how the message will be delivered. *Push methods* are those that get the message out to people who are not necessarily looking for it. Some of these methods are given in the table below.

Table 10-2. Push Communications Methods

Channel	Usage	Notes
Executive email usually sent to all of org	Establish management support Efficient way to establish broad awareness for larger audiences Provide a guiding vision or com-mon directional statements to ref-erence	Readership is probably less than 50% for one email Often creates no real commitment Usually, it is a building step to create a foundation for later methods. Little change will happen unless the call to action is very specific and backed up by tight controls
Personal email to one person or small group	Use personal influence, establish management support Can create commitment if sender is trusted and agreements are made	Greater readership and acceptance if people know and trust the individual
Webinar	Efficient for large-scale communi-cations of foundational ideas Can provide good poll or feed-back opportunity at the same time	It is a push method when distributed through a calendaring tool like an Out-look invite; otherwise, it is a pull method if listed on website Can draw 100s of people Takes time and organization to pre-pare and run effectively

Channel	Usage	Notes
All-hands meetings	Builds awareness Demonstrates management support Offers limited Q&A opportunity Can give limited overview information for broad consumption	Variable attendance
Staff meetings	Demonstrates management support Offers significant opportunity for discussion that can help improve the idea Discussion can build commitment	Needs to be well facilitated Can be fed by "cascaded" PowerPoint slides but managers may need prep to do that well
Standing forums	Connects to specific audience Enables opportunity for discussion, which can build commitment	Participants have varying backgrounds and commitment Channeled through the communications team
Blog or social media post	Personal or group post	Pushes to your followers

Pull methods require people to take the initiative to find the message. These methods can be more impactful than the push methods, but they may need to be combined with push methods to reach the stakeholders.

Table 10-3. Pull Communications Methods

Channel	Usage	Notes
Blog, wiki, or web Page	Provide more detailed information and references	Still a writing project—takes time and skill to do well
Discussion Board	Interactive Q&A format	Can be a push method if there is a community that "watches" it

Channel	Usage	Notes
		Requires vigorous action to monitor, respond, and maintain it
Videos—professional	Virtual experience More impactful and emotional messaging Provide better instruction or how to in some cases	Well done videos take a lot of time, skill, and at times money
Videos—webcam style	Provide more personal or emotional appeal, which can build more commitment	Easier to make for some change leaders who prefer talking to writing
Web-based Training	Cheaper way to do large-scale training for relatively straightforward (not complex) topics	Can be expensive and time consuming to develop
Live Training	Necessary for complex or highly impactful topics Cheaper and faster to develop for small stakeholder groups where core team leads the training	Expensive and time consuming to develop and deliver to large audiences Can be developed iteratively, customized, and evolved

Once a draft of the plan is created, use your understanding of the key critical success factors to determine if the plan is robust:

- Does it have effective reach? Are you using communications channels that will reach the intended audience?

- Will it get their attention? Will the themes be interesting? Will it be delivered by trusted sources? Is there enough repetition?

- Are the messages targeted to the audience (stakeholder) groups, so they are relevant?

- Are messages varied with different slants? Sometimes the

same basic message can be conveyed with variations in theme. This will lessen message fatigue and increase the chance of catching attention from the stakeholder group.

Develop Core Content

Once communications deliverables and channels are identified, the content must be developed. Like most things, a better result is achieved if the content is developed according to a solid process. You should try to adhere to a process like the following:

1. Create a draft.

2. Review the draft with the team one or more times.

3. Review the draft with a wider audience.

4. Test the material on a few sample audience members.

5. Get approval. It may also be necessary with some kinds of content to get approval from management, especially if they are going to send it or deliver it.

Creating effective content is critical to success. So, the content must not only be relevant to the reader, but effective in delivering the message. The following sections give some angles to consider.

Connecting

Content is useless if it does not get attention. The challenge with change communications is people have many habitual ways of filtering information. Emails are automatically deleted or filed in a split-second decision, or perhaps even by an automated rule in the mailbox. Similarly, ideas are dismissed or ignored based on instantaneous review of certain key features. The rule of thumb is that you have 7 to 10 seconds to get their attention.

Professional marketers know that in email this means you must get the reader's attention in the subject line or upper right corner of the message. This is especially important with people reading their messages on mobile phones and twitter feeds, where all they see is the subject line of first few lines of the message.

A lot of email wastes the first lines by saying things like,

- Back in 1982…
- Our mandate has been to rationalize all services…

Compare those with these professional first lines

- Free….
- Act now to….

That said, there are few caveats. First, of course, companies like Nike spend millions of dollars on quality ads, so this doesn't have to be that. Your message may be going to a few hundred or a few thousand people, not millions. It is going to go with other context and engagement, so it doesn't have to do everything. You probably aren't going to invest millions in print ads and promotions, so it is more flexible and can be adjusted along the way.

The content used in the communications campaign is high-level in nature and normally should focus on a few common, core concepts and methods, at least in the initial phases. Some guidelines are given below.

Content Mix

Messaging in the early phases usually focuses on the case for change, the nature of the change, and how the stakeholders will be involved. Notice how Figure 10-2 shows these items along with relative percentages of how much of the content they should occupy.

As shown in the figure, the case for change and roles and behaviors are recommended to be 60% of the communication. Yet, it is often the case that much more time is spent on talking about the future state than these factors.

This communication content should be forthright and honest. Make sure to reduce anxiety and uncertainty by painting a picture of the future that is as complete and exciting as possible. The more they know,

Figure 10-2. The Mix of Communications Content

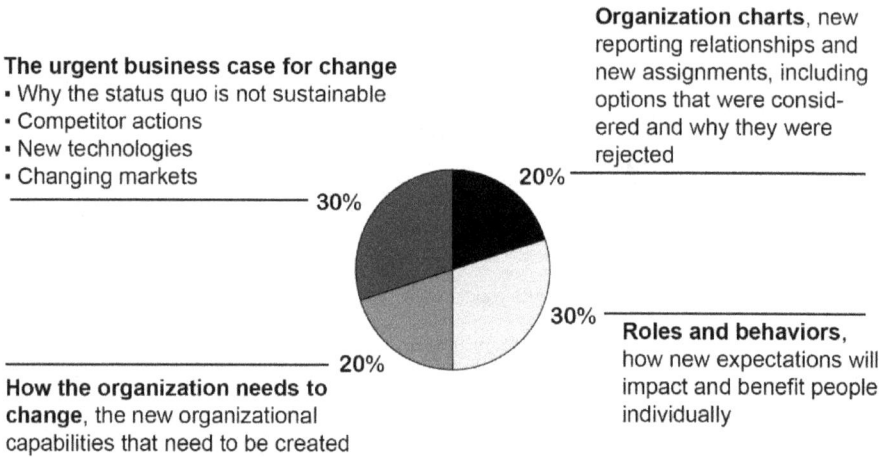

The urgent business case for change
• Why the status quo is not sustainable
• Competitor actions
• New technologies
• Changing markets
————————————— 30%

Organization charts, new
reporting relationships and
new assignments, including
options that were consid-
ered and why they were
rejected
20% —————————————

**How the organization needs to
change**, the new organizational
capabilities that need to be created
————————————— 20%

30% —————————————
Roles and behaviors,
how new expectations will
impact and benefit people
individually

the more they will commit to the process and embrace the vision. Change planners often err on the side of too little communication. They fear it will raise questions, create confusion, or imply unfulfillable commitments. These notions lead to little or no communications, which creates a vacuum of information where people often fear the worst. A better approach is to communicate a lot, but just be sure to set the right context. Let people know that things are still being figured out and may change. Invite feedback and let them know you will do your best but cannot be sure to use it.

There are several things that can be done to improve the effectiveness of the content. These are described below.

Reducing Anxiety

People react to messages that are threatening numerous ways. After Emperor Hirohito's original message, many Japanese simply went about their business, essentially ignoring the change. Others gathered in a large crowd in front of the Imperial Palace and wept. Some military officers committed suicide, disgraced by their defeat. Other soldiers attacked and hacked to death over a dozen POWs. Some Japanese soldiers in remote locations — unlike Hiroo Onoda who kept fighting — believed they would be blamed and disappeared into the jungle.

A key purpose of change messaging is reducing anxiety about the change. When changes start, people become uncertain about the future. They can try to ignore it, have grief, become angry, get depressed, or even lash out. Change messaging can ease this in a couple of ways.

First, simply recognizing the ambiguity can help. People would like for the change planners to tell them exactly what is in mind, but this is often impossible because it is simply unknown. Regularly, leaders should reduce uncertainty by assuring people that feeling confused or uncertain about what to do is natural. Provide ways for them to participate in helping define and understand the changes rather than simply wait.

Second, offer what information you can. Many times, too little communication is done because change leaders believe they need to have everything worked out before they communicate. As a result, stakeholders are left in an information vacuum and feel confused and anxious. There is generally a level of information that can be communicated, and it is fine to be transparent about what is and is not figured out.

Perception of Justice

Whether a change is perceived as fair or just is a considerable influence on attitudes toward the change. If the change effort is viewed mainly benefitting people who have relationships with the boss, then people become much more reluctant.[6]

Consequently, change initiatives should try to maintain the perception of justice. There are several kinds, as listed below.

- **Distributive.** The outcomes are fair. People did not receive preferential treatment based on relationship, gender, national orientation or similar factors.

- **Procedural.** The implementation process is fair.

- **Interactional.** The treatment from decision makers is fair.

Seven Levers or Factors (Rs)

When you are seeking to create a shift of mind, it is important to craft messaging that engages people in rethinking their stories about the world. Howard Gardner, in his book *Changing Minds*, offers seven key levers, or factors, of change, based on his research. These are listed below.

- **Reason.** The change story should be rational and make sense.

- **Research.** It should be based on research that people accept. This information should be data-based and be compelling.

- **Resonance.** The change should be aligned to their personal goals and situation.

- **Representational re-description.** When information about the change is presented in diverse ways, it is more convincing.

- **Resources and rewards.** The change effort should offer sufficient resources and rewards. The messaging should make this clear.

- **Resistances.** The concerns of stakeholders, both imagined and real, must be dealt with.

- **Real world events.** The overall context and situation can affect the viability of the change. For example, during wars or recessions, people will have their focus elsewhere. Change efforts should consider this timing and acknowledge those pressures and factors.

Cognitive Processing Modes

People process information differently. Although logic is more influential to earlier adopters than later adopters, you should still mix styles in these messages. Some people are more influenced by authority, others by logic, others by peers, some by values, and so on. Other people are procedural and like timelines and sequences of events, and still others are conceptual and like models and analogies.

While everyone is influenced by these factors to some extent, most people put more emphasis on one style over another. So, it is advisable to include a mix of these in the communications content.

- **Structure.** Giving a picture and breakdown of it. Some people like to see models, classifications, and drawings that give the structure of things.

- **Data.** One type of person prefers to see the data and draw their own conclusions from the data, or at least see how conclusions that are being offered are connected to the data.

- **Process.** Other types of people like to see timelines and know when events are planned to happen. They want to see process flows and other descriptions or representations of the sequences involved.

- **Metaphor.** Another common way people understand information is through a metaphor or other type of comparison. They understand the new idea by relating it to something they already know. For example, large companies often name their internal education departments as a "University" to make it sound like higher education. But, of course there are many differences between a corporate internal education group and a full-fledged university, such as in the granting of degrees and offering a rounded or universal education.

Analyzing Communications Effectiveness

Getting feedback about communications is an important part of the process. It is very difficult to know what communications will be effective without sharing them with people and getting their feedback. So, at first, feedback is gathered from a subset of the audience, prior to sending communications on a broad scale. This minimizes confusion. Later in the campaign, you may want to set up indicators to know how effective the communications are in achieving the goals.

Socializing

The first step of gathering feedback on drafts is socializing them with likely stakeholders. This is a little different than a review process, which is often done with other experts in the communication team or the Core Group.

The socialization of communications involves showing them to actual stakeholders to discover how they will react. What other questions do they have? Is the message engaging? What is their reaction to change? What should be better explained?

This can be done in various ways. For example, it could be done individually or through group presentations. The messaging could also be shared with pilot audiences, like the ambassadors discussed in Chapter 13.

A/B Testing

Another form of testing often used by professional marketers is called "A/B testing." In this form of testing, two or more versions of the same messaging are created. Then each version is sent to a different stakeholder group to see which version gets the best response.

There are several ways to track the responses. If available, specific software like MailChimp will enable tracking of links that are clicked in emails. Or, if you do not have that kind of technology, you could put different links in each message so that clicks on those links can be tracked as hits to a web page. Or, there could also be other different calls to action, such "call here for more information" to determine which channel gets more responses.

Indicators

At the start of the campaign, of course, the overall awareness of the change is nearly zero. There is little reason to measure it at first, but as the communications campaign moves forward, you should periodically collect feedback and adjust as needed. Methods for doing this include effectiveness surveys, spot interviews, and getting feedback in various meetings.

Cheat Sheet

The communications strategy describes how large groups of stakeholders are broadly made aware of the change initiative. It establishes a fundamental, positive understanding of the initiative. To accomplish this, it usually employs mainly one-way, mass media communications. While mass media is frequently not enough on its own to ensure adoption, it can be an efficient way to mobilize first adopters and lay a foundation for strategies discussed in later chapters.

The communications strategy must meet three critical success factors:

- **Reaching people.** Large-scale audiences can be difficult to reach and require a systematic approach often involving several channels.

- **Getting attention.** People habitually tune out messages they are not seeking, so the messaging must get their attention. Methods involve creating sticky messages, using trusted people to deliver them, and repetition.

- **Relevancy.** The stakeholder must understand how the message is relevant to them. It needs to supply the necessary information to confirm its relevancy and reduce the reasons for rejecting it.

Developing a plan for effective messaging through these phases is facilitated by using a good process and applying best practices. This process includes

1. Translate core messages to stakeholder groups.

2. Develop the plan. This is often done using the communications planning matrix.

3. Create the communications pieces. Developing effective messaging content is facilitated by using a good process and applying best practices. This process includes,

    a. Create a draft.

    b. Review the draft with the team one or more times.

    c. Review the draft with a wider audience.

    d. Test the material on a few sample audience members.

    e. Get approval from management, if necessary.

    f. Test the content on pilot stakeholder groups. Use A/B testing and create ways to understand the reach and impact of the content.

The communications strategy is the first of five key strategy areas. It can usually be started quickly while other strategies are still being developed. It establishes awareness and a base of knowledge for other efforts. The other four strategies will be developed in the following chapters. Particularly, the leadership of an organization can play a vital role in communicating the big picture of the change, which is discussed in the next section.

11

Change Leadership

Every conversation is an intervention.

—An oft-spoken organizational change maxim

There is usually a power differential in an organization where some people exercise more influence than others. Commonly, this situation stems in part from having a formal hierarchy of managers and employees. While formal authority is often not sufficient alone to create change, it is an important influence, and many stakeholders will not adopt a change unless they see leadership is involved and behind the change. Moreover, there is also informal power, the result of personal influence due to high skills, knowledge, authority, or contacts. Whenever there is organizational power in a system, this power affects relationships and their susceptibility to change, so we must engage these power players when seeking to create change.

Considerable research has suggested that lack of change leadership is a leading cause of failure in change initiatives. While the causes of failure are complex and diverse across initiatives, it is certainly true change leadership is a crucial factor. However, it is also the case that many changes are launched by executives and then go nowhere. So, even when a direction is set from top leadership, considerable planning and organizing is needed to get it implemented.

Planning and organizing is needed to support and encourage the formal and informal power players in the organization to use their power to forward the change. This may require establishing some overt roles and structure, but the act of exercising change leadership is often quite subtle: In the right moment, change leaders ask insightful questions, provide key information, make connections for people, and help them understand the importance of the change. This is not usually through formal presentations but in casual conversations that occur intermixed with other activities.

This kind of change leadership addresses one half of an important dynamic in change. Over the years in change management research, it has been common to talk of change as being "top-down," or driven by upper management versus "bottom-up," or driven by employees and people lower in the organization who are passionate about the change. The latest research has shown it is not one or the other. Rather successful change needs both top down and bottom up efforts, as shown in the figure below.

Figure 11-1. Simultaneous Top Down and Bottom Up Change

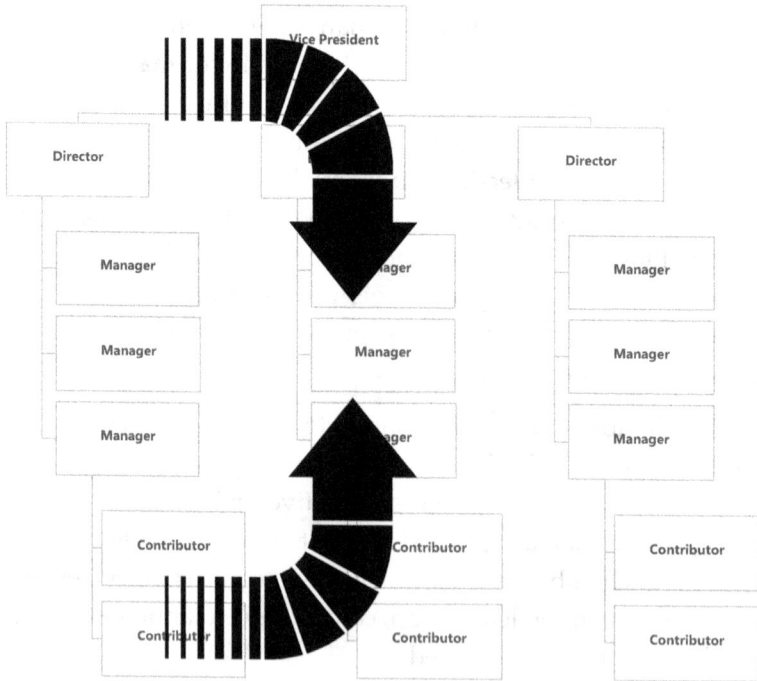

In this chapter, we will discuss the role of change leaders, including the typical ways of structuring them and setting them up to use their
influence. The corresponding "bottom up" action will be discussed later in
Chapter 13.

Roles by Phase

Change leadership occurs throughout the change process, not just
in one function of the Generating Change Model. However, in each function there are different priorities and levels of activity, as summarized in
the graphic and corresponding subsections below.

Figure 11-2. Change Leadership by Function

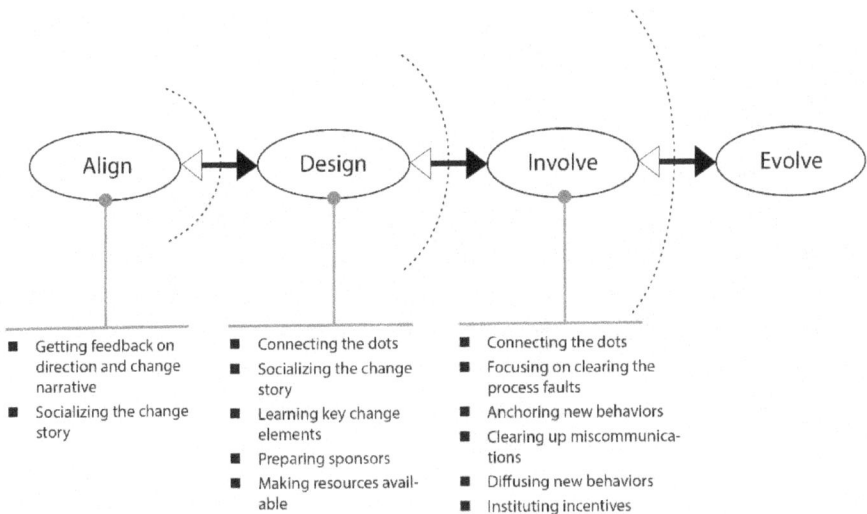

Align	Design	Involve	Evolve
■ Getting feedback on direction and change narrative ■ Socializing the change story	■ Connecting the dots ■ Socializing the change story ■ Learning key change elements ■ Preparing sponsors ■ Making resources available	■ Connecting the dots ■ Focusing on clearing the process faults ■ Anchoring new behaviors ■ Clearing up miscommunications ■ Diffusing new behaviors ■ Instituting incentives	

Align Function: Socializing and Shaping the Change Story

In the Align function, the Core Group engages the change leadership community to align on the change story, as described in Chapter 4. At
this point, socializing the story individually and in small groups may be
enough. The leadership community helps shape the change story.

Based on those conversations, the leadership community is also typically engaged in learning the basic change story and socializing it with their interpersonal networks. This is to prepare stakeholders for the change and to create a first layer of mental alignment. The goals are to empower the leadership community, have them help shape the story, and begin early identification of potential issues.

Design Function: Preparing to Lead the Change

In the Design function, the focus of change leadership is on preparing the way for when the change is ready. It involves knowing the tangible outcomes of the change and understanding the ways for stakeholders to be involved and to get key information.

At this point, a valuable tool for mobilizing managers is setting up a series of working sessions with them. They become one aspect of a change agent network for the organization, as will be discussed in Chapter 13.

These working sessions should be timed to begin in the weeks preceding the launch point and should prepare leaders to support the change as it rolls out for several weeks to months after the launch. It is usually best to schedule the sessions more intensely in the period directly preceding and following a roll out, until an adoption level of around 65% is achieved, or learning communities have been firmly established. Then, meeting frequency may be decreased. These working sessions are designed to give them a more specific role in supporting the change as it rolls out. The topics of the working sessions should include the following:

- Current resources available to aid stakeholder adoption
- Feedback from change leaders on potential issues they see
- Any changes needed to adapt the change program to what is truly happening
- Key messaging to be forwarded out to their staffs, via staff meetings and so on

Involve Function: Accelerating Success and Removing Barriers

In the Involve function, change leadership should be out in force. They continue to meet regularly and check in to get updates about the change and provide feedback. Some of their key responsibilities in this phase are as follows:

- Recognizing and rewarding people for doing new behaviors.

- Inquiring if people are aware of and understand key points.

- Looking for places where adoption of the change is stalled or breaking down and working with the Core Group and designers to clear the obstacles.

- Helping people connect the dots of how the change affects them and supports the company's goals.

- Supporting change ambassadors and related learning communities (as will be discussed in Chapter 13).

Evolve Function: Embedding the Change in the Way People Work

In the Evolve function, change leaders should continue supporting the change and using their interpersonal influence to encourage later adopter groups. Metrics can be monitored, and adjustments can be made. Change leaders should particularly focus on the following levers of forwarding the change:

- Identify and evangelize best practices and success stories.

- Discover break points and work to clear them.

- Encourage embedding incentives, automating, and putting hooks into processes and tools to facilitate making the change part of the way people work.

Leading in Every Conversation

The practice of developing change leadership is primarily one of educating members of the leadership community how they can move the change forward by making the appropriate response. Beyond learning the accurate information and terminology to support the change, there are few specific tasks or items. Rather, change leaders must be aware that every conversation they have is an opportunity to lead the change — by making connections, asking questions, and clarifying the direction.

In this role of supporting the diffusion of the new behaviors, managers might find themselves in a role that is contrary to their usual behavior. Normally, managers seek to maintain order and control. They often discourage critique or expression of issues and problems. They try to communicate in a way that encourages people to continue "business as usual." But in the creation of organizational change, their role is more as a steward who seeks to support the change and create the conditions for diffusion to occur. This involves purposely finding and exposing obstacles, clearing them, and focusing on perpetuating new behaviors rather than the old ones.

Members of the leadership community could also be stakeholders themselves; that is, they could be asked to adopt behaviors such as participating in governance, analyzing reports, and providing resources for the new process. Still, besides adopting certain behaviors to support the future system, managers need to exercise a role as change leaders to help forward the diffusion of change.

The change leadership role is not a set of tasks to be checked off. Instead, the manager must be a high-level change champion by engaging as much as possible with stakeholders and having productive conversations with them. Being a change leader is about creating the direction and tone for the change. This could be done by people at various levels in the organization. It could be done by executives or by any other group of people who decided to initiate a change. Regardless, the people who "hold the flame" for the change effort need to provide enough leadership.

Success in change leadership is greatly dependent on the energy the individuals put into it. The key idea here is that leaders (should be) always talking to people, and every conversation is an opportunity to forward the change. Especially, they should hold a positive perception and communicate it to others. If they perpetuate negative talk about the change, people will lose interest and take the change less seriously. If they talk positively, help people make connections, sort out misconceptions, invite them to be involved and raise issues, then a very different outcome can happen.

This activity can have big results. While researching the customer perceptions of various IT services a few years ago, I found that one formerly much-maligned service had made a dramatic turnaround, going from a service with poor customer satisfaction to one of the best. The cause? It turns out the manager had a practice of personally answering every complaint or concern that was raised on email lists, even doing this late into the night. Numerous people attributed his responsiveness and openness as the reason for their change of attitude about the service. While he could have passed the job off to subordinates, his willingness to handle complaints showed he was serious about improving the service.

Change leadership is not so much a process as the consistent application of key skills. Here is a list I have compiled over many years.

- **Communicate a simple, compelling vision.** Understand the basic change story and be able to frame it in one's own words, emphasizing both the benefits for the organization as well as the effect on the individual. For example, clearly and consistently remind people that transformation is required to gain a competitive advantage.

- **Use the right language.** It is important for change leaders to know the terminology and basic concepts. They should clarify these for others and straighten out misconceptions.

- **Challenge others to get on board with the change.** Interact with individuals and groups in the organization to explain the who, what, when, where, why, and how of the change.

Confront colleagues when they are not supporting the change. Keep colleagues honest by connecting back to group decisions. Mediate strong conflict among key people in the organizations.

- **Use questions.** Ask critical questions that discover whether the new behaviors are being adopted and where the fault lines exist. Utilize every opportunity to interact with others and encourage challenges and answer questions.

- **Face up to people's expressions of negativity.** People could be negative about the change. The change leader must avoid falling into the trap of colluding with them and agreeing. Change leaders should support the change, and when negativity occurs they should seek to understand it and work with it. This could be by clearing up misconceptions or acknowledging the challenges and channeling the feedback to the right people on the change team.

- **Recognize and reward people who are demonstrating the new behaviors.** This does not have to be monetary. It could be just saying "thank you" or mentioning them to others. It could be taking them to lunch or any number of other possibilities.

- **Notice small wins and celebrate them.** Momentum is maintained by noticing small wins and celebrating them. Even just having a moment of congratulations is good. Or, you could have a celebratory lunch with the team or go to a movie together.

- **Identify success stories and popularize them to others.** Propagating success stories has several advantages. First, they build on the learnings of one group to benefit others. Second, they create the sense of momentum, which encourages later adopters to adopt. Third, practical examples are often more compelling to people who are struggling to understand how to adopt the change.

- **Support other change agents.** As will be discussed in Chapter 13, if the change effort uses change ambassadors, then effective change leaders will support them by helping make connections, inviting them to speak at staff meetings, and helping communicate key messages.

Symbolism

Change leadership actions are influential in part through their symbolism. At the most basic level, the act of change leadership is itself symbolic and communicates leadership support. It demonstrates leadership confidence in the change program. However, the way in which actions are done can be supportive or detrimental, because they are always interpreted symbolically.

For example, here are some real examples that I have seen:

- A vice-president at a company meeting declared employees are empowered and then told a story about how it was a good thing he reviewed expenses over $25 because he found an employee wasting money.

- A company closed their project management office while declaring support for the discipline of project management.

- A vice-president proclaimed the values of diversity and opportunities for women but had all white male direct reports.

- Employees organized diversity and women's empowerment activities, but the leaders did not participate.

- Management said the people and a culture were valued but removed employee perks like free coffee, free popcorn, company paid broadband, and company paid mobile phones.

Any or all these items could have been well meaning and cost effective. But as the maxim goes "actions speak louder than words." The symbolism of these actions spoke louder than the justification that was given.

Commensurately, it may be valuable to brainstorm and execute purposeful symbolic actions that will have a positive effect. For example, some CEOs take $1 pay when their companies are in trouble. Other symbolic actions might include

- Having skip-level meetings

- Getting an executive to show up and voice support at the start of important meetings

- Putting a person in charge of a certain key area (sometimes called a "czar")

- Getting rid of ostentatious executive perks like planes and cars

Change Leadership Structures

Depending on the size of the organization and the characteristics of the change effort, it may be necessary to deploy a structure for mobilizing the change leadership. Just asking people to be a good change leader is not usually enough. There are four common methods for doing this, as follows:

- Basic sponsorship

- Cascade

- Outside into the middle

- Inside out

Sponsors

The sponsor is a high-ranking individual who can make key strategic decisions for the direction of the change effort and can be perceived as speaking for the highest levels of management in the organization. The goal is also to be able to bring on board other sub-organizations, so the sponsor should have the ability to also engage other high-level managers who might control affected resources.

A sponsor is a more formalized leader in the change process. They are not necessarily a stakeholder who is affected by the change, although it is possible. But, the sponsor role is a formal role as part of the change infrastructure. Thus, an individual playing a sponsor role should be an active evangelizer. They may even control resources.

The sponsor is someone who

- Is not involved in the day-to-day operation of the change program
- Has responsibility for all the affected groups
- Acts as a champion across the company

The responsibilities of the sponsor could include the following:

- Ensure the organization is aligned with the change: identify cross functional interdependencies and help ensure gaps are closed.
- Visibly convey strong organizational commitment to the change.
- Meet privately with individuals or groups to assert strong personal support for the change. Ensure necessary resources are available.
- Reward those who support the change or express displeasure with those who resist the change.
- Assess progress.
- Remove obstacles.

Sometimes, even though sponsors are assigned, they become just a "name in a box," and the sponsors are not effective. It is normally a little dicey, since usually they are persons who are relatively high in the hierarchy and this makes it tough for you to tell them what to do and to hold them accountable for their role. However, you will have to set up the sponsors so that they understand their role, which may transition them from simply representing their organization in committee meetings to actively championing the change in their respective organizations.

These are some approaches that often work to engage sponsors more effectively:

- Meet with them individually and explain your role and their role.

- Set up a regular session to meet with them. Use these sessions to

  o   Discuss feedback to them and from them.

  o   Work to alleviate them of logistical details.

  o   Ask them when they can present things and where.

  o   Work with them to think through their role sponsor. Where can they communicate the vision? Who can they reach out to for feedback?

  o   Provide them with ready to use materials, such as PowerPoint slides on the change that they can do.

- Use a sponsorship contract. This can be a little sensitive, but some change practitioners have used a formal contract to get their sponsors to commit publicly and in writing to how they support the program. For example,

  o   Arrive at least one team meeting per quarter to show support.

  o   Recognize the project in an all-hands meeting and any other opportunity they might find.

  o   Reward key players periodically by inviting them for breakfast or some similar event.

  o   Coordinate with other sponsors to get them enthused with sponsorship behaviors.

  o   Display a symbol on their desk (metaphor for the project).

  o   Receive feedback on a regular basis about some aspect of the change effort.

- Sponsorship scorecard. Another instrument that has been used effectively in some situations is the sponsorship scorecard. The change maker put some key categories like visibility, proactiveness, and accessibility of the sponsor and then compiles feedback from selected stakeholders about the categories. The feedback is then shared in shared in a scorecard format with sponsors to give them a sense of how they are doing according to others.

A variation is having more than one sponsor, where a small group of sponsors is formed into a *steering committee,* as depicted in Figure 11-3. This is especially important when the change affects several independent organizations and there is a need to make joint agreements. The steering committee then includes a sponsor or senior representative from each organization who can participate in this and speak for their organization.

Figure 11-3. Steering Committee

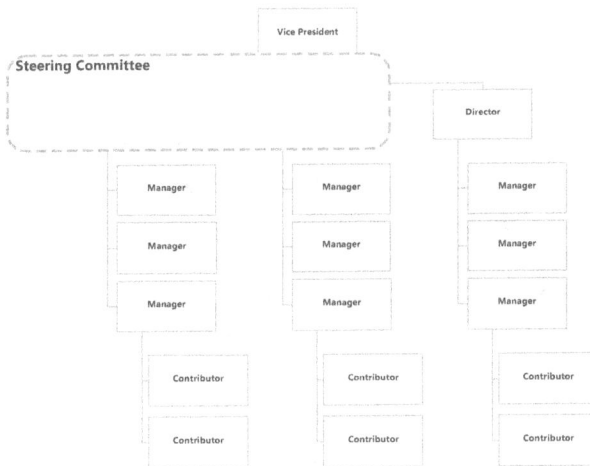

Cascade

Sponsors can be used to engage with the organization in several ways. First, especially with highly top-down changes, it may be possible to use them to generate a management cascade. This involves the sponsor and change team leveraging each layer of management to influence the next level lower, as shown in Figure 11-4.

Figure 11-4. Management Cascade

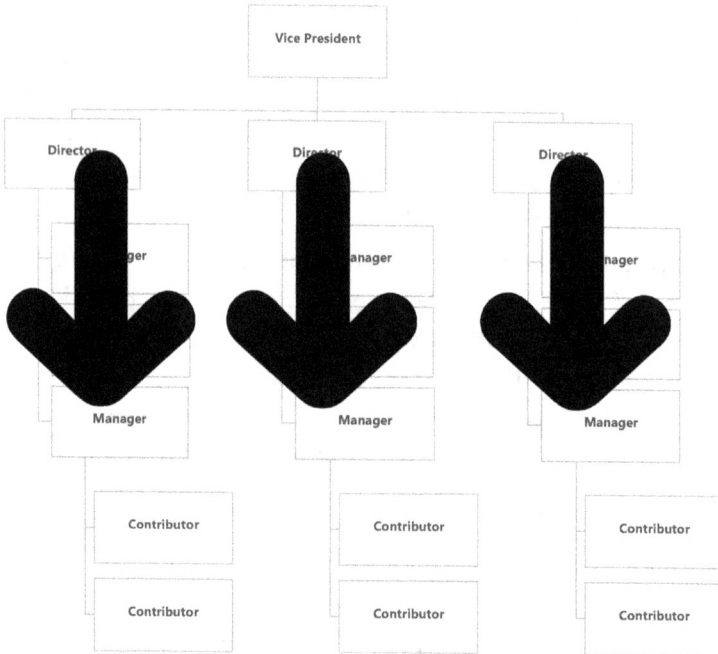

For example, if there is a company-wide decision to enter skills in skills inventory, the managers may be asked to communicate this decision to their staff. This method theoretically engages the influence of the direct manager and allows for interactive question and answer, so it can be powerful. But, the method often falls apart because it results in a presentation being emailed to managers with a request to discuss it with their staff. But this often fails. Some managers do it well. Others forget. Some just forward the presentation in email to their staff.

When the cascade is done well, it usually involves the change team holding one or more meetings with the managers where the material is explained to them, and the managers are trained to deliver it. In the case of sensitive issues, such as restructuring, the manager may need to be partnered with a facilitator or human resources manager who helps them deliver it. Then, there should be follow up with the managers to ensure it was done and gather feedback.

Lateral Influence Network

Especially in larger, more complex environments, there are often changes that need to be driven that do not warrant intensive top management involvement. These are usually lower level changes to processes and tools, often ones that need to be standardized across organizations. These often do not rise to the level of being able to get substantial attention from the top, but they still benefit from leadership.

In these cases, the sponsors can be organized to support a lateral network of management of influence. This requires establishing management level champions who then use their influence both upward and downward, as shown in Figure 11-5.

Figure 11-5. Lateral Influence Network

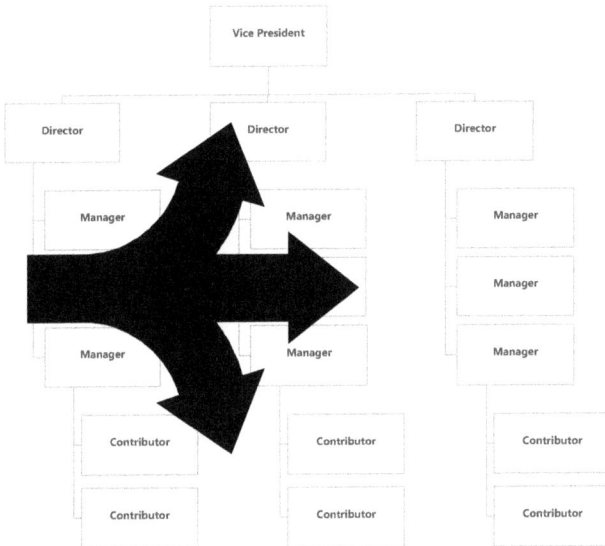

As shown in the lower part of figure, they will normally connect with an ambassador network as described in the Chapter 13. Operating committees are often used in conjunction with steering committees, described previously.

These managers may be organized into a form of an *operating committee*. The role of the operating committee is to make more day-to-day decisions about how the changes will be rolled out. The operating committee may have relationships with the steering committee.

The operating committee can be started using these steps:

1. Identify key managers to include.

2. Hold a kickoff.

   o   Give an overview of the change and gather their feedback.

   o   Review the expectations of being an operating committee member.

   o   Ask the operating committee to evaluate the situation in their respective area and report back next time.

3. Hold periodic meetings.

   o   Respond to their previous feedback.

   o   Provide updates.

   o   Gather feedback.

   o   Discuss challenges they are finding and how to resolve them.

Inside Out

More complex and foundational changes probably require more of an inside-out approach, especially in large organizations with many departments. The inside-outside out change enables the many business units of an overall organization to be engaged in the change yet still handle the change according to their specific needs. This means there is an overall framework intended to establish consistency across the organizations, but within each organization there is a largely independent change effort guided by their own change team as shown in Figure 11-6.

Figure 11-6. Inside Out Change Structure

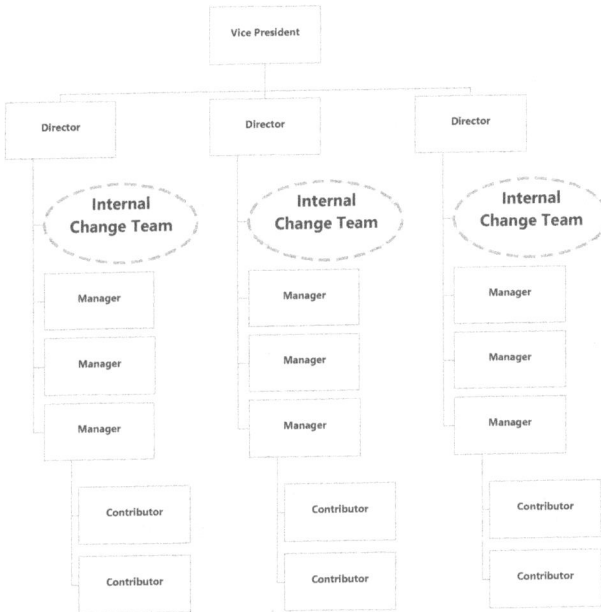

This entails similar leadership workshops as described in Chapter 6, but a common framework is brought into the sessions so that they align with the plan. These sessions should be used to accomplish the following:

- Review change leadership principles.

- Develop the vision/end state for the organization that is consistent with the overall vision and framework.

- Agree on the types of metrics and indicators that they want to see to know it is successful.

- Reach agreement on the plan, including how it will be staffed and monitored.

Cheat Sheet

The establishment of change leadership behaviors by members of the leadership community is an important driving force for the change effort. Change leadership is the type of soft skill that is hard to get established in an organization. It often sounds like you are trying to tell them how to do their job, and they feel like they have heard it all before. It is also difficult because there often are no concrete examples on when and how to do it, so they must motivate themselves to find them. Since they are busy, they often do not, although they can be motivated to an extent through personal contact and peer pressure.

Change leadership occurs in all the Generating Change Model phases, but the vigorousness intensifies during the Mobilization phase. At that time, it is particularly important that change leaders be enrolled and trained to use the following behaviors:

- Communicate a simple, compelling vision.
- Use the right language.
- Challenge others to get on board with the change.
- Use questions.
- Face up to people's expressions of negativity.
- Recognize and reward people who are demonstrating the new behaviors.
- Notice small wins and celebrate them.
- Identify success stories and popularize them to others.
- Support other change agents.

When sponsors are used, having structure is important to operationalizing this influence. Generally, this starts with identifying and engaging the them. Then, the Core Group can help them mobilize their influence through the formation of steering and operating committees.

Besides sponsors, additional related influencing networks may be formed based on one or a combination of the following strategies:

- Cascading

- Lateral Influence Network

- Inside out

Usually, this change leadership will connect with a change agent or ambassador network as described in Chapter 13. While the change leadership network establishes management support, keeps people connected to the overall company strategy, and clears roadblocks, the managers often do not have the time or the direct knowledge of the change to be the point of contact or the role model. This will be the essential function of the change ambassadors, who the managers will support.

12

Training

We spend very little money on marketing and more money on training our people than advertising.

—*Howard Schultz, CEO Starbucks*

For people to adopt notable change, they often need to develop additional skills. If they do not believe they have the skills or can acquire them, they may not even be willing to try the change for fear of either failing or simply wasting time. Even if they attempt it, the result might be unsuccessful due to their lack of skills or knowledge, and they may reject the change as something that does not work. For example, if the change initiative is to improve collaboration, then employees may need to be trained on methods and skills to collaborate successfully.

Training can also be a way of accelerating the change by helping them experience the new behaviors in a safe environment. Changing the way people interact with others may at first be uncomfortable and counterintuitive, until experienced. If their initial attempts do not result in a positive experience they will revert to simply working together in the original way.

The Training strategy contains the activities of developing and delivering vehicles for people to acquire those skills. This could include such methods as web pages, videos, webinars, live trainings, simulations, video consultations, sandbox environments, mentoring, and certification. Which methods are used depend on the type of change and your analysis of the stakeholder needs.

While the overall communications strategy can lay a foundation of awareness and basic understanding of the change effort, training develops the skills needed to perform the new behaviors. Thus, the training is a formal program focused on developing skills, and this frequently involves developing different skills sets for different stakeholder groups.

In this section, we will discuss taking the stakeholder analysis developed previously and analyzing it for skills that must developed. We will then turn the analysis into requirements that form the basis of an effective training plan.

Task Analysis

The first step is to identify which tasks the stakeholders need to perform. This is called *task analysis*. Drawing on the stakeholder analysis performed earlier, you analyze the required behaviors needed by the various stakeholder groups for necessary skills that must be developed.

While it might be tempting to assign this analysis to a training professional, experience has shown the core team more likely has the basic knowledge needed to begin the task analysis. This can be developed in collaboration with training professionals, but the core team usually needs to drive it. Once the task analysis is underway, it can be deepened and continued by training professionals. This is best because training personnel normally are not familiar enough at first with the intended change. If the change team organizes the task analysis, this creates a nice point to align on shared understandings.

The essential activity of the task analysis is centered on using an organizing framework like that shown in the Figure 12-1. The stakeholders are listed as column heads, and the required behaviors for each are decomposed into sets of tasks in the first column. Then, the cells are used to indicate the level of training needed for the task.

The numbers in the cells indicate the level of training needed. There are three basic types, as given in Table 12-1.

Table 12-1. Example Task Analysis for Portfolio Management

No	Task	Executive	Managers	Prodi. Mgrs.	Analysts	Engineers	Vendors
1	**Reporting**						
1.1	Create and review high-level summaries	1	1	2	2	2	NA
1.2	Create and review standard detailed reports Costing Schedule Resources usage	1	1	2	2	1	NA
1.3	Create customized reports	NA	NA	2	2	NA	NA
2	**Process**						
2.1	Understand the flow of work, who to contact, where to direct action	1	2	3	2	2	2
2.2	Make prioritization decision according to established guidelines and strategic plan	2	3	1	1	1	1
2.3	Understand and use engagement of infrastructure resources	NA	1	3	2	2	1
2.4	Ensure work goes through the approved development process	NA	2	3	3	3	2
2.5	Approve gate reviews	1	3	2	NA	2	NA

No	Task	Executive	Managers	Prodi. Mgrs.	Analysts	Engineers	Vendors
2.6	Follow the development process for all programs	NA		3	3	3	1
3	**Data Capture and Maintenance**						
3.1	Enter and maintain schedule data	NA	1	3	2	2	1
3.2	Update cost information	NA	2	3	2	2	1
3.3	Initiate requests for gate reviews				1		
3.4	Upload and maintain project documentation			1	3	3	2
3.5	Enter time spent on the project			1	1	1	1

1. **Informational**. This level of training is content that can be understood through one-way content delivery. This could be documents, books, videos, podcasts, or other media.

2. **Interactive**. Other kinds of skills, such as consulting, web development, or collaborating, cannot be fully learned by one-way communications. These kinds of skills usually require feedback and modeling by other more experienced people for a period.

3. **Formative**. Other skills, such as managing, presenting, and selling require continuous learning and practices. Expertise in these areas is developed over time, through many forms of learning applied to real situations.

The common, unskilled way to develop training is to make a list of possible content and then package it up. However, this tends to create training that is overly conceptual and not focused enough on developing useful skills. The task analysis grid enables you to determine more accurately how to identify the optimal training modules.

Identify Modules

Once the task analysis is performed, the next step is to group the skills needed into the appropriate modules. A module is a collection of material intended to develop a specific skill or a specific stakeholder or set of stakeholders.

Looking at the grid, try to identify important groupings that will do the following:

- Put similar content in a single module. This makes it more efficient to develop and maintain.

- Keep modules focused and as small as possible. This facilitates being able to replace modules without having to re-work everything if things change in the future or as the training is evolved.

- Focus modules to meet the needs of stakeholder groups as closely as possible. Stakeholders do not want to have to learn irrelevant information.

For example, examine the Figure 12-1 and notice the groupings. Of course, things are never perfectly delineated. You will have to group content to make it efficient and manageable. This might mean some stakeholder groups get a little more depth than they need. But, the goal is to target the skills development as well as possible so that stakeholder groups get what they need and little else.

These groupings in our example might be addressed as shown in table 12-2. Once the content is grouped into the optimal modules, ask "what is the appropriate way to deliver the modules?" In the past, options were mainly limited to print publications and classes, but social media and technology are completely transforming what is possible.

Modularization

Content will be much more effective in modularized, smaller, more targeted pieces. As consumers, we are familiar with one form of this through the vast array of "how to" videos available on the Internet. Whether preparing the Thanksgiving turkey, perfecting your golf chip shot, or replacing the toilet, a short video is usually findable on the Internet within a few minutes.

Figure 12-1. Grouping of Task Analysis

No	Task	Executive	Front line Managers	Project Managers	Analysts	Engineers	Vendors
1	Reporting						
1.1	Create and review high-level summaries	1	1	2	2	2	NA
1.2	Create and review standard detailed reports • Costing • Schedule • Resources usage	1	1	2	2	1	NA
1.3	Create customized reports	NA	NA	2	2	NA	NA
2	Process						
2.1	Understand the flow of work, who to contact, where to direct action	1	2	3	2	2	2
2.2	Make prioritization decision according to established guidelines and strategic plan	2	3	1	1	1	1
2.3	Understand and use engagement of infrastructure resources	NA	1	3	2	2	1
2.4	Ensure work goes through the approved development process	NA	2	3	3	3	2
2.5	Approve gate reviews	1		2	NA	2	NA
2.6	Follow the development process for all programs	NA		2	2		1
3	Data Capture and Maintenance						
3.1	Enter and maintain schedule data	NA	1	3	2	2	1
3.2	Update cost information	NA	2	3	2	2	1
3.3	Initiate requests for gate reviews				1		
3.4	Upload and maintain project documentation			1	3	3	2
3.5	Enter time spent on the project			1	1	1	1

Table 12-2. Training Modules in Portfolio Management Example

Group	Module	Description
A	A web page or video for general distribution.	General reporting methods
B	A small handbook.	Detailed reporting needs, mainly of interest to program and project managers
C	Live sessions with managers to cover examples and handle questions.	Management decision-making
D	Process documentation and embed in appropriate areas of the workflow tool.	Process information for program and project managers
E	A short video showing how to enter the data.	Data capture for program managers
F	A short video showing how to enter the data.	Task entry

This modularization enables just-in-time delivery of more targeted content. A video clip or pop-up instruction can be offered at the point someone must fill out a form. Stakeholders can select languages and levels of detail according to their personal preference or role. This provides much greater flexibility.

This kind of modularization also enables content to be kept more current. When user information is broken into smaller modules, an individual module can be more easily replaced or updated. For example, it is much easier to re-record a one-minute video how to generate a custom report than it is to re-record a 10-minute video about producing all the possible reports.

Interactivity

These days, content can also now be more interactive and customized to the need and this improves learning retention and efficiency. Studies have consistently shown when people interact with the material—such as by matching up related categories or using new knowledge to respond to simulations — their retention level is dramatically improved.[1]

There are many ways to add interactivity to almost any level of presentation or information delivery. You can take questions, poll the audience, do small group activities, and so on.

It also can help to make it fun. While interactivity itself makes it more fun, with a little creativity, you can also create more fun circumstances. For example, you can create simulated press conferences or talk shows as a way of creating a question and answer format rather than the traditional slide presentation.[2,3]

Gamification

Because of technology and greater understanding of the importance of how engagement is produced, we are seeing a rise in *gamification* or the use of game play mechanics to create different incentives.

Gamification has many far-reaching aspects. Not only is it being used to help sell products and do marketing, but it is widely used in corporate training. It is also being considered by some as an approach to total engagement of employees.

Research by Gartner indicates the gamification trend is on the rise. By 2015, over 50% of major companies had gamified some aspect of their process. [4] There are many examples of successful gamification available. For example, the Deloitte Leadership Academy provides leadership classes to busy professionals. Rather than force them into a classroom, the material is offered in small modules of 10 to 60 minutes in length that can be consumed while on the move. Points and badges are awarded for course completion, and there is a leaderboard where people can compare their progress with others. [5]

This has the effect of creating more engagement with the content by providing a wider array of available incentives. Small pieces can be delivered much more on demand and gamification methods can be employed, such as the following:

- **Points**. Just assigning points to completion of activities and keeping score can be motivating to some people. Some people are motivated to achieve a perfect score regardless of what others do.

- **Leader boards.** To amplify the competitive nature of assigning points, leader boards can be used to publicly show who is ahead.

- **Badges or certificates.** Accomplishment can be denoted by assigning virtual badges that people can display. This is like giving certificates.

- **Challenges.** People like challenges that require some skill, but not an overwhelming amount of skill.

- **Levels.** Once a challenge is accomplished, players may have increased their skill level, so having successive levels can inspire them to keep playing. There is a sense of accomplishment and challenge to progress through the various levels.

- **Group challenges.** In trying to enact a gamification system, some people found it was less about getting individual recognition and more about participating with the team.

- **Small rewards.** Small cash rewards such as gift certificates, hats, t-shirts, and so on can be used.

- **Virtual goods.** Sometimes, the reward does not even have to be real. Games like FarmVille have shown that giving people virtual property can lead to great interactivity.

While technology is increasingly becoming available to implement these kinds of games, the games do not have to be that sophisticated. For example, a web page can be posted showing the status of competitors. I once attended a speech by artist Erik Wahl, who created a game by hiding one of his pictures in Los Angeles and then offering to give it to anyone who could find it. He conducted the game using his Facebook page, so it was a very simple set up and lightweight, cost-effective administration of the game.

As a final note on gamification, you should ensure there is mean-ingful interaction in the game. That is, just applying a points system or a leaderboard does not make it into a game. There needs to be a real compe-tition, fun, or accomplishment that is being tracked with points or a lead-erboard. These incentives and tracking mechanisms should augment in-terrelationships that are rewarding in themselves.

Training Content Development Strategies

Once the optimal modules have been identified, the next activity is determining how they are best developed. There are at least three pos-sible strategies for deploying training, as described below. These could be used together.

Prepackaged. In some cases, especially where tools or standard-ized methodologies are to be deployed, there is a vendor training already packaged up to be delivered. This can be useful, but of course it is usually generalized to apply to many companies and may be of varying quality. You will have to review it and determine if it is suitably focused for the intended stakeholders and is of sufficient quality.

Professional Design. In large-scale changes, you might want to have the training content developed by training professionals. Large com-panies often have departments staffed with training professionals, or there are many companies who do this work. Professional training developers have sophisticated processes and extensive education, and this can be im-portant in developing a training that is going to many people.

When you work with an outside training group to do this, there are always some tensions and trade-offs:

- Training professionals will have a learning curve to under-stand the changes. It is easy to underestimate this time, be-cause the core team has learned so much through all the planning meetings and other discussions.

- It is often expensive. In a large-scale change, where small er-rors and confusion can disrupt the productivity of many people, the expense may be worth it. It is very difficult to correct inaccurate or confusing training information once it is released to a large audience.

- The best time to engage professional training is after the content is fairly stable. This often means it has be used in one or more pilots and refined first.

Role modeling. Some skills such as coaching or facilitating, are learned well by watching role models. This could be used in conjunction with a formal class and mentoring.

Roll your own. It is often the case that the change team must put together the training plan themselves. This may be for speed reasons—to avoid the learning curve of engaging a professional training developer— or to avoid the cost. It often makes sense to have the training developed by the change team themselves, now that there are many tools available like Captivate and so on. This makes sense for small audiences and cases where the training may be evolving or highly customized for each audience.

It also often makes sense to develop the training yourself first when you are using a pilot rollout method. You can then gather feedback and customize it on the fly as you go and improve the training after the first two or so groups (early adopters or use by ambassadors). Once the content is stabilized, then have a training development organization make it into a more professional program that can be scaled.

Developing your own training though has some serious implications that should not be overlooked. Firstly, it takes considerable time and energy away from what the Core Group could otherwise being doing. Secondly, even with the tools that are available, making good training takes skill and is not really just a matter of putting some PowerPoint slides together. Sometimes this is sufficient, but not always.

The Training Plan

Using the preceding information, you should be able to put together a training plan. Unlike the communication plan, this will probably involve more of a Gantt style format, due to the needs for content development and specific deliveries. See the example below.

Study the example plan carefully and note the preparation that is required to do that training in terms of preparing instructors and uploading content, as well as the connection to the communications plan around the messaging. A beautiful training module is a waste of time if no one goes to it and getting people to access a self-service training requires its own marketing effort which should be incorporated in the communications plan.

Module Development

Whether you are developing modules yourself or project managing the development by training professionals, it is useful to understand that, like communications content, training modules are rarely perfect after the first draft. They should be reviewed and piloted before rolling them out to large audiences. Follow a process like that below.

1. Work with subject-matter experts and users to more fully understand what skills the stakeholders need to learn.

2. Create a draft.

3. Review the draft.

4. Create final draft.

5. Pilot training.

6. Revise and expand the training.

Figure 12-2. Example Training Plan

	Task	Target Audience	Start	End	Dur	%	2014					
							Feb	Mar	Apr	May	Jun	
	Example Training Development Plan for Portfolio Management		2/25/14	6/17/14	80							
1	Module F: Task entry video and web page	Team Members	2/25/14	3/4/14	6							
2	Module E: Data Capture Virtual Training	Team Members	3/6/14	6/17/14	73							
2.1	Development		3/6/14	4/7/14	23							
2.2	Piloting		4/8/14	4/21/14	10							
2.3	General Distribution		4/22/14	6/17/14	40							
3	Module D: Portfolio Process 1-day live training for Project Managers	Project Managers	3/5/14	6/3/14	64							
3.1	Development		3/5/14	3/21/14	13							
3.2	Piloting		3/22/14	4/7/14	11							
3.3	General Delivery		4/8/14	6/3/14	40							
4	Module C: Project Prioritization and Management	Managers	3/5/14	6/3/14	64							
4.1	Development		3/5/14	3/21/14	13							
4.2	Piloting		3/22/14	4/7/14	11							
4.3	General Delivery		4/8/14	6/3/14	40							
5	Module B: Advanced Reporting Virtual Training	Project Managers	3/5/14	6/3/14	64							
5.1	Development		3/5/14	3/21/14	13							
5.2	Piloting		3/22/14	4/7/14	11							
5.3	General Delivery		4/8/14	6/3/14	40							
6	Module A: Basic Reporting Video and Web Page	All	2/26/14	3/25/14	20							

Training Module Guidelines

While creating professional training content takes considerable education and experience, there are few tips below that you can use if you are "rolling your own."

- **Avoid "death by PowerPoint."** The goal of training is not to go through as much as content as possible. People have limits on how much content they can absorb at a time. So, the goal should be to go through the content at a speed and manner where the content can be effectively learned.

- **Be interactive.** Adult learners often learn better from being given tools and experimenting, so they can figure out how to achieve their own objectives. People do not recall as much from straight presenting as when they are being lectured to or when simply told what to. There are some good books on training games that you can use for inspiration.[6,7]

- **Mix it up and use different modalities.** Ask questions, show videos, give informational quizzes, change speakers, and any number of other means of delivery to keep the pace moving.

- **Start and end with a bang.** People tend to remember the beginning and the end the most.

- **Follow through.** Whichever the strategies you use, you should also bear in mind that just conducting the sessions is only part of the journey. Modern training practice recognizes that training rarely sticks if people just attend it and leave. The ability of the training to stick is partly enhanced by superior design, which is usually interactive and relevant to the learner's goals. But the retention of the material is also enhanced by creating an environment where they can use the training afterward. This is why timing is important. It should be delivered just before it is needed and then some kind of follow up should be designed, such as the following:

- **Mentoring program.** Students are assigned practice projects and are paired with an experienced mentor who can work with them through their initial efforts.

- **Peer support.** Students are organized into dyads or triads that continue to meet with each other in the future to support each other in peer learning.

- **Learning communities.** Students can be connected into learning communities, as described in future chapters.

Cheat Sheet

Training is an activity that formally seeks to develop the skills stakeholders need to be successful with the new behaviors. Training is not always needed, and there can be quite a bit of variation in what is needed from a simple web page or YouTube video to a complete set of courses leading to certification. Depending on the type and scale of the change effort, a lot of training may be needed or just a little.

The basic methodology of training development is given below.

1. **Conduct task analysis.** Training should be organized using the task analysis method.

2. **Identify modules needed.** Once the task analysis is done, appropriate decisions can be made about which training modules are needed and how they can be best developed from a cost.

3. **Create a training plan.** Identify how the modules will come together, how they will be reviewed, who will communicate their availability, and how they will be maintained.

4. **Determine the best way to get modules developed.** It may be suitable to develop the training yourself but developing high quality training for large audiences probably requires training professionals and a significant investment.

5. **Ensure there is follow up.** Communications, training, and change leadership only go part of the way for most significant organizational changes. These comprise a primarily top-down, expert-driven, largely mass media salient of the change effort that will likely engage first adopters only in making the change. It should also build up knowledge across other stakeholder groups, if done well, but they will not likely adopt straight away.

Well-crafted training can be an efficient way to develop the skills your stakeholders need to perform the new behaviors successfully. In some cases, training is enough. But, in other cases the training will just develop basic skills that need to be refined and honed with guidance from peers and mentors. Organizing this interaction is covered in the next chapter.

PART V: Evolve

The activity of continuing to mobilize the change and scale it by gathering feedback and providing a suitable framework.

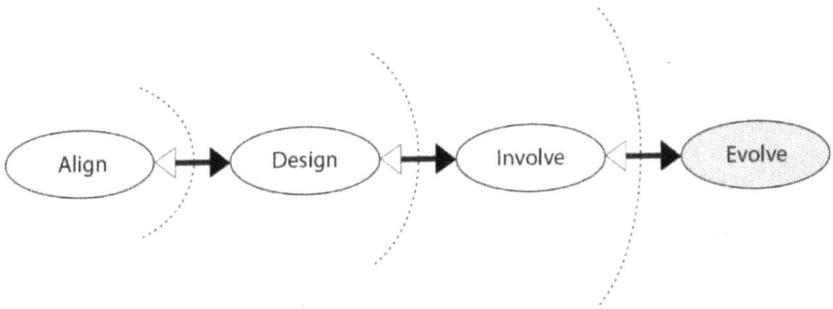

Align → Design → Involve → Evolve

13

Organizing the
Ground Campaign

*Success in securing the adoption of innovations by clients is positively related to
extent of change agent effort in contacting clients.*

—Everett Rogers

In many applications of strategy — such as football, politics, or military — winning requires a strong ***ground game***. This ground game is per-
son-to-person contact. In football or combat, it is physical conflict. In politics and organizational change, it is through personal influence.

Former U.S. President Barack Obama's election victories were
widely attributed to the strength of his ground game. I saw the sophistica-
tion of it upfront once when I attended an Organizing for Obama workshop. They had donor and prospective donor databases, their own social
media site, intensive trainings for organizers, and incentive programs for
not only raising money but for also getting the message out. This resulted
in the essence of a ground game for creating change — people connecting
with people.

Change programs often fall flat after the initial roll out because the
concept of the ground game is not well understood in business organizations. Many people have too much confidence in authority, mass emails,

or the power of a vision statement. As an example, a few years ago, a major technology company where I was consulting decided to roll out a program to improve processes by teaching everyone to use DMAIC. Executive communications were made to the whole division. A one-day training was rolled out and taken by many people. A center of excellence was established, and many people were trained as black belts and farmed out to change programs. Several major change programs were told to follow the DMAIC methodology.

Faced with having to report status according to progress along the DMAIC methodology, some of the change programs made substantial progress. Others, which had difficulty properly defining their programs and measuring the problem condition, struggled and eventually fell apart or shifted to a different approach. In the broader population, the DMAIC approach was picked up haphazardly. Some programs did it, while some did not.

I obtained some personal insight a few months into it when a team contacted me for change consulting on a program they were working on. As they described the program to me, I realized that it was essentially a process improvement program. So, I asked, "Did you go to DMAIC training?" and they confirmed they had. I said, "This is the time to use it." I asked them why they did not make this connection, and they conceded it simply did not occur to them or seem like a practical idea. Yet, it was exactly what they needed.

In a similar example, I once worked with a director in charge of deploying a mobile application to a large enterprise. One day, I happened to ask the director if he had installed the application himself. He had not, and I mentioned I had recently installed it easily. He then installed it on the spot. These kinds of examples are countless and illustrate one of Dr. Rogers' basic findings, that most people adopt a change only after another trusted person encourages it. We just don't see this effect in front of us and assume the mass communications are causing it.[1]

Interpersonal influence is critical in all kinds of large-scale, viral change. When the content is very compelling, like videos of cats playing pianos, then people pass it on spontaneously. But, since organizational change is often not that compelling, we add motivation by purposely mo-bilizing interpersonal interaction. This chapter discusses how to decide on an appropriate structure, kick it off, and transfer ownership to it.

Mobilizing Interpersonal Influence

Intentionally mobilizing interpersonal influence requires structure that leverages interpersonal influence. Fundamentally, the goal is to get a *change agent*, or *ambassador*, to influence someone who trusts them. The structure is needed because a social change often does not spread as easily as a funny video. Social and organizational change programs need a little structure to facilitate the forwarding of influence, as was shown in the fig-ure re-presented below from Chapter 1, where we discussed diffusion the-ory.

Figure 13-1. Change Diffusion

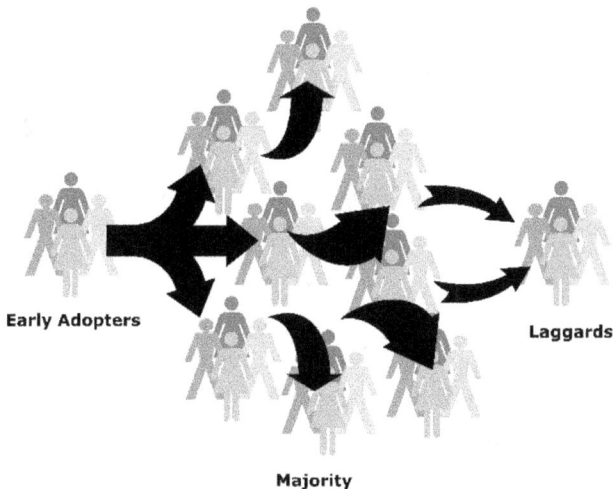

Early Adopters

Laggards

Majority

To accomplish this, the Core Group should set up what I call *learn-ing communities*. They are called this because they are generally informal, composed of people with an interest in the change or who have volun-teered to help, and because they participate in evangelizing the change. This creates a learning cycle These communities are the foundation for forming new interpersonal relationships. They provide the vehicle for self-organizing evolution of the ideas. In this setting, stakeholders can discuss issues and make new agreements with each other.

There are several types of learning communities that can be used to facilitate organizational change. Although they have similarities, each also has its own unique structure and purpose.

- Forums

- Ambassador Networks

- Communities of Practice

- Cascade Teams

- Participative Design Teams

Forums

The easiest learning community to start and run is the forum. The *forum* is a periodic meeting of the community around a certain theme. The purpose is primarily to inform the community members and create shared ideas around certain concepts and skills. There is often no explicit expectation that community members will attend every forum meeting or have any responsibilities other than showing up and following guidelines for participation.

In a forum, the organizers generally arrange for the content to be delivered. These meetings can be interactive but are driven primarily by the presentation of content that the community is interested in. The organizing team solicits ideas for topics, arranges the presenters, sends out the invites, controls the registration, and manages all aspects of the delivery of the forum.

In a forum, especially where technology such as video or audio bridges is used, the number of participants can be quite high, in the hundreds or even thousands of people. These can be done "virtually" using webcast or webinar type approaches. This is often a useful vehicle for supporting change communications. While this type of community has the lowest influence on adoption—because of its relatively low level of involvement by participants—it can be a springboard to other, more involved forms. The basic stages of forum usage are as shown in the Figure 13-2.

Figure 13-2. Stages of a Forum

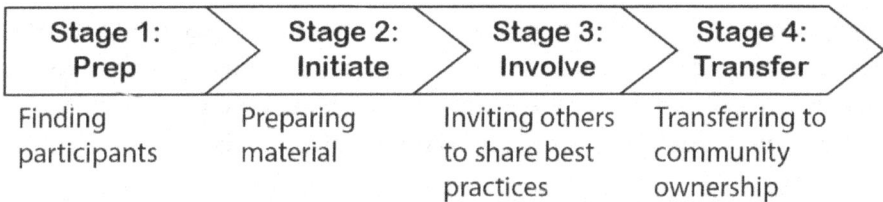

Stage 1: Prep	Stage 2: Initiate	Stage 3: Involve	Stage 4: Transfer
Finding participants	Preparing material	Inviting others to share best practices	Transferring to community ownership

Cascade Teams

The **cascade team** involves a more hierarchical and mandatory flow of change-related engagement. This is intended to drive specific changes down the hierarchy (thus the cascade). While forums involve general voluntary and educational content, the cascade assumes the commitment of managers in the management chain to continue the cascade to their direct reports.

This type of approach is often used when a strategy or new vision

Figure 13-3. Cascade Style

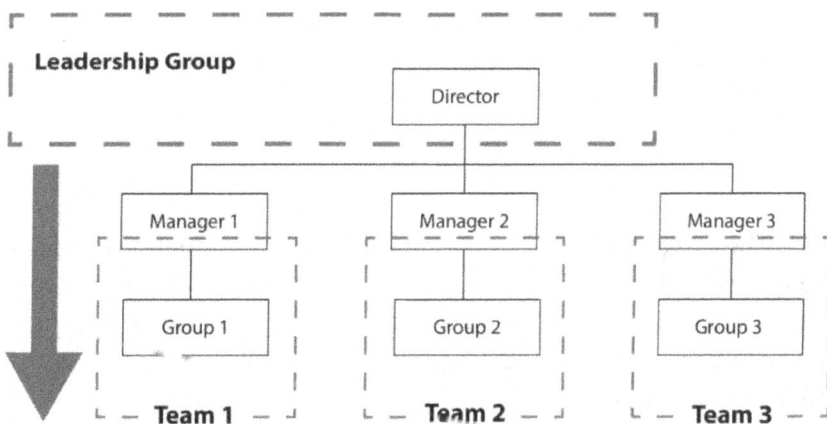

is set at the top. Upper level managers are engaged in forming the fundamental direction and structure. These decisions are then passed to subordinates to figure out at their level, as shown in the Figure 13-3.

This approach like the leadership cascade method discussed in Chapter 11 but involves the Core Group or other a functional change team working more closely with the various levels of management to ensure the engagement happens, not just relying on standard management practices to accomplish it. This converts the cascade from a messaging exercise to an engagement activity where people discuss issues, feedback is gathered, and the initiative is potentially evolved to address the issues.

The critical success factor of the cascade is the meaningful engagement of immediate managers to subordinates. Too often, the application is simply sending PowerPoint slides to managers with a request to pass down to their teams. This is rarely enough. Rather, the cascade method requires considerable focus and involvement from all levels of the management chain, so the issues must be of high importance. Moreover, organization is required to prepare and support the managers in properly running the cascades with their teams. This might have a flow as shown in Figure 13-4.

Figure 13-4. Stages of Cascade Teams

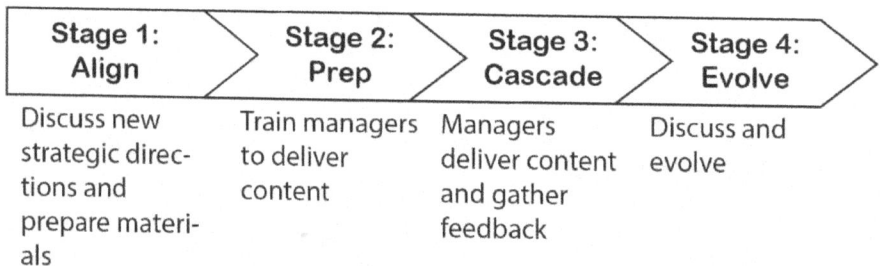

Stage 1: Align	Stage 2: Prep	Stage 3: Cascade	Stage 4: Evolve
Discuss new strategic directions and prepare materials	Train managers to deliver content	Managers deliver content and gather feedback	Discuss and evolve

The cascade method can be effective in some situations, generally those following from a more directive design strategy. This is not appropriate for changing culture or management style, as the cascade approach is going to be reinforcing and improving the existing hierarchy and implied functional alignment.

With more pervasive change in modern organizations, there is much more change that is lateral, or cross-functional, and does not rise to the level of intensive top-level involvement. This is particularly the case in large organizations. For these, the ambassador network is often used.

Ambassador Networks

As emphasized throughout this work, the diffusion of a change is mostly spread through interpersonal networks. In the cascade-style change, the personal influence flows from the immediate manager to subordinates. But in lateral changes, a structure of influence must be established using recognized opinion leaders. For this reason, one of the most popular and useful types of learning community in organizational change is called an *ambassador network*.

The ambassador network involves carefully selecting and deputizing influential individuals to act as champions of the change. They play the role of the first adopter in the diffusion process but use their interpersonal influence to forward the change.

The ambassador network is useful where there is a clear set of new behaviors that must be introduced to a target stakeholder population. Ambassador networks (sometimes called change agent networks) are communities formed to influence the adoption of specific changes.

Like forums, ambassador networks are coordinated through regular meetings where the agenda is set and facilitated by a core organizing team. However, rather than simply participating in the meeting, ambassadors have additional commitments to go out into their assigned communities between meetings to evangelize and role model the change.

Ambassador Role

The ambassador's role includes

- Being knowledgeable about the change, including the correct terminology.

- Reaching out to constituents, keeping them informed about the change, answering their questions, and influencing them to adopt the change.

- Role modeling the change — letting others know they are doing it and demonstrating how it is done.

- Gathering feedback. Finding the fault lines of the change and bringing them back to the program team so that change planning can be refined.

It should be noted that the role of the ambassador is different than a representative. For this reason, people who are already representatives for another organization should be considered carefully for whether they are appropriate as ambassadors or not. Representatives tend to advocate for the view of their represented organization and thus feel obligated to defend their interests. Ambassadors should have allegiance to the Core Group and the change effort. So, it is important this distinction be established early on and the ambassadors are also incentivized accordingly.

Still, the ambassadors are part of their communities, not the change team, so they should be trusted advisors to their constituency. This is a little like the strategy of the Incas when they conquered new territories: They moved part of the population back to the homeland and replaced them with Incas who then lived as neighbors in the conquered areas!

Ambassador Selection

Because of their role, ambassadors usually should have the characteristics of being highly influential and motivated. They should also be drawn from a large cross section of the organization, both hierarchically and laterally. They do not need to have position power, but they should have personal influencing power.

Generally, it is preferable to engage many ambassadors to create high coverage of the target population. However, because ambassadors bring feedback and updates to the coordination meetings, specific meetings are normally kept to an attendance of 20 or less. Thus, multiple concurrent ambassador communities may be needed.

The ambassadors should have the following characteristics:

- Self-motivating
- Keenly interested in the change
- Good communicators
- Well-connected and respected

Basic Phases

There are five basic stages, although these may vary somewhat based on the community.

Stage 1: Selection

There are several ways to find ambassadors. These include the following:

- Asking for nominations from managers
- Seeing who participates most effectively in forums and other activities related to the change
- Asking around
- Asking for volunteers

Stage 2: Engagement with Management

A connection needs to be made to the manager(s) of the ambassadors. If the manager is asked for names, this will occur early on. If names are gathered using a different method, then you will have to approach the managers separately.

The manager must be enrolled to support an ambassador who works for them or will be engaging with their staff. The manager will need to give the ambassador opportunities to attend and present at staff meeting, to gather feedback from the manager about what he or she is hearing, and so on. The manager should also do what is possible to route questions to the ambassador and create openings for the ambassador to engage.

The manager should also help the ambassador by prioritizing people's time, clearing roadblocks, and providing incentives and rewards to both the team and the ambassador to recognize the changes taking place.

Stage 3: Preparation and Feedback

To get things going, you will need to set up the ambassadors properly. These are things to be done:

- Have their managers or a sponsor of the change effort send them a note stressing the importance of their participation.

- Potentially meet with them ahead of time and establish personal relationships.

- Hold a kickoff meeting. This meeting should cover:
    o   The role of the ambassador
    o   An overview of the change and the change effort
    o   Getting their feedback on the change effort
    o   A task for them to go out and talk about the change effort in their local constituencies and get feedback for the next meeting

- Establish a cadence for the meetings. Initially, this might be one or more times a week, then later extending out to every other week or monthly.

In subsequent meetings, information can be delivered to them for obtaining their feedback and getting their questions answered. Use their feedback to improve the basic information and planning. Perhaps even send them out to inquire with their constituents.

Stage 4: Developing and executing local plans

A key part of the process of shifting ownership is to start having team members take on their own responsibilities. They should go out and make their own plans about how they will evangelize and be champions.

Stage 5: Transfer of ownership

As problems are being worked out and ambassadors are working their own engagement plan, the focus of the regular meetings shifts from the core team organizing material and presenting to the ambassadors bringing back feedback and status.

Large Ambassador Networks

One coordinator can manage perhaps 30-40 ambassadors, so in large ambassador networks, especially ones that might span several business units, it may be necessary to have "super" ambassadors who form their own ambassador network in their own business unit or constituency. This is shown in the diagram below.

Figure 13-5. Large Ambassador Network

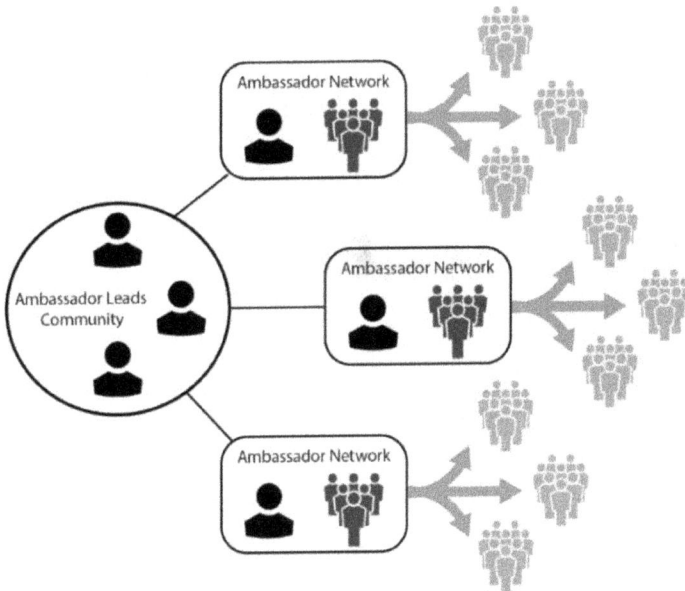

This may require individual meetings with each of the super ambassadors. In general, a full- time coordinator can coordinate 20 other ambassadors.

Multi-Level Ambassador Networks

In large organizations, it may also be valuable to have a multi-level network. This brings together several of the structures discussed previously. One level is the direct ambassadors for the change in each functional group, as we have been discussing, and a second level is the change leadership, or management level. Another level might be sponsors, as shown in Figure 13-4. How many levels is appropriate depends on the size of organization.

Having a leadership-level ambassador group becomes important to ensure the managers are good supporters of the functional-level ambassadors. That is, there are certain management behaviors needed to support the ambassadors, and if there are many managers you will not be able to influence them all personally. So, having a cohort, or first adopters, at the manager level builds the support needed to provide good change leadership.

Figure 13-6. Multi-Level Stakeholder Group

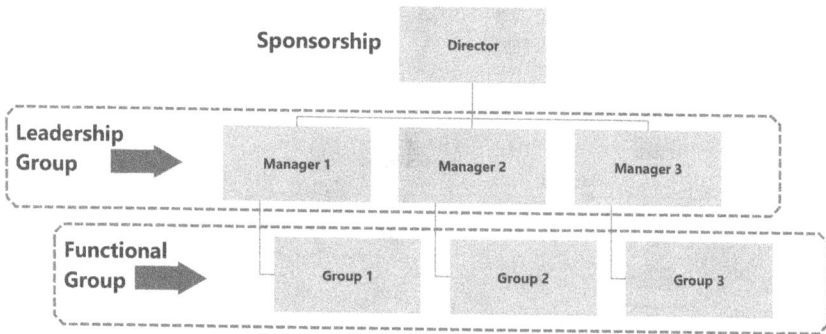

Communities of Practice

A *community of practice* is a regular meeting of people who share common interests. The group is almost always volunteers who are passionate about the topic. This enables both sharing knowledge and creating new knowledge collaboratively, which is especially important in situations where new, more innovative ways of operating are sought.

The purpose of the meeting is to share best practices and insights brought by the members. They have no defined task or objective, and there is no requirement to create specific deliverables. The "deliverable" is the shared understanding of best practices that is built up among the community.

Meeting participants attend voluntarily and are commonly expected to bring some depth of their own knowledge and experience. Usually the number of people in a single meeting is kept smaller, perhaps less than 20, so that everyone can talk and share. Like ambassador networks, there could be a network of small communities of practice.

Although a community of practice is usually started by the Core Group, the meeting ownership in a community of practice should ultimately be shared by all the members. For example, a common structure is rotating the facilitation responsibility among members. One way to start such a community is given below.

1. Put out a call for people who are potentially interested.

2. Hold an initial meeting to go over how the group would work and answer questions.

   o There is no required deliverable or end date, but it is a useful practice to a) set a timeframe of a few months after which the program is re-evaluated, and b) define a default output, such as a panel presentation to the public. Other options are viable as well – publishing papers, presentations at conferences, and so on. These definitions help people feel more comfortable about their commitment and the value.

   o Establish a cadence – weekly to several weeks apart. A month is probably too long.

   o Meeting roles such as facilitator, timer, and process guardian may be used.

o   Have a rule that everyone must take a role (perhaps as one of a rotating facilitator).

3.   Generate and prioritize a list of topics the group might be interested in discussing.

4.   Choose an initial facilitator and an approach for discussing the chosen topics.

> A useful approach is to use the "Five Whys" exercise. The group takes an issue and lists the causes for it. Then, the group lists the causes for them. The process is repeated until root causes are found. In practice, this takes on average five iterations, hence the name of the activity.
>
> Exercises like the Five Whys take some time, so allow for that and resist the urge to decide quickly. The benefit is in the exploration and learning from each other. The group needs to get past the surface explanations to new insights. Spend some time getting to know each other and building relationships. Maintain collegial ground rules.

5.   Go on for a few weeks or even months, until the conversation seems to wind down, and then move on to organizing the report out.

Communities of practice have a lot of flexibility. This format is just one way to do it. The primary goal should be to have an enriching conversation.

Cheat Sheet

The learning community is often overlooked in the change processes. It is incorrectly assumed that once employees have received an executive communication and training, they fully understand the change and have everything they need to move forward with it. But when the employees resume their regular work, they find there are many questions, misinterpretations, and even genuine issues about how to apply the change effectively. Sometimes, if the change is inspiring enough or there is proactive management, the community will begin to learn and integrate the change on their own. But usually this is not the case.

The purposeful creation of learning communities sets up a regular interaction of the target stakeholders so that they meet and discuss how to integrate the change in their work environment. This community interaction over a time creates the mindshare, peer expectations, and, ultimately, ownership to keep the change alive. By discussing and resolving the issues that the change introduces, the members of the community develop the understanding they need to make a sustainable change.

Table 13-1. Types of Stakeholder Communities

Type	Led by	Characteristics
Forum	Change team	• Purpose is to inform and educate attendees • Change team selects content and facilitates meeting • Attendees choose to attend and have no follow up responsibilities • Useful for disseminating information and building commitment when stakeholders are initially ambivalent
Cascade Team	Manager	• Driven by agenda from upper management • Team facilitated by management • Improves the dissemination of management-driven information
Ambassador Network	Lead Ambassador with guidance from project team	• Purpose is to implement specific behavior changes in the organization • Ambassadors have responsibilities to evangelize the change effort • Ambassadors provide the content

Type	Led by	Characteristics
		• Change team provides the frame-work • Useful for building commitment and understanding laterally for high-touch or complex changes
Community of Practice	Members	• Driven a topic of interest • Members share facilitation of the meetings • Useful for generating grass-roots support and for embedding change in an organization

It is possible to evolve learning communities. Depending on the environment, it may be easiest to start a forum to get some level of participation and then transform it to another form, such as a community of practice.

As described above, each learning community has specific purposes, uses, and advantages. It is important to apply the appropriate community to the change situation, which primarily depends on assessing the culture. Additionally, in some cases, the ideal community might be one that the organization is not yet ready to adopt and use. Sometimes there is not the management alignment to use cascade teams or ambassador networks for example. In those cases, it is often possible to get things rolling with one type of community and evolve it into another type.

14

Embedding the Change

For changes to be of any true value, they've got to be lasting and consistent.

—Tony Robbins

Perched on a high platform overlooking a large lake was what appeared to be a giant papier-mâché stork with rudimentary aircraft wings riding on a bicycle. Spectators wait with anticipation as a team of handlers pushed the contraption off the platform. Was it a parade float or an aircraft? Did it fly? How far? The spectacle is part of a regular competition called a *Flugtag*, which is hosted at various locations around the world by the Austrian energy drink maker Red Bull. In a Flugtag, contestants are invited to build human-powered flying machines and launch them off a high platform into the ocean or a large body of water to compete for the record in how far the invention will fly. The intrigue for spectators is of course whether the contraption will fly far or spectacularly crash on launch.

Similarly, in change efforts, even after much expense and time is put into designing them and rolling them out, there is the period of wondering if the change effort will be viable and become embedded in the organization. Frequently though, like one of the homemade planes in a Flugtag, change efforts that are not built on solid principles soar off the launch ramp, fly weakly, and crash.

There are several reasons why this happens. One common reason is that once the pressure created by the Core Group driving the change is removed, the adoption is dropped. So, to prepare for the withdrawal of the temporary pressure created by the Core Group, the change must be embedded in the organization. Embedding means the change is integrated into the structures, incentives, metrics, tools, and other fabric of the organization.

For the change to remain embedded, or sustained, it must inherently create a payoff for the users, as we have been discussing throughout this book. However, at rollout time, this payoff is often not completely implemented: For example, computer interfaces still need refinement; processes require streamlining; and conflicting behaviors between different stakeholders still exist. So, the Core Group must use methods described previously as well as some that will be covered in this chapter until the change is sustainable on its own.

Accordingly, one of the chronic dilemmas in an organizational change initiative is the difficulty in knowing when the effort is truly complete. This leads us to the question "When can the Core Group stop?" Change efforts often seem to go on indefinitely until they lose momentum and are called done, without ever any formal recognition or evaluation that they have achieved their objectives.

While it is impossible to say for certain if a change effort will be sustained and for how long, we can decide whether it is likely to be sustained based on a set of key indicators. So, again, we will evaluate certain critical success factors. In this section, I will outline a lightweight but effective, evidence-based approach for understanding whether critical success factors are in place and thus whether the change effort will likely be sustained. These critical success factors are the following:

- Metrics trending
- Systemic incentives
- Governance
- Ongoing training (or renewal of skills or capability)
- Continuous learning

This chapter pertains to establishing the conditions for these critical success factors to be put in place. These are based on being able to observe certain tangible evidence that gives confidence the change will be sustained for the foreseeable future and the Core Group can disengage.

Metrics Trending

Fundamentally, the change should produce an improvement in business outcomes. As we discussed in Chapter 8, the direct improvement is often difficult to measure; however, you should have established some success indicators that, if they move in the intended direction, give confidence that the business outcomes are, or will be, realized.

A useful rule of thumb is if those success indicators are trending in the desired direction for six to eight months, then there is a reasonable level of confidence they will continue, all other things being equal. While you never know for sure, you can have some confidence from knowing how people systems work. That is, as we have discussed, people work in relationships with each other and tend to maintain stability in those relationships. So, if they have had a chance to become accustomed to working together in the new way, and there are payoffs and support as will be discussed in the next sections, then the same dynamics that tend to resist change will come to propel the change forward after it is established.

The challenge is to get through the transition from the old system to the new system. So clearly, if the business value and other success indicators are not being met, then continued work is needed to evolve the change approach or perhaps even modify the design. This is the fundamental work of the Core Group—to review the progress to date and evolve the change approach as needed. This may require continued effort to reach out to stakeholder groups, adjustment of messaging, interface improvements, process refinement, incentive development, and any number of other methods as we have discussed throughout this book.

Systemic Incentives

When the Core Group leaves the situation, it often also removes some of the incentives that were present. That is, while it is operating, the Core Group is holding meetings, collecting status reports, facilitating messaging, and organizing champions. This creates incentives for others to be involved that will no longer be present if the Core Group moves on. So, this needs to be accounted for in the way the system works.

While it would be nice to have the change intrinsically pay off for everyone just by doing it, there are numerous types of behaviors that are beneficial to the company but not necessarily directly and immediately to the individual. Of course, people get paid, and some will argue that should be enough. But recall that the employee's world is not nearly so clear cut. Stakeholders have many options and choices about how to achieve their tasks and tend to choose the ones that give more tangible benefits unless there are counterbalancing elements make working for the long term or common good a more tangible benefit.

We will call these systemic incentives. There are many kinds of incentives, as we have been discussing, but these systemic incentives are ones that are part of the fabric of how the organization works. That is, they are part of the ongoing business process, not a special event someone has to organize.

For example, consider the following:

- **Award programs**. Award programs can be created that focus on recognizing people who demonstrate key behaviors. These could be behaviors such as teamwork, customer focus, or collaboration.

- **Performance management.** If there is a company goal-setting program in place, one of the goals could be focused on demonstrating a key behavior.

- **Recognition events.** People who are thought leaders or champions for a specific behavior can be invited to special events, such as summits and off-sites where they get a chance to contribute creatively to continuous improvement initiatives.

- **Levels of achievement.** People who develop the desired new behaviors can receive achievement awards or levels of achievement such as the martial-arts style belts in Six Sigma.

Another key type of incentive will be ongoing creative involvement and empowerment. This is covered in "standing learning communities" later in Chapter 15.

Governance

Ideally, the inherent payoffs in the system propel the change forward. So, in principle, the new behaviors could go on indefinitely without a problem. But, the reality is that things sometimes get off track. This is true in the beginning while employees are getting used to the new ways. The incentives experienced by any person are complex and there are often other hidden and unintended incentives in the system. Later, as people begin to figure out the system, there can be tendencies to either drop activities that are not well incentivized or to optimize (or "game") the system to newly discovered incentives.

Governance provides oversight to monitor if things are getting off track. So, one key function of governance is to monitor indicators and act. Another function of governance is to require approvals for certain things that might require a greater level of expertise, judgment, or visibility. These are decisions that should not be left to chance or the possibility they will be made by employees without the proper credentials. Thus, governance ensures there is adequate visibility to key decisions being made and the risk are known and accepted.

The governance function has the following responsibilities:

- Review the performance of the organization, including success indicators, and act if things get out of compliance. This may include handling escalations or conducting inquiries about success indicators that seem out of whack. It could include corrective action.

- Periodically review and determine if changes are needed to the program itself. As time goes on, conditions may change and thus the implementation may also need to change. To keep process and systems fresh, a review should be conducted.

- Encourage retrospective or post-mortem reviews. It is easy for people to finish the delivery and immediately move on to the next thing. But the needs of continuous improvement call for taking a brief time to review what happened and identify what improvements could be made for next time. Then, it takes focused action to embed those improvements in the system

Governance would typically be put in place by a committee of people who meet periodically, although it could be an entire process in a large organization. The players in the governance system should have the power to hold the relevant functions of the organization accountable and to adjust how the changes are implemented if necessary.

There are many possible examples of this kind of governance, including the following:

- Change review boards
- Operating committees
- Organizational reviews (checkpoints)
- Audits
- Gate reviews, release approvals
- Institutional review boards
- Certification and licensing authorities

Ongoing Training

Commonly, a change effort will be rolled out with accompanying training. Considerable effort will be invested in organizing the training, so one indicator is simply to ensure sufficient people get trained. This may take some time, especially if the training is optional and they enroll themselves, or the training is just in time.

Then, the effort to train everyone often stops. Perhaps the training is made into a course offering or recorded and posted to a website. Then, people who are trained take other positions and new people come in. Typically, they are left to themselves to find the training and mentors who can guide them, and then, over time, the training becomes increasingly out of date as processes evolve and conditions change.

While self-training and learning from peers works in some cases, you should consider whether this is the most effective way. It may be worthwhile to establish a training that new people can take. It could be recorded and placed on the web or it might be conducted periodically in live session. Similarly, new methods could be added into an existing new hire training. At any rate, consistency and efficiency will be improved if new people do not have to figure out new process and expectations or themselves.

The training should also have an owner and be periodically reviewed. This could be a checklist item for the governance team. People who own the rights post or files to update the training often leave, and this should be monitored and resolved.

Standing Learning Communities

For situations involving significant behavior change, you may have put in place some form of learning community, as discussed in Chapter 13. While the time and commitment in the learning community may decrease after a while, some form of learning community might be needed indefinitely. Without some community to explore and review if the practices continue to be effective for all involved stakeholders, the change can become sub-optimized and obsolete.

This especially occurs in change types like the implementation of a practice, such as project management, agile software development, or change management. For example, if a new project management methodology is introduced, the project managers may need an ongoing forum where changes or refinements to the methodology can be discussed. They may go to a change control board for approval, but often there is much discussion and exploration needed to agree on the change.

These communities can become important venues for future changes as well. When there are organized communities of architects or program managers with standing meetings, shared databases, and key contacts, then future changes can be brought to them for review and feedback much more easily.

Scorecard

When there are multiple programs or tracks involved in a change initiative, it may be necessary to track the factors discussed above for each program. One way to do this is using a scorecard, such as the example shown in the table below. The categories can have evidence or metrics associated with them to make it clearer whether it is done or not.

Table 14-1. Progress Report for Financial Reporting Initiative

Financial Reporting 2.0	Metrics	Trained	Incentives	Governance	Learning
Financial analysis process	100	100	75	50	50
Project cost tracking process	100	50	25	0	0
Quarter close process	100	100	50	50	0

Qualitative scorecards have usages. Many people will claim the kind of numbers being collected are subjective, and this is true but overlooks the function of the scorecard. As discussed in Success Indicators, we are not valuing the programs, grading them, or creating a scientific theory. The numbers and indicators are simply a way to ground a conversation. It takes what is quite vague when expressed in stories and words and makes it a little more concrete so that a more productive conversation can be held.

Table 14-2. Sustainability Indicators

Indicator	Evidence
Success indicators trending in the desired direction	• Percent of stakeholders trained. • Metrics reports showing adoption of core, non-negotiable behaviors.
Training	• Affected stakeholders have all been trained. • Report of who has been trained and how new people will be trained.
Governance in place	• Description of governance process.
Incentives operating	• Description of incentive process.
Learning structures in place	• There is a process for adapting and improving the solution over time.

So, in using the scorecard, you will find people give many answers. Some are very vague. These can be accepted and over time the group practices together how to make clearer statements. But having something written down enables a follow up.

Cheat Sheet

This chapter has discussed a framework for deciding when the change can be considered embedded and sustainable in the organization. This point allows the Core Group to disengage. The key is knowing if the critical success factors discussed above have been met. Of course, one never knows for sure, but if the factors discussed in this chapter are in place, then the effort can be considered likely to be sustained.

- **Success Indicators.** Success indicators show improvement over defined period (e.g., 6 months).

- **Training.** A target percent of stakeholders is trained.

- **Governance in Place.** There is a governance process that has been tested.

- **Incentives Operating.** Methods of rewarding the desired behavior been put in place.

- **Learning Structures in Place.** There is a process for adapting and improving the solution over time.

15

Emerging Trends

The art of progress is to preserve order amid change, and to preserve change amid order.

—*Alfred North Whitehead*

As stated early on, the means of applying organizational change are rapidly changing themselves. At the time of this writing, there are several trends and capabilities beginning to take hold that will transform the landscape of organizational change. While the methods discussed in this book will remain viable, as they are based on basic human psychology, recent technologies will increase the scope, speed, and applicability of change methods.

Change Infrastructure

Up to this point, we have been primarily discussing change efforts that are started from scratch. This assumes an organization that was not prepared for continuous change. But, with the increasing acceptance of pervasive change, companies are beginning to put in place structural elements that give them a foundation for integrating changes that come along, saving time and expense in creating the structures from scratch.

This is important because the traditional management structures are built for stability, or to preserve order, as Alfred North Whitehead mentions in the opening quote. With change becoming continuous and pervasive, preserving order can also mean resisting change.

So, the acceptance of continuous change is going to ultimately result in change to the structure of organizations. Rather than starting up initiatives or tiger teams to shepherd a change every time a new initiative comes around, there will be standing teams and committees to facilitate ongoing change. For example, the business units in some large companies have operations groups with the responsibility to integrate change coming to them from other organizations into their organization's workflow. For example, if the finance process changes, the operations group in each business unit will have the responsibility to be the Core Group for that change within their unit. They facilitate standing "inside out" leadership structure as discussed in Chapter 11. Similarly, some IT organizations have standing business readiness teams that continuously work with business counterparts to integrate change in core accounting, sales, and purchasing platforms (ERP systems).

Another approach is to have standing communities of practice around roles. These communities regularly discuss their roles, gather improvement feedback, and facilitate changes for that community. For example, there could be a community of IT architects and IT managers. These groups would meet similar to the communities of practice described in Chapter 13 but would be standing communities for all types of change that might be coming, not just a specific one.

Another form of standing change infrastructure is a cross-functional team with the responsibility to continuously integrate organizational change arising from company strategy. In fact, John Kotter recommends a high-level "second operating system" in his book *Accelerate!* He calls for a network-like structure to co-exist with the traditional hierarchy.[1]

> *The old methodology simply can't handle rapid change. Hierarchies and standard managerial processes, even when minimally bureaucratic, are inherently risk-averse and resistant to change. Part of the problem is political: Managers are loath to take chances without permission from superiors. Part of the problem is cultural: People cling to their habits and fear loss of power and stature — two essential elements of hierarchies. And part of the problem is that all hierarchies, with their specialized units,*

> *rules, and optimized processes, crave stability and default to do-*
> *ing what they already know how to do.*

Kotter proposes that a modification is needed to the traditional hi-
erarchal structure and processes, or operating model, of an organization to
accommodate a world of fast-paced change. His solution is a second operating model that is complementary to the first. He is careful to note that
both operate together; that is, one does not replace the other. And it is different than a matrix organization.

> *The solution is a second operating system, devoted to the design*
> *and implementation of strategy, that uses an agile, network-like*
> *structure and a very different set of processes. The new operat-*
> *ing system continually assesses the business, the industry, and*
> *the organization, and reacts with greater agility, speed, and cre-*
> *ativity than the existing one. It complements rather than over-*
> *burdens the traditional hierarchy, thus freeing the latter to do*
> *what it's optimized to do.*

He claims this does not create more overhead but makes the enterprise easier to run and accelerates strategic change. Kotter's second operating model is composed of a network of leaders who have the freedom
and authority to explore and shape new strategic ideas. They harvest ideas
and practices throughout the organization, and they shape the best ideas
into coherent expressions of potential future directions. The network facilitates the collaboration across multiple levels and functions. It is not
bound to the traditional reporting channels. Kotter says,

> *In the absence of bureaucratic layers, command-and-control*
> *prohibitions, and Six Sigma processes, this type of network per-*
> *mits a level of individualism, creativity, and innovation that*
> *not even the least bureaucratic hierarchy can provide. Popu-*
> *lated with employees from all across the organization and up*
> *and down its ranks, the network liberates information from si-*
> *los and hierarchical layers and enables it to flow with far*
> *greater freedom and accelerated speed.*

Data Science

Organizational change relies heavily on research about stakeholder interests, motivations, and skills. Traditionally, this research has been done by interviews, surveys, and focus groups. But there are new methods coming into play, and these are the methods of big data and data science.

This opportunity arises due to the confluence of several factors, including developments in statistics, distributed processing, and machine learning, as well as approaches to linking and visualizing large data sets. Consequently, there are much better, more viable means of effectively analyzing extensive data sets and doing something actionable with the result—including taking advantage of opportunities to improve business efficiency.

These developments will have profound impacts on how organizational change is conducted. In fact, at some forward-thinking companies such as Google and Facebook, they already are. At Google, the human resources team, called People Operations, is not only concerned with traditional roles of establishing pay grades and resolving disputes between employees and managers. They are continuously collecting data and analyzing it. Consequently, they have built, according to Chris DeRose, writing for *Atlantic*, "one of the most refined performance-management engines in the world."[2]

This performance management-engine investigates many aspects of what contributes to employee performance. For example, they found performance was improved when employees were kept within 150 feet of food and when the cafeteria lines were kept to around a 4-minute wait. In another case, Google management was concerned that mothers who had just given birth were leaving the company at a rate twice the average. They were able to reduce the departure rate back to average and increase employee happiness by offering the new mothers additional time off—at full pay—to spend with their families. But this was not just being altruistic; in fact, Google saved more money on this program than it spent.

One should also note that these findings can be not only good for a company like Google but also good for science. Much of management and organizational change thinking has been shaped by subjective experience and qualitative research methods like surveys and interviews. While these have their place, the introduction of the ability to scientifically research ideas with real-time data is powerful. In many ways, the ability of companies to have these large data sets available and analyze them is providing a new window on science that was previously not possible.

While the applications of these kinds of methods are still in infancy when it comes to how to facilitate organizational change, they certainly paint the picture. There are many key questions that such analysis might routinely improve for organizational change. These include the following:

- Who are the stakeholders?

- Which stakeholders are more influential than others?

- What is the level of adoption?

- What kind of communications will be most effective?

Answering these questions will be profound enough, but big data will also enable us to challenge the very tenants and guiding ideas of organizational change, just as Google's research provided insights into key factors of employee happiness. A lot of organizational change is now about maxims and best practices adopted through experience. For example, there are a lot of well-known guidelines about communications—how it should look, what it should say. But these have been developed largely by practitioners from their experience, not from rigorous study. With data science, we will be able to run experiments to see what kind of messaging resonates best with stakeholders.

That is, beyond relying solely on the rather opaque, subjective experiences and opinions of experts, we can add the dimension of what current evidence is telling us. This may challenge even the opinions of highly regarded experts. For example, Harvard University professor Gary King recounted a contest to predict the outcome of all the Supreme Court cases in a year. He compared a statistical analysis against the judgment of 87 law professors. The result? King states, "It was no contest." He asserted that if relevant data is available, statistics will always win out over experts or even groups of experts. This can be hard pill to swallow in a world where people have established representations as experts based on their accumulated experience.[3]

This kind of finding challenges not only the professions, but the kind of judgments we all make daily. In another example, researchers Wu Youyou, Michal Kosinski, and David Stillwell published a study in early 2015 where they analyzed Facebook friend networks and found computers can often determine your friend's personality more accurately than you can! [4]

Choice Architecture

We often talk about changing behavior to create organizational change, but maybe we should be having a conversation about shaping choices. Recent research has exposed some interesting aspects to human decision-making. While Dr. Rogers' adoption cycle remains valid, the way in which humans make decisions has been shown to be far less logical and much more context-driven than often imagined.

Professors Richard Thaler and Cass Sunstein provide numerous examples in their highly popular book *Nudge*.[5] For example, the order of presenting information counts. That is, if I tell you A then B, you may make one decision; but if I tell you B then A, you may make another. In one experiment, groups of college students were asked two questions in this order: (A) How happy are you? (B) How often are you dating? At first, there was little correlation between the two questions: Happy students were sometimes dating a lot and sometimes not; unhappy students were sometimes dating a little and sometimes not. But the dating question was asked first, things changed dramatically—more than half of students who were dating tended to be happy and of those not dating, more than half tended to be unhappy.

Apparently, getting the college students thinking about their love life tended to influence their outlook on life in general. This seems logical when you think about it. The memory affects their feelings. But what about this one? In another experiment, the professors asked some students to first add 200 to the last three digits of their phone number and write down the result. Then, the students were asked to guess if Attila the Hun sacked Europe before or after the year indicated by the number. What they found was that students with high phone numbers tended to give estimates that averaged 300 years later than students who started with low numbers!

Of course, the student's phone number has nothing to do with when Attila the Hun sacked Europe. So, what happened? The answer concerns how the human mind processes information. In this case, Thaler and Sunstein explain that people estimate using mental anchors as a starting point and then determining a reasonable distance from the anchor.

Similarly, other kinds of context can be important. In Manchester, England, it seems there was a lot of public angst about the slow repair of potholes. They were taking years to get fixed. That is, until a creative person attracted attention to them in a clever way — by drawing chalk outlines of penises around them. The potholes started getting fixed much more rapidly!

These human dynamics introduce new possibilities for organizational change approaches. By thinking ahead about the dynamics of decision-making, we can perhaps find easy tweaks to the plan that subconsciously affect decision-making. We often think that logically nothing has changed for stakeholders, but these examples have shown that even though the reality of the situation was essentially unchanged, the context could affect priorities and judgments in a substantial way.

Thaler and Sunstein call this choice architecture. They explain that a "choice architect has the responsibility for organizing the context in which people make decisions." I suspect this perspective will be much more prevalent as the science of influence and motivation continues to develop.

Gamification of Change

Creating organizational change is heavily reliant on motivating people. Traditionally, this has been done with money — in the form of salary, bonuses, and stock—as well as recognition such as awards, promotions, and new roles. But humans are motivated by a much richer spectrum of things. But other motivations are often difficult to put into practice.

Gamification is the application of game-like dynamics to business issues. This approach and recent research concerning its effectiveness was introduced in Chapter 12 as it pertained to training strategies. But training strategies are just the beginning. We are likely seeing a much bigger emergence of gamification as an important framework in getting work done and in organizational change.

There is an emerging body of work on the gamification of the enterprise itself. It's not really making the work place a game; the value of this perspective is in using the metaphor of a game to keep focused on what is really motivating the system. This puts emphasis on fun, creativity, collaboration, clear goals, feedback and all the things that create a more rewarding workplace. These approaches help remove the innate biases toward command and control and parental type work of organization structures.

Gamification methods have been used for many years, particularly in well-designed workshops. But the opportunities have always been constrained by the mechanics of operating the game. Tallying points by hand is time consuming, as is enforcing the rules. However, advances in technology have now made it much easier to put the supporting frameworks in place to automate many gamification dynamics, making them much more feasible. Thus, gamification methods are being applied to positive effect in many areas, such as those below.

- **Idea generation.** Stakeholders can generate ideas for improvement in the modern form of the "suggestion box." With web-based idea generation, stakeholders not only think up the ideas, they can evaluate them too. For example, the Department for Work and Pension in the United Kingdom created a game called Idea Street, where employees generated ideas as well as commented and voted on others. This was used to prioritize the ideas. An executive with the agency estimated the ideas resulted in $30 million in savings.[6]

- **Wellness and health.** Many companies are offering gamification to improve wellness to their clients. Through the Red-Brick system, employees can get dollars to spend on health care by completing evaluations and health challenges. Many other companies such as Fitbit and Fitocracy also offer gamified solutions where users earn badges and points for completing activities such as walking or drinking target amounts of water.[7]

- **Learning foreign languages.** The wildly popular DuoLingo app and website teach you a foreign language in small chunks, giving you a chime and a small bump in levels as you progress. Many people have found it quite addictive and instructional.

- **Productivity.** There are numerous games available to encourage productivity in various areas. For example, Deloitte constructed a game to reward their consultants for checking in and providing information about who they met.[8] Target created a game played by the cashier during checkout to improve their accuracy.[9]

Going Out to Create Waves

A lot of ground has been covered in this book. The traditional means of organizational change have been disassembled and reassembled to ground them more solidly on the known research in cognitive psychology, diffusion theory, compliance theory, learning theory, and many others. Left behind is much of the mythology and common maxims commonly associated with organizational change derived from consultant experiences and interviews with executives.

The approaches in this book have focused on what is scientifically known to work. Thus, while the methods may be new, uncomfortable, revolutionary, or counterintuitive, to not do them is rolling the dice about whether the change effort will succeed or not – a dice roll that has historically had Las Vegas odds.

There is even more to come in the direction set out here. The confluence of new research in how the mind works along with new computing approaches will enable an environment for creating change that is much less dependent on pushing a core vision from executives down into the organization, and there will be much less deferring to the wisdom or experience of people who hold position power.

Instead, there will be structures embedded in the organization to facilitate continuous change. These structures will foster organizational learning by making data more transparent and by decentralizing power down to the right levels. This is the only way to handle the complexity of modern businesses, non-profits, and communities. The accuracy and advisability of beliefs about productivity, adoption, and other aspects of organizational effectiveness will be questions that are verified or rejected through evidence and analysis from data science. Change initiatives will be much less reliant on executive direction and much more reliant on the choice architecture and setting fun, goal-driven, feedback-providing environments.

The means of creating change are themselves changing. Hopefully this book has given you a basic set of foundational skills and concepts to go out and create something good. In the beginning of this book, I asserted that besides the learning theses basic methods, you need two other things: an unwavering intention to create something good and steadfast determination. In this way, following the opening chapter advice of Mother Teresa, you can be the catalyst for waves of change emanating outward from you. It is now up to you to garner your commitment and focus to influence positive change.

Index

Bibliography

Amnesty International. "The 'Arab Spring': Five Years on." Accessed December 30, 2016. https://www.amnesty.org/en/latest/campaigns/2016/01/arab-spring-five-years-on/.

Arkansas Rice Depot. "Our Story." Accessed October 8, 2016. http://www.ricedepot.org/about-us/arkansas-rice-depot-info/our-story/.

Banathy, Bela H. *Designing Social Systems in a Changing World.* The Language of Science. New York: Plenum Press, 1996.

Baumeister, R. *Meanings of Life.* New York: Guilford Press, 1991.

Bikhchandani, Sushil, David Hirshleifer, and Ivo Welch. *Information Cascades and Observational Learning.* Columbus, OH: Charles A. Dice Center for Research in Financial Economics, Fisher College of Business, Ohio State University, 2005.

Black, Eric. "Why is Turnout So Low in U.S. Elections? We Make It More Difficult to Vote Than Other Democracies." *MinnPost*, October 1, 2014. Accessed July 15, 2017. https://www.minnpost.com/eric-black-ink/2014/10/why-turnout-so-low-us-elections-we-make-it-more-difficult-vote-other-democrac.

Block, Lauren G., Vicki G. Morwitz, William P. Putsis, and Subrata K. Sen. "Assessing the Impact of Antidrug Advertising on Adolescent Drug Consumption: Results From a Behavioral Economic Model." *American Journal of Public Health* 92, no. 8, (2002): 1346–51.

Block, P. *Flawless Consulting: A Guide to Getting Your Expertise Used.* San Francisco, CA: John Wiley & Sons, 2011.

Bono, Edward de. *De Bono's Thinking Course.* [New ed.]. Harlow: BBC Active, 2006.

Bradbury, Matt. "A Brief Timeline of the History of Recycling." Accessed December 28, 2016. http://www.buschsystems.com/recycling-bin-news/2014/05/a-brief-timeline-of-the-history-of-recycling/.

Brown, John S., and Paul Duguid. *The Social Life of Information.* Boston: Harvard Business School Press, 2000.

Caralli, Richard A. "The Critical Success Factor Method: Establishing a Foundation for Enterprise Security Management." 2004. Accessed July 20, 2013.

Cialdini, Robert B. *Influence: Science and Practice*. 4th ed. Boston, MA: Allyn and Bacon, 2001.

Collins, Jim. "Level 5 Leadership: The Triumph of Humility and Fierce Resolve." *Harvard Business Review*, 2001, 66–76.

Denning, Stephen. *The Springboard: How Storytelling Ignites Action in Knowledge-Era Organizations*. Boston, Oxford: Butterworth-Heinemann, 2001.

Derose, Chris. "How Google Uses Data to Build a Better Worker." *The Atlantic*, 2013.

Detert, James R., and Ethan R. Burris. "Can Your Employees Really Speak Freely?" Accessed August 9, 2017. https://hbr.org/2016/01/can-your-employees-really-speak-freely.

Dilts, Robert B. *Strategies of Genius*. Capitola, CA: Meta Publications, 1994.

Dr. Frank Luntz. *Words That Work: It's Not What You Say, It's What People Hear*. New York, NY: Hyperion Books, 2007. Accessed March 3, 2015.

Drutman, Lee. "Simple Ways to Increase Voter Turnout." *Pacific Standard Magazine*, March 31, 2008. Accessed July 15, 2017. https://psmag.com/news/simple-ways-to-increase-voter-turnout-4660.

Duhigg, Charles. "What Google Learned from Its Quest to Build the Perfect Team." *The New York Times Magazine*, 2016. Accessed August 19, 2017. https://www.nytimes.com/2016/02/28/magazine/what-google-learned-from-its-quest-to-build-the-perfect-team.html?mcubz=1.

EPA, U. S., and OSWER. "Advancing Sustainable Materials Management: Facts and Figures." Accessed December 28, 2016. https://www.epa.gov/smm/advancing-sustainable-materials-management-facts-and-figures.

Frankl, Viktor E. *Man's Search for Meaning: An Introduction to Logotherapy*. Rev. and enl. ed. London: Hodder and Stoughton, 1964, ©1962.

"Gamification – the Game and Beyond!" Accessed June 15, 2015. http://blog.gfk.com/2013/07/gamification-the-game-and-beyond/.

Gardner, Howard. *Changing Minds: The Art and Science of Changing Our Own and Other People's Minds.* Boston: Harvard Business School Press, 2004.

Granovetter, Mark. "Threshold Models of Collective Behavior." *American Journal of Sociology* 83, no. 6, (1978): 1420–43. doi:10.1086/226707.

Greencrest. "Advertising Frequency - Is There a Magic Number?" Accessed September 1, 2013. http://greencrest.com/marketingprose/advertising-frequency-is-there-a-magic-number.

Grobart, Sam, and Evelyn M. Rusli. "Cisco Shuts Down Flip, Its Video Camera Unit." *The New York Times*, April 12, 2011. Accessed February 3, 2013. http://www.nytimes.com/2011/04/13/technology/13flip.html?_r=0.

Grunert, Klaus G., and Charlotte Ellegaard. "The Concept of Key Success Factors: Theory and Method." Unpublished manuscript, last modified July 20, 2013.

Hamarie, Juho, Jonna Koisvisto, and Harri Sarsa. "Does Gamification Work? A Literature Review of Empirical Studies on Gamification."

Hanson, Robin. "The Informed Press Favored the Policy Analysis Market." Accessed February 9, 2013. http://hanson.gmu.edu/PAMpress.pdf.

Hepburn, R. W. "Questions about the Meaning of Life." *Religious Studies* 1, no. 02, (1966): 125. doi:10.1017/S0034412500002419.

Herzberg, Frederick. *One More Time: How Do You Motivate Employees?* The Harvard Business Review Classics Series. Boston, Mass.: Harvard Business Press, 2008.

"How Gamification Reshapes Corporate Training." *CIO*, 2013. Accessed February 15, 2014. http://www.cio.com/article/728268/How_Gamification_Reshapes_Corporate_Training.

Kaplan, Robert S., and David P. Norton. *The Balanced Scorecard: Translating Strategy into Action.* Boston, Mass.: Harvard Business School Press, 1996.

Knowledge@Wharton. "From Fitbit to Fitocracy: The Rise of Health

Care Gamification." Accessed June 15, 2015.
http://knowledge.wharton.upenn.edu/article/from-fitbit-to-fitoc-racy-the-rise-of-health-care-gamification/.

Korzybski, Alfred. *Science and Sanity: An Introduction to Non-Aristotelian Systems and General Semantics.* 3rd ed. International Non-Aristotelian Library. Lakeville, Conn: International Non-Aristotelian Library Pub. Co, 1948.

Kotter, John P. "Accelerate!" *Harvard Business Review,* 2012. Accessed August 6, 2017. https://hbr.org/2012/11/acceler-ate%5b5/25/2015%206:41:20%20AM%5d.

Kotter, John P., and Dan S. Cohen. *The Heart of Change.* Boston, MA: Harvard University Press, 2002.

Laxalt, Francois. "The Secret to Increasing Message Frequency without Fatiguing Your Audience." Accessed September 2, 2013. https://blogs.adobe.com/digitalmarketing/email/secret-increasing-message-frequency-fatiguing-audience/.

"Learning Should Be Fun." Accessed August 20, 2017. https://mindhacks.com/2009/01/19/learning-should-be-fun/.

Lerner, Kira. "5 Ways To Fix America's Dismal Voter Turnout Problem." Accessed July 15, 2017. https://thinkprogress.org/5-ways-to-fix-americas-dismal-voter-turnout-problem-6342bc2d1190.

LevelsPro. "Target's Cashier Game – Is It Really a Game?" Accessed June 15, 2015. http://www.levelspro.com/targets-cashier-game-is-it-really-a-game/.

Levinson, Jay C. *Guerilla Marketing Excellence: The Fifty Golden Rules for Business Success.* London: Piatkus, 1993.

Maslow, A. *Toward a New Psychology of Being.* New York: Van-Nostrand Reinhold, 1968.

McFadden, Robert D. "Hiroo Onoda, Soldier Who Hid in Jungle for Decades, Dies at 91." Accessed August 1, 2017. https://www.nytimes.com/2014/01/18/world/asia/hiroo-onoda-imperial-japanese-army-officer-dies-at-91.html.

Miles, R. H. *Leading Corporate Transformation.* San Francisco: Jossey-Bass Publishers Inc, 1997.

MIT Technology Review. "Using Games to Get Employees Think-

ing." Accessed June 15, 2015. http://www.technolo-
gyreview.com/news/425044/using-games-to-get-employees-think-
ing/.

Mitchell, Kimberley. "Like Magic? ("Every system is perfectly designed...")." Accessed August 9, 2017. http://www.ihi.org/commu-
nities/blogs/_layouts/15/ihi/commu-
nity/blog/itemview.aspx?List=7d1126ec-8f63-4a3b-9926-
c44ea3036813&ID=159.

Myers, David G. *The Pursuit of Happiness: Who is Happy - and Why.*
London: Aquarian/Thorsons, 1993.

NTL. Institute. *Effects of Positive Practices on Organizational Effectiveness.* NTL Institute - Sage, 2011.

Paterson, J. M. & C. J. "Organizational Justice, Change Anxiety, and
Acceptance of Downsizing: Preliminary Tests of an AET-Based
Model." 1, (2002).

Prince, Michael. "Does Active Learning Work? A Review of the Research." Accessed August 25, 2017.
http://www4.ncsu.edu/unity/lockers/users/f/felder/public/Pa-
pers/Prince_AL.pdf.

Purser, R. E. a. C. S. *The Self Managing Organization: How Leading
Companies are Transforming the Work of Teams for Real Impact.* New
York: Simon & Schuster Inc, 1998.

Reiss, Spencer. "DARPA's Gambling Man." *Wired,* no. 11.10. Accessed February 9, 2013. http://www.wired.com/wired/ar-
chive/11.10/start.html?pg=14.

Ricouer, Paul. *Hermeneutics and the Human Sciences (J. B. Thompson,
Trans.).* Melbourne, Australia: Cambridge University Press, 1981.

Roberto, Michael A. *Why Great Leaders Don't Take Yes for an Answer:
Managing for Conflict and Consensus.* Upper Saddle River, N.J: Pearson Education, Inc., publishing as Prentice Hall, 2007, c2005.

Rockart, John F. *Chief Executives Define Their Own Data Needs.* Cambridge, MA: Harvard Business School Press, 1979.

Rogers, Everett M. *Diffusion of Innovations.* 5th ed. New York: Free
Press, 2003.

Rosenthal, Caitlin. "Big Data in the Age of the Telegraph." *Mckinsey
Quarterly,* March 2013. Accessed October 27, 2016.

http://www.mckinsey.com/business-functions/organization/our-insights/big-data-in-the-age-of-the-telegraph.

Sherr, Ian. "Apple's Secrets Revealed at Trial." *The Wall Street Journal*, August 5, 2012. Accessed June 20, 2015. http://www.wsj.com/articles/SB10000872396390044368750457756742184074545 2.

Simmons, Annette. *Whoever Tells the Best Story Wins: How to Use Your Own Stories to Communicate with Power and Impact*. Saranac Lake, NY, USA: AMACOM, 2007.

Surowiecki, James. "Damn the Slam PAM Plan!" *Slate*, 2003. Accessed February 9, 2013. http://www.slate.com/articles/news_and_politics/hey_wait_a_minute/2003/07/damn_the_slam_pam_plan.html.

Tamblyn, Doni. *Laugh and Learn: 95 Ways to Use Humor for More Effective Teaching and Training*. New York: AMACOM, 2003.

Thaler, Richard H., and Cass R. Sunstein. *Nudge: Improving decisions about health, wealth, and happiness*. New Haven, Conn., London: Yale University Press, 2008.

"The History of Recycling in America Is More Complicated Than You May Think." Accessed December 28, 2016. http://time.com/4568234/history-origins-recycling/.

Thiagarajan, Sivasailam. *Simulation Games by Thiagi*. Bloomington, IN: Workshops by Thiagi, 2004.

Thompson, Janice. "Improving Voter Participation: Oregon Challenges and Opportunities." Unpublished manuscript, last modified July 15, 2017.

Thurow, Roger. "For Hungry Kids, 'Backpack Clubs' Try to Fill a Gap - WSJ." Accessed October 8, 2016. http://www.wsj.com/articles/SB114909067247767572.

Tribou, Alex, and Keith Collins. "This Is How Fast America Changes Its Mind." *Bloomberg*, June 26, 2015. Accessed December 23, 2016. https://www.bloomberg.com/graphics/2015-pace-of-social-change/.

Shaw, Jonathan. "Understanding Big Data Leads to Insights, Efficiencies, And Saved Lives." Accessed June 14, 2015. http://harvardmagazine.com/2014/03/why-big-data-is-a-big-deal.

Wikipedia. "Recycling in the United States - Wikipedia." Accessed December 28, 2016. https://en.wikipedia.org/w/index.php?oldid=753845119.

Wikipedia. "Chris Crocker - Wikipedia." Accessed December 26, 2016. https://en.wikipedia.org/w/index.php?oldid=754412995.

Wikipedia. "Britney Spears." Accessed December 26, 2016. https://en.wikipedia.org/w/index.php?oldid=756225489.

Yankelovich, D. *The Magic of Dialogue*. New York: Simon and Schuster, 1999.

YouTube's Greatest Hits: The True Stories behind 15 of YouTube's Most Popular Videos. Minute Help Press, 2012.

Youyou, Wu, Michal Kosinski, and David Stillwell. "Computer-Based Personality Judgments Are More Accurate than Those Made by Humans." *Proceedings of the National Academy of Sciences of the United States of America* 112, no. 4, (2015): 1036–40.

Notes

Chapter 1

[1] Arkansas Rice Depot. "Our Story." http://www.ricedepot.org/about-us/arkansas-rice-depot-info/our-story/ (accessed October 8, 2016).

[2] Thurow, Roger. "For Hungry Kids, 'Backpack Clubs' Try to Fill a Gap - WSJ." http://www.wsj.com/articles/SB114909067247767572 (accessed October 8, 2016).

[3] Collins, Jim. "Level 5 Leadership: The Triumph of Humility and Fierce Resolve." *Harvard Business Review*, 2001, 72.

[4] Rosenthal, Caitlin. "Big Data in the Age of the Telegraph." *Mckinsey Quarterly*, March 2013.

[5] Korzybski, Alfred. *Science and Sanity: An Introduction to Non-Aristotelian Systems and General Semantics*, 3rd ed., International Non-Aristotelian Library (Lakeville, Conn: International Non-Aristotelian Library Pub. Co, 1948).

[6] Banathy, Bela H. *Designing Social Systems in a Changing World,* The language of science (New York: Plenum Press, 1996).

[7] Tribou, Alex and Collins, Keith. "This Is How Fast America Changes Its Mind." *Bloomberg*, June 26, 2015.

[8] Wikipedia. "Britney Spears." https://en.wikipedia.org/w/index.php?oldid=756225489 (accessed December 26, 2016).

[9] *YouTube's Greatest Hits: The True Stories behind 15 of YouTube's Most Popular Videos* (Minute Help Press, 2012).

[10] "Chris Crocker - Wikipedia." https://en.wikipedia.org/w/index.php?oldid=754412995 (accessed December 26, 2016).

[11] Rogers, Everett M. *Diffusion of Innovations*, 5th ed. (New York: Free Press, 2003).

[12] Granovetter, Mark. "Threshold Models of Collective Behavior." *American Journal of Sociology* 83, no. 6, (1978).

[13] Gardner, Howard. *Changing Minds: The Art and Science of Changing Our Own and Other People's Minds* (Boston: Harvard Business School Press, 2004).

[14] Compiled from Google Trends.

[15] Bradbury, Matt. "The History of Recycling in America Is More Complicated Than You May Think." http://time.com/4568234/history-origins-recycling/ (accessed December 28, 2016).

[16] EPA, U. S. and OSWER. "Advancing Sustainable Materials Management: Facts and Figures." https://www.epa.gov/smm/advancing-sustainable-materials-management-facts-and-figures (accessed December 28, 2016).

[17] "Recycling in the United States - Wikipedia." https://en.wikipedia.org/w/index.php?oldid=753845119 (accessed December 28, 2016).

[18] "A Brief Timeline of the History of Recycling." http://www.buschsystems.com/recycling-bin-news/2014/05/a-brief-timeline-of-the-history-of-recycling/ (accessed December 28, 2016).

Chapter 2

[1] Kotter, John P. and Cohen, Dan S. *The Heart of Change* (Boston, MA: Harvard University Press, 2002).

[2] Grobart, Sam and Rusli, Evelyn M. "Cisco Shuts Down Flip, Its Video Camera Unit." *The New York Times*, April 12, 2011.

[3] Gardner, 2004.

[4] This is drawn from Nature Conservancy's 2012 California Climate Change program, although greatly simplified for illustrative purposes.

[5] Mitchell, Kimberley. "Like Magic? ("Every system is perfectly designed…")." Institute for Healthcare Improvement, http://www.ihi.org/communities/blogs/_layouts/15/ihi/community/blog/itemview.aspx?List=7d1126ec-8f63-4a3b-9926-c44ea3036813&ID=159 (accessed August 9, 2017).

Chapter 3

[1] Amnesty International. "The 'Arab Spring': Five Years on." Amnesty International, https://www.amnesty.org/en/latest/campaigns/2016/01/arab-spring-five-years-on/ (accessed December 30, 2016).

[2] Sherr, Ian. "Apple's Secrets Revealed at Trial." *The Wall Street Journal*, August 5, 2012.

[3] Detert, James R. and Burris, Ethan R. "Can Your Employees Really Speak Freely?" https://hbr.org/2016/01/can-your-employees-really-speak-freely (accessed August 9, 2017).

[4] Brown, John Seely and Duguid, Paul. *The Social Life of Information* (Boston: Harvard Business School Press, 2000).

[5] Cialdini, Robert B. *Influence: Science and Practice*, 4th ed. (Boston, MA: Allyn and Bacon, 2001).

Chapter 4

[1] Gardner, 2004, p. 82

[2] Reiss, Spencer. "DARPA's Gambling Man." *Wired*, no. 11.10.

[3] Surowiecki, James. "Damn the Slam PAM Plan!" *Slate*, 2003.

[4] Hanson, Robin. "The Informed Press Favored the Policy Analysis Market." http://hanson.gmu.edu/PAMpress.pdf (accessed February 9, 2013).

[5] Ricouer, Paul. *Hermeneutics and the Human Sciences (J. B. Thompson, Trans.)* (Melbourne, Australia: Cambridge University Press, 1981).

[6] Dr. Frank Luntz. *Words That Work: It's Not What You Say, It's What People Hear* (New York, NY: Hyperion Books, 2007).

[7] Simmons, Annette. *Whoever Tells the Best Story Wins: How to Use Your Own Stories to Communicate with Power and Impact* (Saranac Lake, NY, USA: AMACOM, 2007), p. 185

[8] Ibid.

[9] Gardner, 2004, p. 73

[10] Dr. Frank Luntz, 2007.

[11] Kotter and Cohen, 2002.

[12] Block, Lauren G. et al. "Assessing the Impact of Antidrug Advertising on Adolescent Drug Consumption: Results From a Behavioral Economic Model." *American Journal of Public Health* 92, no. 8, (2002).

[13] Denning, Stephen. *The Springboard: How Storytelling Ignites Action in Knowledge-Era Organizations* (Boston, Oxford: Butterworth-Heinemann, 2001).

Chapter 5

[1] Personal communication.

[2] Purser, R. E. and Cabana S. *The Self Managing Organization: How Leading Companies are Transforming the Work of Teams for Real Impact* (New York: Simon & Schuster Inc, 1998).

[3] Brad Plumer, "Why 50 million Americans won't vote Tuesday, in two charts," accessed July 14, 2017, https://www.washington-post.com/news/wonk/wp/2012/11/05/why-50-million-americans-wont-vote-to-morrow-in-two-charts/

[4] Rockart, John F. *Chief Executives Define their Own Data Needs* (Cambridge, MA: Harvard Business School Press, 1979).

[5] Caralli, Richard A. "The Critical Success Factor Method: Establishing a Foundation for Enterprise Security Management." 2004.

[6] Grunert, Klaus G. and Ellegaard, Charlotte, "The Concept of Key Success Factors: Theory and Method" (unpublished manuscript, July 20, 2013)

[7] Lerner, Kira. "5 Ways To Fix America's Dismal Voter Turnout Problem." ThinkProgress, https://thinkprogress.org/5-ways-to-fix-americas-dismal-voter-turnout-problem-6342bc2d1190 (accessed July 15, 2017).

[8] Drutman, Lee. "Simple Ways to Increase Voter Turnout." *Pacific Standard Magazine*, March 31, 2008.

[9] Black, Eric. "Why Is Turnout So Low in U.S. Elections? We Make It More Difficult to Vote Than Other Democracies." *MinnPost*, October 1, 2014.

[10] Thompson, Janice, "Improving Voter Participation: Oregon Challenges and Opportunities" (Common Cause, August 2009) (unpublished manuscript, July 15, 2017)

Chapter 6

[1] Block, P. *Flawless Consulting: A Guide to Getting Your Expertise Used* (San Francisco, CA: John Wiley & Sons, 2011).

[2] Roberto, Michael A. *Why Great Leaders Don't Take Yes for an Answer: Managing for Conflict and Consensus* (Upper Saddle River, N.J: Pearson Education, Inc., publishing as Prentice Hall, 2007, c2005).

[3] Bikhchandani, Sushil, Hirshleifer, David and Welch, Ivo. *Information cascades and Observational Learning* (Columbus, OH: Charles A. Dice Center for Research in Financial Economics, Fisher College of Business, Ohio State University, 2005).

[4] Cialdini, 2001.

[5] Yankelovich, D. *The Magic of Dialogue* (New York: Simon and Schuster, 1999).

[6] Duhigg, Charles. "What Google Learned from Its Quest to Build the Perfect Team." *The New York Times Magazine*, 2016.

[7] Dilts, Robert B. *Strategies of genius* (Capitola, CA: Meta Publications, 1994).

[8] Bono, Edward de. *De Bono's Thinking Course*, [New ed.] (Harlow: BBC Active, 2006).

[9] *Effects of Positive Practices on Organizational Effectiveness* (NTL Institute - Sage, 2011).

[10] Tamblyn, Doni. *Laugh and Learn: 95 Ways to Use Humor tor More Effective Teaching and Training* (New York: AMACOM, 2003).

[11] Banathy, 1996.

[12] Bono, 2006.

[13] Ibid.

[14] Duhigg, 2016.

Chapter 7

[1] Rogers, 2003.

[2] Maslow, A. *Toward a New Psychology of Being* (New York: VanNostrand Reinhold, 1968).

[3] Herzberg, Frederick. *One More Time: How Do You Motivate Employees?* The Harvard Business Review Classics Series (Boston, Mass.: Harvard Business Press, 2008).

[4] Baumeister, R. *Meanings of Life* (New York: Guilford Press, 1991).

[5] Hepburn, R. W. "Questions about the Meaning of Life." *Religious Studies* 1, no. 02, (1966).

[6] Frankl, Viktor Emil. *Man's Search for Meaning: An Introduction to Logotherapy*, Rev. and enl. ed. (London: Hodder and Stoughton, 1964, ©1962).

[7] Baumeister, 1991.

[8] Ibid.

[9] Myers, David G. *The Pursuit of Happiness: Who Is Happy - And Why* (London: Aquarian/Thorsons, 1993).

[10] "Learning Should Be Fun." https://mindhacks.com/2009/01/19/learning-should-be-fun/ (accessed August 20, 2017).

[11] Paterson, J. M. & C. J. "Organizational Justice, Change Anxiety, and Acceptance of Downsizing: Preliminary Tests of an AET-Based Model.", (2002).

Chapter 8

[1] Kaplan, Robert S. and Norton, David P. *The Balanced Scorecard: Translating Strategy into Action* (Boston, Mass.: Harvard Business School Press, 1996).

Chapter 9

[1] Miles, R. H. *Leading Corporate Transformation* (San Francisco: Jossey-Bass Publishers Inc, 1997).

Chapter 10

[1] McFadden, Robert D. "Hiroo Onoda, Soldier Who Hid in Jungle for Decades, Dies at 91." https://www.nytimes.com/2014/01/18/world/asia/hiroo-onoda-imperial-japanese-army-officer-dies-at-91.html (accessed August 1, 2017).

[2] Greencrest. "Advertising Frequency - Is There a Magic Number?" Greencrest, http://greencrest.com/marketingprose/advertising-frequency-is-there-a-magic-number (accessed September 1, 2013).

[3] Levinson, Jay Conrad. *Guerilla Marketing Excellence: The Fifty Golden Rules for Business Success* (London: Piatkus, 1993).

[4] Laxalt, Francois. "The Secret to Increasing Message Frequency without Fatiguing Your Audience." https://blogs.adobe.com/digitalmarketing/email/secret-increasing-message-frequency-fatiguing-audience/ (accessed September 2, 2013).

[5] Grice, Paul. "Logic and Conversation". In Cole, P.; Morgan, J. *Syntax and Semantics: Speech acts* (New York: Academic Press,1975).

[6] Paterson, 2002.

Chapter 12

[1] Prince, Michael. "Does Active Learning Work? A Review of the Research."

[2] Tamblyn, 2003.

[3] Thiagarajan, Sivasailam. *Simulation Games by Thiagi* (Bloomington, IN: Workshops by Thiagi, 2004).

[4] Hamarie, Juho, Koisvisto, Jonna, and Sarsa, Harri. "Does Gamification Work? A Literature Review of Empirical Studies on Gamification."

[5] "How Gamification Reshapes Corporate Training." *CIO*, 2013.

[6] Tamblyn, 2003.

[7] Thiagarajan, 2004.

Chapter 13

[1] Rogers, 2003.

Chapter 15

[1] Kotter, John P. "Accelerate!" *Harvard Business Review*, 2012.

[2] Derose, Chris. "How Google Uses Data to Build a Better Worker." *The Atlantic*, 2013.

[3] "Understanding Big Data Leads to Insights, Efficiencies, and Saved Lives." http://harvardmagazine.com/2014/03/why-big-data-is-a-big-deal (accessed June 14, 2015).

[4] Youyou, Wu, Kosinski, Michal, and Stillwell, David. "Computer-Based Personality Judgments Are More Accurate than Those Made by Humans." *Proceedings of the National Academy of Sciences of the United States of America* 112, no. 4, (2015).

[5] Thaler, Richard H. and Sunstein, Cass R. *Nudge: Improving Decisions about Health, Wealth, and Happiness* (New Haven, Conn., London: Yale University Press, 2008).

[6] "Using Games to Get Employees Thinking." MIT Technology Review, http://www.technologyreview.com/news/425044/using-games-to-get-employees-thinking/ (accessed June 15, 2015).

[7] "From Fitbit to Fitocracy: The Rise of Health Care Gamification." Knowledge@Wharton, http://knowledge.wharton.upenn.edu/article/from-fitbit-to-fitocracy-the-rise-of-health-care-gamification/ (accessed June 15, 2015).

[8] "Gamification – The Game and Beyond!" http://blog.gfk.com/2013/07/gamification-the-game-and-beyond/ (accessed June 15, 2015).

[9] "Target's Cashier Game – Is It Really a Game?" LevelsPro, http://www.levelspro.com/targets-cashier-game-is-it-really-a-game/ (accessed June 15, 2015).

Thank You

Thank you for taking the time to read this book. I hope you found it valuable. Here are some final take-aways you might find useful for further advancement.

- For more detailed information and templates, please check my website here:

    https://www.empowerbase.com

- You can also find service offerings and contact information on empwerbase.com if you would like coaching or consulting.

- We are always adding material to the site, so if you don't find what you need, do make sure to check back or send me a note.

- To be kept informed, you can **join our mailing list**.

- For future publications, also check

    https://www.dougwalton.com

Finally, if you found this book valuable, would you **please leave a review on Amazon or Goodreads?**

My commitment is to add as much value as possible for you to achieve your personal and professional goals. Your interest in my materials is hugely appreciated, and I hope you will consider these options and future publications.

Best wishes,

Doug Walton

www.ingramcontent.com/pod-product-compliance
Lightning Source LLC
Chambersburg PA
CBHW062048270326
41931CB00013B/2981